D1528097

MARXISM, SOCIALISM, FREEDOM

MARXISM, SOCIALISM, FREEDOM

Towards a General Democratic Theory of Labour-Managed Systems

RADOSLAV SELUCKÝ

St. Martin's Press · New York

Library of Congress Cataloging in Publication Data

Selucký, Radoslav.
    Marxism, socialism, freedom.

    Includes bibliographical references and index.
    1. Marxian economics.   2. Communist state.
3. Socialism.   4. Liberty.   5. Democracy.
I. Title.
HB97.5.S42 1979   335.4   79-14913
ISBN 0-312-51855-2

FOR KATEŘINA AND MICHAL

I take the view that we can think either of a perfect society or of a society in which life is liveable, but not of both at once.

L. KOLAKOWSKI

The political problem of mankind is to combine three things: economic efficiency, social justice and individual liberty.

J. M. KEYNES

It is possible to conceive a community in which the necessary diversity of economic functions existed side by side with a large measure of economic and social equality, and in which, therefore, while the occupations and incomes of individuals varied, they lived, nevertheless, in much the same environment, enjoyed similar standards of health and education, found different positions according to their abilities, equally accessible to them, intermarried freely with each other, were equally immune from the more degrading forms of poverty, and equally secure against economic oppression.

R. H. TAWNEY

Contents

Introductory Note

This book deals with a question which is not only of general theoretical interest but which also reflects one of the most topical political and ideological problems of our time: can socialism be democratic in the sense of guaranteeing individual freedom? As the most influential socialist theory was formulated by Karl Marx and Friedrich Engels, the first part of the book is devoted to a detailed analysis of the Marxist concept of socialism, particularly to the cleavage between Marx's perception of the economic and the political liberation of man. While Marx's economic concept of socialism consists of a single social-wide factory based on vertical (hierarchical) relations of superiority and subordination, his political concept of socialism consists of a free association of self-managed work and social communities based on horizontal relations of equality. Whoever accepts in full Marx's first concept has to give up the latter, and vice versa: they are mutually exclusive. Paradoxically enough, Marx's unhumanistic vision of one social-wide factory resulted from his humanistically motivated rejection of the market for which he is nowadays praised not only by many socialist humanists but also by some liberals. This is why I start my inquiry with a re-examination of the Marxian concept of the market to establish where Marx made the theoretical mistake which turned his ideal society into a nightmare.

The second part of the book deals with revisionism. In particular, it offers a new interpretation of Lenin's revision which superseded the cleavage of Marx's concept by having added to Marx's hierarchically structured socialist economy an equally hierarchically structured political system; a critical appraisal of the Yugoslav attempt to extend the principle of self-management to macropolitics; my own democratic revision of Marxism; and finally also an analysis of structural links between the market and freedom with regard to the democratic theories of Karl Polanyi, Milton Friedman and C. B. Macpherson. The concluding chapter of the second part also discusses specific features of the socialist market and proves the impossibility of a non-market democratic theory.

In the third part of the book I offer a general model of democratic socialism and a general democratic theory of labour-managed systems. If socialism is redefined, stripped of its utopian features, enriched by valuable liberal principles and based on a synthesis of the market and social planning, it is possible to construct a theoretical model combining socialism, individual freedom and political democracy, as well as a democratic theory maximising both social welfare and liberty. While the model and the theory deprive Marxist socialism of its revolutionary spirit and doctrinal purity, they may restore its appeal to those disappointed by its present ideological sterility, theoretical impotence and practical inability to deal effectively with relevant human, social, economic, political, ethnic and moral problems of our time.

RADOSLAV SELUCKÝ

Acknowledgements

This book was started with a grant from the Ford Foundation in 1969, partly written during my short stay at the Institute of International Studies of the University of South Carolina, Columbia, in 1970, and completed thanks to a grant from the Canada Council in 1974 as well as technical support given me by Carleton University, Ottawa, in 1977. I wish to express my deep appreciation to all these institutions whose assistance enabled me to give the text the attention the topic required. I wish also to thank all those of my colleagues and friends whose comments and suggestions helped me to improve the quality of the manuscript.

R.S.
Paris, June 1978.

Part One

Marx's Concept of Economic and Political Liberation of Man: A Critique

1 The Market

1.1 THE GENERAL CONCEPT OF THE MARKET

My interpretation of the Marxist concept of the origins and development of the market can be briefly summed up in the following manner:

The process of production is a contradictory unity of human and material factors. In the economic sphere of any social organism, the human (subjective) element clashes with the external conditions of its existence, i.e. with Nature which appears to man both as the object of his work and the environment in which he works. Human needs can be satisfied only within the framework of Nature and only through its medium. Nature is an object of human needs, man is an objectified being and labour is a process of objectified activity in which man mediates, regulates and controls the material interchange between himself and Nature. The labour process, however, differs from other natural processes in that it is not merely a result of the workings of the laws of Nature; it goes beyond the realm of the interacting laws of Nature because man has brought into it a particular cause of the preceding changes: conscious human need, purpose, interest, aim.

The human being is composed of two mutually contingent elements, physical and rational, which together form man. In his biological substance, man is a part of Nature and subject to its laws. In his rationality and in his thinking, man continuously transcends the realm of Nature and subjects it to his own needs. Labour, as a condition of human existence, contains both these elements within itself. As human civilisation has developed, the importance of the subject has increased: more and more, man has subdued Nature and acquired a better understanding not only of the laws of Nature but also of those governing his social existence. In this sense, man has come to stand apart from Nature and has become a *conscious* maker of his own history.

Econqmic growth is just another expression for the development of the productive forces which, in turn, may be expressed as the development of the technology of production, transportation and exchange; as the development of human experience, skills and intellectual capacities; as a growing knowledge of the qualities of Nature; as the development of the sciences. The development of the productive forces has its own regulator. At a certain (capitalist) stage of the development of the social division of labour, it is the market mechanism.

Men become economically active in order to satisfy their needs. In the initial stages of the development of human society, the incentive for economic activity was immediate. But as soon as people began to work in a specialised manner, each permanently concentrating on a single type of economic activity, they had to start exchanging, first their surpluses and, later, all the products of their labour. An intermediary appeared between production and consumption – i.e. exchange.

From the moment when the social division of labour begins to operate as the determining economic factor, the volume of use-values which an individual can consume depends on the equivalent which he obtains for the product of his labour on the market. If there is to be an incentive for economic activity now, in the conditions of the social division of labour, there has to be a mechanism which constantly transposes the private, specialised concrete labours of the individuals into abstract social labour. The mechanism which continuously solves the contradiction between private (concrete) and social (abstract) labour is the market.

Since the single producer now does not produce all the use-values needed to satisfy his needs, but specialises only in producing one use-value (or a part thereof) through the exchange of which he obtains the necessary goods and services, he ceases being concerned with the use-value of his economic activity and, of necessity, begins to concern himself with the exchange-value of the results of his labour. The relations in which the producer exchanges his goods for the goods needed to satisfy his needs depend on the level of both his individual and social productivity of labour and on the ratio of supply and demand of the goods concerned.

The development of production and exchange based on the operation of the market mechanism is spontaneous and automatic: the law of value regulates production and exchange according to the relation of supply and demand whereby it allocates both capital and labour in certain proportions into individual branches of economic activity.[1] Both capital and labour flow in the direction of those branches whose goods are in sufficient demand, and away from branches whose goods are not in sufficient demand. If the mass of capital and labour increases in the branches whose goods are in great demand, an increase in production follows in due course; thus, after a certain period of time, supply exceeds demand. On the other hand, in the branches where the mass of capital and labour has diminished the volume of production will decrease, thus lowering the volume of supply which begins to lag behind demand. The value mechanism leads through prices to competition not only within every branch but also among the branches which produce substitutive goods or provide substitutive services.

The market mechanism forces producers to make goods (regardless of their use-value) which yield an equivalent. Thus the economic activity of men is not realised directly but in a roundabout way, through the market. The market is the only element linking the separate producers, the principal integrating economic force, the place where the producers can ascertain whether their work is social labour, i.e. whether it is being socially recognised, whether its product is exchangeable. Products which, for whatever reason, are not realised on the market as exchange-values are, from the social point of view, redundant. This also means that the labour expended on their production has been expended needlessly. From the market point of view, such labour must be considered as not having been undertaken at all.

It is this feature of the market mechanism (i.e. that individual producers verify the social usefulness of their labour not directly but through an intermediary; not *ex ante*, at the very start of the production process, but *ex post facto*, only when the product has reached the market) which causes contradictory social effects. It leads, on the one hand, to economic growth, to efficiency and to eventual increase in the productivity of labour. On the other hand, since the producers work for an unknown market guided only by their own estimate, and frequently expending labour and capital needlessly and to no purpose, it may lead to a waste of both labour and capital. Although the market mechanism does organise proportional production in society, it does so *ex post* (and through disproportions) rather than *ex ante* (and in a planned manner).

The market mechanism, along with the law of value, works spontaneously. It is the integral, primal, natural and automatically operating regulator of the economy. This mechanism as such has no aim: it regulates economic processes as an intermediary for the achievement of aims set by man. The aim for this self-regulator must be provided from the outside. But whatever the aim is, it can be reached – in the conditions of scarcity – only through the material interest of the producers, the material advantage of the economic units. If this internal self-regulator of the economy is to be constructed in a manner which promotes the achievement of desired goals, a human intervention is necessary – an act of will, a decision by a subjective factor.

The market mechanism has four basic shortcomings. As it operates spontaneously and organises the proportions *ex post*, it causes disharmony between supply and demand, creates an economic imbalance and gives rise to economic crises. The second shortcoming of the market mechanism is that it increases social inequality. Left to operate spontaneously, it leads to a sharp social differentiation which disturbs the stability of the community. The third failure of the self-regulatory mechanism is that it encourages only economic activity which yields profits and is advantageous for the producers. Therefore, it is hardly applicable to production of goods and services which, though needed by the community, are not subject to the criterion of profit. And finally, if not tamed by an outside (social) intervention, the market leads inevitably to monopoly.

My interpretation of the Marxist concept of the market leads to eight conclusions:

1. The market is a product of the social division of labour, autonomous producers and scarcity. (The term 'scarcity' means that it is not possible to satisfy *all* social and individual needs.)
2. It allocates production factors, organises economic processes and regulates exchange.
3. It continuously solves the contradiction between private (concrete) and social (abstract) labour.
4. It is the mediating link and, at the same time, the feedback between production and consumption.
5. It creates objective criteria through the price mechanism for comparing the costs of production.
6. It is based on a horizontal type of economic relations among the agents of economic activity.
7. It operates spontaneously, has no internal aim and regulates economic proportions *ex post*.
8. Its four shortcomings can be superseded only if the market is combined with a social plan.

1.2. THE MARXIST CRITIQUE OF THE MARKET

Capitalism is the only known economic system in which the market has become the universal regulator of the economy and market relations have extended over the entire society. That is why a traditional Marxist critique of capitalism is, at the same time, a critique of the market.

The Marxist critique of commodity, market and money relations has three sources: moral, philosophical and economic. Money as the universal commodity (and gold as its material substance) is the universal form of capital which is *the* cause of human misery. The fetish of money – even more obvious than the fetishism of commodities – is an expression of the dominance of things over people, of the objectification and reification of human relations. The moral condemnation of gold (and money) was expressed by Marx in words as fiery as those used by some early utopian socialists;[2] Engels condemned trade as 'immoral', 'inhuman', 'legalised fraud';[3] and Lenin prophesied a fate for gold similar to that which Thomas More assigned to it in his Utopia: it shall be used – after the victory of the world proletariat – as building material for public lavatories.[4]

The moral condemnation of commodity, market and money relations is irrelevant from a scholarly point of view, and it should be noted that it does not represent the substance of the Marxist critique of market society. There is one exception, however. When Marx had successfully constructed his theory of surplus value within the strict framework of equal exchange,* one would have it that he was proud of this scholarly achievement. He was instead exasperated, however. The reason? By the *market* standards, the exchange between the worker and the capitalist is equal. By any *human* standards it is unequal. Hence, because the market standards are at odds with human standards, the market must by all means be eliminated from any really human society.

Marx's philosophic and economic condemnation of the market is of much greater importance. The core of the philosophic condemnation consists in Marx's concept of alienated labour. Alienation of labour caused by commodity and market relations lies in the fact that the producer ceases to be concerned with the use-value which he has created, with the concrete existence of his product, with its meaning, significance and usefulness, and is concerned merely with its *exchange-*

---

* The worker sells his labour power whose value is determined by the value of the necessary means of life. Hence his wage (the price paid for his labour power) is equal to the reproduction costs (value) of the labour power. From the point of view of the market, the exchange is equal. However, the capitalist may yet appropriate the surplus-value because the *use-value* of the labour power is able to produce a surplus over its own value. Since it was the capitalist who bought the labour power, it is he who employs its use-value and, consequently, appropriates the surplus.

value, primarily from the quantitative point of view. Thus the aim of labour, its content and quality are alienated from the producer and human labour is reduced to a mere abstraction reflected in exchange-value.

In a market society, the bonds between people are provided by things (commodities). By exchanging commodities, people obtain the means of their existence. The fate of a producer depends on whether or not a thing (commodity) is exchanged. A product, quite simple as long as it was a mere thing, turns into a mystery and a fetish as soon as it becomes a commodity. This mystery is caused not by its use-value but by its exchange-value as the exclusive form of its substance, i.e. value. Why is it that the same thing yields the equivalent in one instance and fails to do so in another? Why are the same things (commodities) sometimes exchangeable and sometimes not? Why does man's fate depend on the market situation rather than on his skills and performance? Marx's answer to these and many other related questions is simple: it is caused by the circumstances which prevail over people, by the things now being produced as commodities which are no longer under the producer's control and, consequently, appear to him as alien, unknown, mysterious and all-powerful forces.

This alienation grows even deeper as the division of labour works its way into a workshop and transforms the producer into a *detail*-worker who no longer creates an end (final) product but only a part of it, and carries out one partial task in which he specialises and acquires a degree of virtuosity. If human labour was meaningful earlier (man was a maker of the use-value, of the end-product), its meaning is now lost. The immediate producer is no longer interested in what he produces, he loses his interest in a concrete profession and is interested only in a job. Since his labour has ceased to be an inner need of his self-expression and self-fulfilment, it becomes merely the source of his livelihood, a prerequisite of his physical existence. It stands apart from man since he carries it out not because of the need to create but under the pressure of necessity, in order to make his living.

Thus the alienation of man from his labour goes hand in hand with the externalisation and objectification of man and his labour. Social division of labour and market (commodity) relations dehumanise labour which used to be the basic mark distinguishing man from other animals.

There is, however, yet another dimension of alienated labour caused by the very existence of the market. As far as wage labour is concerned, the worker creates values not for himself but for the capitalist who has purchased his labour power (a commodity being sold and bought on the labour market) and who, therefore, appropriates the result of the work. The product of exploited labour (surplus-value) is alienated from the worker: it does not belong to him but to a capitalist. Since capital relations loom as superstructure over the commodity and market relations, no exploitation of wage labour could be possible without the existence of the latter. That is why Marx suggests that only when the capital relationship growing out of the market is abolished, will the capitalist form of alienation vanish; only when the market relationship is superseded and commodities again become mere products without mystery, will the market form of alienation disappear; and only when things cease to rule over man will the market form of the externalisation and objectification of man disappear.

Marx's economic condemnation of market relations is based on the fact that the market allocates production factors both spontaneously and *ex post*, i.e. not only blindly but, above all, uneconomically, through disproportions. Market allocation of production factors is the wasting of social labour. In the conditions of capitalism it is accompanied by periodical economic crises.[5]

This critique of commodity and market relations appears and reappears throughout the entire body of the work of Marx and Engels. The conclusion that Engels draws from it is that 'no society can for any length of time remain master of its own production and continue to control the social effects of its own process of production unless it abolishes exchange among individuals'.[6]

1.3. THE MARXIST CONCEPT OF DIRECT ALLOCATION AND DISTRIBUTION

If commodity production and market organisation of the national economy work as obstacles to a rationally functioning society which would be humanistically organised and develop without crises, there seems to be no way out but to abolish the market and replace it by direct allocation of production factors and direct distribution of national income. Instead of using the *ex post* regulator of the market, the *ex ante* regulator of a plan should be introduced to create 'a community of free individuals, carrying on their work with the means of production in common, in which the labour-power of all different individuals is consciously applied as the combined labour-power of the community'.[7]

In order to abolish the market, however, it would be necessary to abolish some of its prerequisites: social division of labour, scarcity and autonomy of producers.

Marx and Engels have never formulated a clear concept of social division of labour. On the contrary, they used the term interchangeably and were recurrently giving various meanings to the phenomenon. For instance, the following passage suggests that as long as there is a qualitative development of productive forces, there has to be also a further development of social division of labour: 'Each new productive force, insofar it is not merely a quantitative extension of productive forces already known (for instance the bringing into cultivation of fresh land) causes a further development of the division of labour.'[8] Another passage seems to suggest quite the opposite: 'In a higher phase of communist society . . . subordination of the individual to the division of labour, and therewith also the antithesis between mental and physical labour, has vanished . . . . '[9]

On another occasion, the division of labour is identified by Marx and Engels with private property;[10] on yet another, the concept of division of labour is formulated by Engels in a different manner: 'Division of labour is direct domination of the labourer by the instrument of labour, even if not in the capitalist sense.'[11]

Be that as it may, Marx and Engels wanted to abolish division of labour. It clearly follows from their various notes, propositions and constructions. The most famous example can be found in *The German Ideology*:

For as soon as the division of labour comes into being, each man has a particular, exclusive sphere of activity, which is forced upon him and from which he cannot escape. He is a hunter, a fisherman, a shepherd, or a critical critic, and must remain so if he does not want to lose his means of livelihood; whereas in communist society, where nobody has one exclusive sphere of activity but each can become accomplished in any branch he wishes, society regulates the general production and thus makes it possible for me to do one thing today and another tomorrow, to hunt in the morning, fish in the afternoon, rear cattle in the evening, criticise after dinner, just as I have a mind, without ever becoming hunter, fisherman, shepherd or critic.[12]

There is nothing communistic in such an arrangement: any farmer can afford to organise his life according to the suggested pattern even in present-day society. The pattern is inapplicable universally, however. One could hardly invent computers in the morning, perform neurosurgery in the afternoon, repair a jet in the evening and conduct a symphonic orchestra after dinner without becoming respectively computer engineer, neurosurgeon, jet-mechanic and conductor.

Unlike in *The German Ideology*, Marx was reasonably realistic in his *Capital* when suggesting how to abolish the old division of labour within the factory. His idea is based on a kind of polytechnic education which would enable the workers freely to change their place within industries. He quotes approvingly from a French author[13] and praises Robert Owen 'who has shown us in detail the germ of the education of the future, an education that will, in the case of every child over a given age, combine productive labour with instruction and gymnastics, not only as one of the methods adding to the efficiency of production, but as the only method of producing fully developed human beings.'[14] But even if this were accomplished, it could not abolish the division of labour within society.

As to a supersession of scarcity, the prospects are not too promising either. Marx and Engels knew only too well that human needs, even if some of them are determined by Nature, are always social and historical. Hence they are, in the last analysis, determined by man himself. 'The satisfaction of the first need', they told us, 'leads to new needs.'[15] 'The communists have no intention of abolishing the fixedness of their desires and needs, an intention which Stirner, immersed in his world of fancy, ascribes to them and to all other men; they only strive to achieve an organisation of production and intercourse which will make possible the normal satisfaction of all needs, i.e. a satisfaction which is limited only by the needs themselves.'[16] Being an optimist, Marx had believed that man would someday achieve mastery over Nature, free himself from his role as the principal agent of the production process and put himself alongside of it rather than within it. Of course, this would require an abundance brought about by full automation and other as yet unknown scientific discoveries and technological innovations.

I may conclude that Marx had in mind neither an egalitarian determination of individual needs nor a social-wide rationing of goods and services, but a *genuine* supersession of scarcity in the future communist society. One may agree with him (in principle) that a relative (or particular) overcoming of scarcity might be possible in some distant future. One should be rather sceptical, however, of an absolute supersession of scarcity. As long as one discusses prospects for an *immediate* future, scarcity should be recognised as a realistic limitation by any suggested model of socialist society.[17]

If, therefore, the social division of labour as the foundation of commodity production and market relations cannot be abolished by a conscious human intervention, and if, furthermore, the scarcity of resources and goods cannot be superseded in the foreseeable future, then it becomes necessary to abolish at least the third prerequisite of the market, the autonomy of producers. The traditional Marxist way of abolishing the autonomy of producers is the expropriation of private ownership of the means of production through nationalisation.

Thus, a solution does exist. But what to do with the social division of labour which has not disappeared? What is there to replace the market relations and bonds among producers? How to create a new system of communication and a new feedback between suppliers and customers?

Here, too, a way out seems to be offered by Marx which appears to be very persuasive. The division of labour exists not only within society but also within every economic unit. If the bonds *between* economic units are those of the market, the bonds among the producers within economic units are deprived of their market content. The organisation of work in a shop is direct, not mediated: the hierarchy progresses from the top downward controlling both labour and the production process according to the consciously elaborated plan. Marx compares the capitalist owner of a factory to a commanding general, technicians and engineers to officers, foremen and supervisors to NCOs and workers to privates.[18] The management of economic units, as in an army, is based on hierarchy and relations of superiority and subordination. Given the specialisation and compartmentalisation of the work process in detail operations, the end-effect depends on the co-ordinated efforts and on the united interest of all those participating in the production. Only the end-product resulting from the activities of various individuals and machines gives a meaning to the common work, only the use-value of the jointly produced commodity can be realised on the market as an exchange-value.

Thus, the bonds among people within the production units are distinct from those within the society. The former do not operate through the medium of market and exchange but are managed directly: only the production unit as a whole can face other production units as one independent (autonomous) producer faces another. While the only authority for the production units is the market where exchange is carried out and the results of their economic activities are realised, the authority within a production unit is its owner (manager) who controls and organises this unit by his power and in his interest. If a production unit is to assert itself successfully on the market, the necessary prerequisite is that the interest of the production unit becomes the interest of each of its employees, that the production unit as a whole appears, vis-à-vis other production units, as a representative of one particular interest vis-à-vis other particular interests.

If the division of labour within a production unit is supported by the authority of the organiser, by direct management of both the labour and production process, by the exact plan and the conscious co-ordination of employees with the exclusion of the intermediary market mechanism – why, then, should it not be possible to apply these patterns of enterprise management to the entire national economy? Above all, the absence of commodity and market relations within the production unit is due to the fact that these are relations within one ownership. If the ownership of all the means of production is taken over by the state, then there is no reason why the bonds among various production units should be those of exchange and market.

Though Marx did not say this explicitly (it was only Kautsky and Lenin who deduced the one nation, one factory concept from Marx's implicit suggestions), he touched upon the problem in his polemics against Proudhon:

> Society as a whole has in common with the interior of a workshop that it too has its division of labour. If one took as a model the division of labour in a modern workshop, in order to apply it to a whole society, the society best organised for the production of wealth would undoubtedly be that which had a single chief employer, distributing tasks to the different members of the community according to a previously fixed rule.[19]

It follows from Marx's statement that this arrangement would be only welcome. But what about the increased authority in society? Would it be in accord with Marx's humanistic intentions? It seems that Marx would not mind:

> The *a priori* system on which the division of labour, within the workshop, is regularly carried out, becomes in the division of labour within the society, an *a posteriori*, nature-imposed necessity, controlling the lawless caprice of the producers, and perceptible in the barometrical fluctuations of the market prices. Division of labour within the workshop implies the undisputed authority of the capitalist over men that are but parts of a mechanism that belongs to him. The division of labour within the society brings into contact independent

commodity producers who acknowledge no other authority but that of competition, of the coercion exerted by the pressure of their mutual interests; just as in the animal kingdom, the *bellum omnium contra omnes* more or less preserves the conditions of existence of every species. The same bourgeois mind which praises division of labour in the workshop, life-long annexation of the labourer to a partial operation, and his complete subjection to capital, as being all organisation of labour that increases its productiveness – that same bourgeois mind denounces with equal vigour every conscious attempt to socially control and regulate the process of production, as an inroad upon such sacred things as the rights of property, freedom and unrestricted play for the bent of the individual capitalist. *It is very characteristic that the enthusiastic apologists of the factory system have nothing more damning to urge against a general organisation of the labour of society than that it would turn all society into one immense factory.*[20]

Thus, the famous one nation, one factory concept was born. Though Marx was not its explicit author, he was certainly its spiritual father.

1.4. THE TYPES OF THE MARKET

The market is not a product either of private ownership of the means of production or of capitalism. It came into being and evolved with the development of the social division of labour. In all pre-capitalist production forms, the market existed only where we find the three prerequisites: scarcity, social division of labour and autonomous producers. The first historically known form of exchange took place among tribes producing distinct use-values on the basis of their common (tribal, communal) ownership of property. This collective form of property, while preventing an exchange within the tribe (community), enabled the exchange among the tribes (communities). Thus, the autonomy of producers (economic units, tribes, communities) may or may not coincide with private ownership. It is not private ownership but the independent (autonomous) position of economic units which is relevant in this respect.[21] Only an abolition of private property which is accompanied by the abolition of the autonomous position of producers may bring the existence of the market to an end.

The basic form of the *pre-capitalist* (or non-capitalist) market can be expressed by the formula C–M–C (commodity–money–commodity).

This type of market is typical for small producers interested in use-values rather than in the exchange-value. The exchange-value (money) plays only the part of an intermediary and serves not as capital but merely as the medium of exchange. This is the simplest form of the circulation of commodities (mediated by money) whose purpose is selling in order to buy. Commodity is both the point of departure and the end of this particular market.

The general formula for the *capitalist* market (M–C–M') is reversed. The circulation starts with money (M) which is exchanged for commodity (C) and transformed again into money (M). While the pre-capitalist market (C–M–C) finds its justification in that the commodity at the beginning and at the end is represented by a different use-value, the capitalist market (M–C–M') finds its justification only if the sum of money at the end exceeds the sum of money at the beginning: the whole purpose of such a circulation is buying for (less) money (M) in order to sell for (more) money (M'). While the pre-capitalist market (C–M–C) can exist without agents making profit, the capitalist market would be absurd if an agent did not make a profit.

The full formula for the capitalist market reads as follows: M–C . . . production process . . . C'–M'. Money at the beginning plays the part of capital which is used for buying both the means of production and labour power. Then, the process of circulation is interrupted by the process of production which results in an end-product which is sold for money enriched by a surplus-value. This full formula applies to *productive* capital; the formula M–C–M' applies to *trading* capital and the formula M–M' applies to *banking* capital. This is the first reason why the capitalist market is universal; it covers all fields of economic activity, i.e. production, trade and banking. The second cause of its universality lies in the fact that labour power becomes a commodity being regularly sold and bought on the labour market. And thirdly, the capitalist market goes beyond economics, captures all spheres of human activity and transforms almost everything into commodities.

This universal capitalist market is based on either free competition or on monopolistic (oligopolistic) organisation of the economy. Free competition historically precedes the monopolistic stage of capitalism. Although free competition and monopoly are, by definition, mutually exclusive, they may coexist: while a number of industries, trades and services could be oligopolised or monopolised, a number of industries, trades and services may be working under free competition. From the historical point of view, however, *economic* monopoly is a logical outcome of the free competitive market. Both concentration and centralisation of capital serve as the vehicle transforming capitalism from free competition into its monopolistic (oligopolistic) stage.[22]

There are several types of monopoly. The basic one stems from *Nature* and is caused by the scarcity of land suited for the production of specific items, e.g. gold, rare wines, etc. A *legal* monopoly could rely either on an exclusive patent or on an exclusive privilege to produce, transport or distribute certain products or provide a certain kind of service. Such a privilege is usually granted to its holder by a legal act. Finally, a monopoly can be derived from *economic might*. If one (a monopoly) or a few big producers (an oliogopoly) control the entire market or most of the market, they could control all market conditions including prices, terms of supply and quality of commodities. While the market of free competition is dominated by the buyer, a monopolistic (oligopolistic) market is dominated by the seller. It is worth noting that both monopolistic and oligopolistic markets may be found in pre-capitalist, capitalist and post-capitalist societies.

The position of economic units within the (free competition) market is characterised by three specific features: (1) economic units make decisions autonomously; (2) they compete with each other; (3) they are dependent on the exchange-value of their production. According to Marxist theory, the terms 'autonomy' or 'autonomous decision-making' should be interpreted as an economic independence or isolation. In other words, every individual economic unit chooses its production of a specific use-value independently of any superior authority except the market. This choice is a private matter of the production unit influenced solely by information coming from the market.

Secondly, once the economic unit has chosen its production pro-gramme, the continuity of its production process depends on the social (market) recognition and acceptance of its use-value. Only after the use-value has been socially recognised can the exchange value be appropriated by the producer and serve as the point of departure for a new phase of the reproduction process.

If one takes the writings of Marx and Engels unhistorically, it may seem that the producer's decision about what is to be produced should always be blind and accidental. Such a belief is not quite correct, however. The producer's decision is blind and accidental only in certain circumstances. More precisely, it is blind and accidental only when economic units produce for an unknown market. This was neither the case of local small producers' markets prevailing in the late stages of feudalism, nor is it the case of contemporary oligopolistic and monopolistic markets. The local pre-capitalist markets were well known to local producers: both the demand and supply were stable for relatively long periods of time. Contemporary oligopolistic and monopolistic markets are not only controlled but even created by big corporations. As a matter of fact, the notion concerning blind and accidental decisions should be applied mainly to the market of free competition prevailing during the lifetime of Marx.

This notion can be examined from yet another point of view. The market may be either absolute or limited. It may be limited by exempting various (economic) activities (e.g. public services and utilities) from the profit criteria. Another kind of market limitation exists when key macroeconomic decisions are made by political means through a social plan while the market allocation applies only to the microeconomic level. Such a limited market relies upon conscious political interference in the economic sphere which either eliminates blind and accidental decisions completely or reduces them to a minimum.

A limited market is usually combined with social planning. Some Marxists still maintain that market and plan are mutually exclusive. They argue that planning is conceivable only within the framework of a single ownership of the means of production. Since a capitalist economy consists of many privately owned economic units, planning may be introduced within each of them but not at the national or social level. According to this concept, the necessary precondition of any social, nation-wide planning is the abolition of private property by virtue of nationalisation of the means of production. Only if the state directly owns and controls the nationalised enterprises could it make them subject to its national planning.

This argument did not pass the test of history. A state, even the liberal state, may interfere not only with the market, but also with privately owned enterprises. Some of the advanced capitalist countries combine the market with long-term central planning (e.g. France) or short-term central planning (e.g. The Netherlands). At least two socialist countries, Yugoslavia and Hungary, combine their social central planning with a limited and regulated market. Even the classical non-market Soviet-type command economic systems consciously use some market elements. It would be rather difficult to find any single system relying either on the *pure* market or on the *pure* planning system.

A combination of the market with a central plan finds its expression in so-called indicative planning. Economic units preserve their autonomous position vis-à-vis the national planning board as well as their right to decide what is to be produced. Production decisions may be influenced either by the producers' knowledge of the market or by the information coming from the central planning board. Economic units are told by the planners that if they want to get a guaranteed return for their investment they should follow governmental guidance. If they accept the social guidance, their decisions still remain autonomous since the planning board has no authority to issue binding orders. On the other hand, the decisions made by the economic units are no longer private since the social guidance has been accepted. This guidance consists of reliable information about both the present and *future* terms of credit, taxation, subsidies, rates of depreciation, etc. Since the reliability of this information is guaranteed by the government, it would be against the interest of economic units not to follow such advice. In the circumstances, economic units behave as commodity producers: they produce for the market and pursue their material advantage. The market, however, is fashioned by the central plan. Since the planning board does not control economic units directly through binding orders but indirectly through its economic policy, the plan does not replace the market; it merely supplies the market mechanism with the social objectives and utilises the market to meet certain social priorities.

A market can not only be limited and/or combined with central (indicative, indirect) planning. It can also be strongly controlled and permanently regulated. Intervention may concern, for instance, price subsidies. Control may concern wages, prices, rents and dividends. Regulation may affect import and export of both commodities and capital. Despite all these limitations, the market does not cease to exist. Though it functions neither spontaneously nor blindly, it is still self-regulating: only some of its regulators (e.g. prices) are regulated by the extra-economic, conscious political decisions.

I have already used the terms 'pre-capitalist' and 'capitalist' market. One may quite legitimately use the term 'socialist market' as well. Almost all types of market described above may be applied to socialist economies: use-value-oriented market; planned market; limited market; controlled and regulated market; oligopolistic or monopolistic market. There is one exception, however: no legitimate socialist system may subscribe to a *laissez-faire* universal market operating within the framework of the private ownership of the means of production.

Two conclusions may be drawn from what has been developed so far: (1) to avoid confusion, the general term 'market' must not be identified with 'capitalist market'; (2) whenever the term 'market' is used in theoretical discussion, the type of market should be specified. Unless stated otherwise, I understand under the general term 'market' an exchange of commodities among autonomous producers.

1.5. MARX'S DILEMMA

Exchange is the core of the market. Unlike other economic relationships among people (e.g. between masters and slaves, lords and serfs), the very essence of exchange is that of *equality* and *equivalence*. Any agent of the exchange must have the right to act in his self-interest; therefore, he must be personally *free*. He must have the right to dispose of his particular commodity, too; therefore, in his capacity as the agent of exchange, he must be *independent* of any superior authority. He is – from the economic point of view – *equal* to his counterpart in the process of the exchange. Though the exchange is carried out by people, their interrelations are quite *impersonal*.

All relations mediated by exchange are horizontal and therefore in opposition to vertical relations based on personal dependence. Within the framework of exchange there is no room for any extra-economic coercion which served as the base for two major pre-capitalist modes of production, slavery and feudalism. Exchange rests on *contract* which, from the formal point of view, presumes voluntary consensus.

All these characteristics of the market have been explicitly recognised by Marx himself. In *Grundrisse* he devoted a long passage to this particular topic:

> Each of the subjects is an exchange; i.e. each has the same social relation towards the other that the other has towards him. As subjects of exchange, their relation is therefore that of *equality*. It is impossible to find any trace of distinction, not to speak of contradiction, between them; not even a difference.[23]

> Therefore, when the economic form, exchange, posits the all-sided equality of its subjects, then the content, the individual as well as the objective material which drives towards the exchange, is *freedom*. Equality and freedom are thus not only respected in exchange based on exchange-values but, also, the exchange of exchange-values is the productive, real basis of all *equality* and *freedom*.[24]

Since money is only the realisation of exchange-value, and since the system of exchange-values has realised itself only in a developed money system, or inversely, the money system can indeed only be the realisation of this system of freedom and equality . . . A worker who buys commodities for 3s. appears to the seller in the same function, in the same equality – in the form of 3s. – as the king who does the same. All distinction between them is extinguished.[25]

Under *capitalist* conditions, however, the market equality of people is rather formal and one-sided. It concerns a mere equality of men as exchangers in the economic sphere and, if reflected in politics, a mere equality of men before the law in the political sphere. It does not concern either the distribution and use of property or the distribution and use of power. Workers selling labour power are only formally equal to capitalists who buy it. In fact, they are unequal as compared with the bourgeoisie: the very existence of the proletariat stems from the fact that this social class is the only one within capitalist society which is denied the right to private property. If proletarians owned the means of production, they would cease to be proletarians and would become private producers. Thus, the denial of private property to the proletariat is a principle which turns market equality into inequality for the working class.[26]

In order to extend the market principle of equality and freedom to *all members* of the society, it would be necessary (1) to create a market consisting exclusively of small producers, and (2) to prevent the development of exchange-value into capital and the development of labour producing exchange-value into wage labour.

These two requirements are both naïve and utopian. At the point when the creation of the universal (capitalist) market has been completed, all the means of production have already been distributed unequally. Any attempt to redistribute them in an equal manner would have been possible only by virtue of revolution. It would have to be a conservative revolution going *back* from the capitalist market (M–C–M') to its rudimentary point of departure (C–M–C).

Let me for a moment assume that this curious revolution has worked out. All producers are equal; there is no use of capital and wage labour. What is present, however, is the market of small private producers (C–M–C). All producers are autonomous and face the same criteria of competition. As a result of the latter, some of them would gain an advantage: those using better land; those applying more productive technology; or simply those who are more able than others. Within a certain period of time, a surplus of exchange-value in the hands of a few would turn into capital while the labour of the non-competitive producers would turn into wage labour. The fact that any market based on private property and left to operate spontaneously leads to sharp social differentiations would inevitably turn the non-capitalist market of small private producers into the capitalist market.

Since any uncontrolled market leads to the gradual concentration of wealth in the hands of a minority while pushing the majority into the ranks of wage labour, it seems to be quite logical to suggest, as *the socialist* remedy, the abolition of the market. But here lies the main problem of the Marxist approach: the abolition of the market is, at the same time, the abolition of the economic base for equality and freedom. Since the market creates an economic structure consisting of the horizontal relations of formal equality, equivalence and freedom, any non-market socially planned economy resting on the division of labour and scarcity would create a structure consisting of vertical relations of personal dependence, superiority and subordination. *Tertium non datur*. Therefore, the concept of a non-market socialist system cannot turn the formal and partial equality and freedom of the capitalist market into real and universal equality and freedom. By abolishing the market without destroying its roots, especially the social division of labour and scarcity, the social foundation of equality and freedom disappears.

This dilemma was not solved by Marx, although he recognised it. On the one hand, he appreciated the causal relation between exchange and freedom. On the other, he knew all the negative effects of the *laissez-faire* market. In particular, he was well aware of the inequality of the proletariat within the framework of the capitalist market. Instead of trying to construct a socialist market, which would eliminate inequality while preserving the general foundation of equality and freedom, he decided in favour of a non-market socialist system. The evils of the capitalist market bothered him much more than the virtues of the market as such.

Marx's philosophical objection against the market ('that the individual has an existence only as producer of exchange-value, hence the whole negation of his natural existence is already implied')[27] is irrelevant as long as man produces within the framework of the social division of labour and scarcity. Even if man's product ceases to be an exchange-value, it will remain, as long as the social division of labour prevails, a product for others. And conversely, the products of other men will become, owing to the same social division of labour, products for him. If this barter is to be equal (and Marx would agree that it should be equal), its distinction from exchange-value would be rather formal and the negation of man's natural existence would be implied as well.

Another of Marx's concepts is of much greater relevance, however. Unlike in his famous *Preface to a Contribution to the Critique of Political Economy* in his *Grundrisse*, he distinguishes not five but only three great social forms:

> Relations of personal dependence (entirely spontaneous at the outset) are the first social forms, in which human productive capacity develops only to a slight extent and at isolated points. Personal independence founded on *objective (sachlicher)* dependence is the second great form, in which a system of general social metabolism, of universal relations, of all-round needs and universal capacities is formed for the first time. Free individuality, based on the universal development of individuals and on their subordination of their communal, social productivity as their social wealth, is the third stage. The second stage creates the conditions for the third.[28]

If one translates this complex language into more simple terms, one would find that Marx tried to characterise three different general qualities of social relationships in the course of the development of history. The first quality is common to all pre-capitalist societies, the second is typical for the capitalist stage of social development and for universal (civil) society, while the third will be characteristic of the post-capitalist (socialist, communist) system. The relationships of personal dependence in the first stage, of objective (*sachlicher*) dependence in the second and of general independence in the third are the three degrees through which mankind progresses from the realm of necessity to the realm of freedom.

Gradualism in liberating the individual from the shackles, first of personal dependence and, later, of objective dependence became the basis of the Marxian non-market concept for the post-capitalist society in which people would shed their dependence on exchange-values and money. Or, in other words,

> Individuals are subsumed under social production; social production exists outside them as their fate; but social production is not subsumed under individuals, manageable by them as their social wealth. There can, therefore, be nothing more erroneous and absurd than to postulate the control by the united individuals of their total production, on the basis of *exchange-value*, of *money*. . . .[29]

Marx suggests that 'the *private* exchange of all products of labour, all activities and all wealth stands in antithesis not only to a distribution based on natural or political superiority and subordination of individuals to one another' – i.e. that exchange is the basis of personal independence, equality and freedom – 'but also to free exchange among individuals who are associated on the basis of common appropriation and control of the means of production'.[30]

Why does an exchange stand in antithesis to free exchange among individuals who are associated on the basis of common appropriation and control of the means of production? Though exchange freed producers from all the forms of personal dependence, it created their objective dependence on exchange-value. The market has destroyed relations of superiority and subordination but is unable to serve as the foundation of equality. First, says Marx, the relations between the worker and the capitalist *within* the factory are still based on an unequal relation of superiority and subordination. Though the very signing of the contract meets all criteria of (formal) equality, the *consummation* of the contract assumes the form of inequality (master-servant relations). Second, the market never functions according to its pure principle of equivalence. On the contrary, it always finds its way through the law of value and, consequently, through the prices oscillating around their essence, i.e. values. Because capitalism tends to create permanent unemployment, labour supply tends to exceed demand for labour. Hence, wages tend to approximate a mere subsistence level. (This is an objective economic tendency which could be reversed by extra-economic means, e.g. through trade unionisation, labour legislation, etc.)

What follows from Marx's logic is this: on the one hand, the market (objective dependence) destroys personal dependence; on the other hand, personal independence is based on objective dependence. Free individuality, according to Marx, could be based only on the universal development of individuals which presupposes the abolition of objective dependence (the market). Marx is not concerned with the fact that by overcoming the *objective dependence* of man through the abolition of the market he at the same time destroys the very foundation of man's *personal independence*. He fails to answer *positively* the question how free individuality may be created and preserved without a preservation of its personal independence which, under the conditions of scarcity, stems from its objective dependence.[31]

Here one is again facing the same dilemma of Marx: without the abolition of the market there is no way to free man from his objective dependence. By abolishing the market there is no way to preserve man's personal independence. Had it not been for Marx believing that the economic base determines (or at least conditions) the political super-structure, one could suggest that personal independence, once estab-lished by the market, is capable of survival despite the fact that its economic foundation had been abolished. However, such a suggestion would be contrary to Marx's method of scholarly analysis as well as his conception concerning the three great social forms:

> The less social power the medium of exchange possesses . . . the greater must be the power of the community which binds the individuals together, the patriarchal relation, the community of antiquity, feudalism and the guild system. Each individual possesses social power in the form of a thing. *Rob the thing of this social power and you must give it to persons* to exercise over persons.[32]

If there is only the alternative between personal dependence and objective dependence, then everyone must make a choice. The in-capability of a social scientist to identify with either of these two possibilities had led and must lead to utopia.[33] Marx himself decided in favour of utopia. His synthesis rests on the following assumption: *at the moment when the division of labour and scarcity die out*, the commodity production with market relations would die out as well while the independent (autonomous) position of producers as the foundation of their personal independence, equality and freedom could be preserved.

While this proposition is very appealing as a long-term humanistic and rather utopian objective, it does not offer a realistic programme either for the period following the socialist revolution or for the entire lower phase of communism. Since it is quite obvious that a mere abolition of private property cannot bring the division of labour and scarcity to an end, any attempt to eliminate the market must, under the circumstances, be based on the abolition of the independent (auto-nomous) position of the producers. *While such an artificial abolition of the market destroys the very foundation of personal independence, it cannot eliminate the objective dependence.* To prove this proposition, I must re-examine the Marxian concept of direct allocation of resources and direct distribution of social wealth.

2 Marx's Non-Market Model of Socialism

2.1. INDIVIDUAL LABOUR AS IMMEDIATELY AND DIRECTLY SOCIAL LABOUR

From the theoretical point of view, Marx's concept of direct allocation (non-market model of socialism) has at least two shortcomings. The first consists in the assumption that the mere collectivisation (socialisation, nationalisation) of the means of production makes the concrete labour of each individual *a priori* social labour. Says Marx:

> Within the co-operative society based on common ownership of the means of production, the producers do not exchange their products; just as little does the labour employed on the product appear here *as the value* of these products, as a material quality possessed by them, since now, in contrast to capitalist society, individual labour no longer exists in an indirect fashion but directly as a component part of the total labour.[1]

Engels is even more explicit:

> From the moment when society enters into possession of the means of production and uses them in direct association for production, the labour of each individual, however varied its specifically useful character may be, is *immediately and directly social labour*.[2]

Neither Marx nor Engels assume, in the above quotations, that division of labour and scarcity have been superseded. The only thing assumed is a supersession of an autonomous position of both the individual producers and the economic units. To understand the ease with which Marx and Engels arrived at their conclusion, I have to follow Marx's logical construction aimed at a *formal* solution of the problem:

25

Further, the division of labour also implies the contradiction between the interest of separate individuals or the individual family and the common interest of all individuals who have intercourse with one another. And indeed, this common interest does not exist merely in the imagination, as the 'general interest', but first of all in reality, as the mutual interdependence of the individuals among whom the labour is divided . . . . Just because individuals seek *only* their particular interest which for them does not coincide with their common interest the latter is asserted as an interest 'alien' ('*fremd*') to them and 'independent' of them, as in its turn a particular and distinctive 'general' interest; or they themselves must remain within this discord, as in democracy. On the other hand, too, the *practical* struggle of these particular interests, which *actually* constantly run counter to the common and illusory common interests, necessitates *practical* intervention and restraint by the illusory 'general' interest in the form of the state.[3]

In a market system, says Marx, the individuals are connected only very loosely with each other. Therefore, their labour is posited as general labour only through exchange. To be posited from the outset as a link in general production, another assumption has to be accepted, namely the communal (rather than private) character of production determined by communal needs and communal purposes:

In the first case, which proceeds from the independent production of individuals . . . mediation takes place through the exchange of commodities, through exchange-value and through money; all these are expressions of one and the same relation. In the second case, the *presupposition is itself mediated*; i.e. a communal production, communality, is presupposed as the basis of production. The labour of the individual is posited from the outset as social labour. Thus, whatever the particular material form of the product he creates or helps to create, what he has bought with his labour, is not a specific and particular product, but rather a specific share of the communal production. He therefore has no particular product to exchange. His product *is not an exchange-value*. The product does not first have to be transposed into a particular form in order to attain a general character for the individual. Instead of a division of labour, such as is necessarily created with the exchange of exchange-values, there would take place an organisation of labour whose consequence would be the participation of the individual in communal consumption.[4]

These lengthy quotations are indispensable for an understanding of Marx's logic. In no other place did Marx reveal his reasoning for the non-market arrangements so explicitly: the division of labour denoting specialisation of producers is now called an *organisation* of labour; the social character of labour previously established only *ex post* through the market exchange is now *presupposed* and, therefore, established *ex ante* through communal planning. What is needed, suggests Marx, is not a real supersession of the social division of labour but rather an elimination of the producers' mutual independence and autonomy, a substitution of the *community*-type organisation of labour for the previous *society*-type division of labour.

The proposition that individual labour becomes directly social labour is not acceptable for at least three reasons:

(i) As long as scarcity prevails, a necessity remains to exchange various use-values according to their production costs and to distribute the common wealth among the people according to their work. Since the mere nationalisation of the means of production is unable to eliminate divergences between the individual and the social productiveness of labour, there must exist quantitative differences between the socially necessary labour and individual labours. If the society cares for a rational use of scarce (limited) resources, it should permanently compare all individual labours with the socially necessary labour. This is the first reason why Marx's and Engels' suggestion that every individual labour is directly social labour does not hold either theoretically or empirically.

(ii) A use-value produced in a nationalised enterprise according to a social plan may not satisfy either the social or individual needs simply because of its unacceptably low quality which turns it into spoilage and, consequently, into a non-product. This is the second reason which makes the theory of the *a priori* social character of concrete labour in a socialist society unworkable.

(iii) The use-values are produced in accordance with the social plan. There is no guarantee, however, that the production proportions set by social planners reflect the proportions of the demand. Hence, every redundant use-value fails to be directly recognised as social labour.

Owing to the social division of labour and scarcity, the permanent contradiction between individual and social labour does exist even in fully nationalised and centrally planned economies. Since this contradiction testifies to the presence of commodity production, all hitherto known socialist societies have had to recognise, sooner or later, that the objective basis for the production of commodities has not yet been eliminated. Moreover, since the contradiction between individual and social labour could be solved only through the (market) exchange, it was necessary to build into all the non-market command socialist economies a substitute which would simulate the market mechanism. To supply the theoretical arguments with empirical evidence, I have chosen the Soviet case of the credit reform in 1930:

> The incorrect concept of the planned forms of relations which need no intermediary levers of stimulation led in the past more than once to unhappy consequences. The credit reform of 1930 can serve as an illustration. It was carried out according to the following principle: All enterprises were to deliver their products to other enterprises according to a plan and, in return, were to receive automatically and again according to a plan, money from the State Bank regardless of what was the buyer's attitude to their production . . . . As a result, most enterprises began to fulfil their plans only in a formal manner. The consumers had no way of influencing the suppliers. The State Bank was expending enormous sums of money for low-quality production which was *below the value* shown in the vouchers submitted to the bank. There was a danger that the circulation of money would be seriously disturbed. The Communist Party . . . pointed to the necessity of abandoning the planned automatism in credit-making, of introducing *contractual* relationships among enterprises and of subjecting the enterprises to the *khozrashchot* system, i.e. the principle of paying their expenses out of the yield of their production. It proved necessary that the enterprises be reimbursed not according to what the plan had provided for but according to what they actually produced, actually *realised (sold)*.[5]

Since, within the framework of the social division of labour and scarcity, the concept of direct allocation of resources and direct distribution of products cannot work either rationally or efficiently, intermediary levers, i.e. a market exchange or a kind of simulation of it (e.g. the *khozrashchot*), must be introduced. Under these circumstances, *men as producers cannot be freed from their objective dependence, i.e. from their dependence on exchange-value.* Whether the exchange-value be determined by the market or by the plan is of little importance. What matters is the fact that the socially necessary labour must be determined in quantitative terms and all economic units should adjust the productivity of their individual labour to social requirements. If they fail to do so they cannot obtain from society the full equivalent for their products. Provided their individual productivity is lower than the social average, they could obtain only the equivalent *less* the difference between the social productivity and their individual productivity. Thus, their objective dependence on exchange-value remains.

Within the framework of the distribution according to work, 'the same principle prevails as in the exchange of commodity-equivalents: a given amount of labour in one form is exchanged for an equal amount of labour in another form . . . This *equal right* is an unequal right for unequal labour. It recognises no class differences, because everyone is only a worker as is everyone else; but it tacitly recognises unequal individual endowment and thus productive capacity as natural privileges. *It is, therefore, a right of inequality, in its content, like every right.* Right by its very nature can consist only in the application of an equal standard . . . Right can never be higher than the economic structure of society . . . .'[6] This quote from the famous chapter of Marx's *Critique of the Gotha Programme* deals with the position of man as an individual in the lower stage of communist society in which the market has already been abolished and 'individual labour no longer exists in an indirect fashion but directly as a component part of the total labour.' One can see, however, that the mere abolition of private property and the market did not contribute much to the supersession of man's objective dependence. To make the desired supersession of objective dependence real, it would be necessary to overcome 'the enslaving subordination of the individual to the division of labour and therewith also the antithesis between mental and physical labour; labour should become not only a means of life but life's prime want; the productive forces should increase with the all-round development of the individual'[7] – in short, it would be necessary to overcome, in a positve way, both the social division of labour and scarcity.

At this point, one may ask a quite legitimate question: why did both Marx and Engels believe that the abolition of private property could eliminate the production of commodities and therewith also the market? The reason behind this belief may be found in *Das Kapital*: 'Only such products can become commodities with regard to each other, as result from different kinds of labour, each kind being carried on *independently* and for the account of *private* individuals.'[8]

On the one hand, the independence (autonomy) of producers is here rightly recognised. On the other hand, the existence of commodities is linked to *private* individuals whose autonomous position stems from private property. The causal connection of an autonomy of producers with private property is both a methodological and a theoretical error. It is a methodological error because it adds to one of the necessary preconditions of the market (autonomy of producers) its historically transient and therefore unnecessary form (private property). It is a theoretical error since the essence of the phenomenon (autonomy of producers) is not distinguished from the phenomenon's appearance (private property).[9]

2.2. CONFUSION OF DIFFERENT TYPES OF THE DIVISION OF LABOUR

The second shortcoming of Marx's concept of direct allocation and distribution consists in identifying the division of labour within society with that within production units (enterprises). Paradoxically enough, it was Marx who recognised, at one point, a distinction between the social division of labour in general, in particular and in detail. By quoting from F. Skarbek's *Théorie des richesses sociales*, he fully accepted Skarbek's concept of the division of labour between agriculture, industries, etc., as *general*, the splitting-up of these sectors into species and subspecies as *particular* and, finally, the division of labour within the workshop as *singular* or *detail*.[10] He was mainly interested, however, in one aspect of the distinction: whether it causes commodity production or not. 'But what is it that forms the bond between the independent labours of the cattle-breeder, the tanner and the shoemaker?' he asks on one occasion. 'It is the fact that their respective products are commodities. What, on the other hand, characterises division of labour in manufactures? The fact that the *detail labourer produces no commodities. It is only the common product of all the detail labourers that becomes a commodity.*'[11] This is what makes it possible to overcome commodity production and therefore the market relations within the factory. By analogy, if the society as a whole were organised as one production unit subject to the single state ownership of property, it would be possible to overcome commodity production and therefore the market relations within the society-wide factory.

This conclusion could hardly be correct. What distinguishes a single autonomous economic unit from another is that each unit specialises in one end-product which enters the market. If all single economic units turn into workshops of the nation-wide trust, each of them, no doubt, loses its former autonomous position vis-à-vis the central management but retains, first, its autonomous position vis-à-vis all other economic units and, second, its production of specialised and, therefore, distinct end-products. Since each workshop works within the framework of the social division of labour in particular and in general, it produces not for itself but for an exchange. A mere organisational change of the management of a national economy (the creation of one nation-wide trust) cannot turn the division of labour in general and in particular into the division of labour in detail. While the division of labour *in detail* remains within each workshop, the division of labour among workshops and branches retains its nature as *particular* and *general* respectively. If the activity of workshops is to retain any meaning, then the individual workshops must mutually exchange their goods. Some kind of exchange cannot be avoided.

When people work in order to make a living, and when the economic units in which they work must form an organisationally unified entity from the point of view of the production aim, it is necessary, for both the worker's individual output and the collective output of the economic unit, that they receive a material incentive. Those who create the wealth of society must be economically compelled to work (if the society decides in favour of an extra-economic compulsion, then it ceases to be an 'association of free producers') because their labour is neither free nor life's prime want but merely a labour in detail which has a meaning only as a sum total of the work of the collective producers making the final use-value.

Thus, when there are technologically separate economic units specialising in the production of various use-values; when there are producers who work under the pressure of necessity, i.e. in order to obtain the means of their livelihood through their labour; when the *technologically* conditioned division of labour in particular and in general does not cease to exist even within the nation-wide syndicate; then there exist the typical conditions of commodity production and market exchange.[12] If a fundamental economic balance is to be maintained under these circumstances, if the principle of distribution according to each individual's labour is to be applied, if there is to be an orderly exchange of human activities, it is necessary that the economic relations among economic units be mediated through the market since it is not the individual but the economic unit which appears as the producer of the use-value which is made not for itself but for others. In this connection, the very existence of two qualitatively different relationships – those within the society reflecting the division of labour in general and in particular, and those within each economic unit reflecting the division of labour in detail – causes quite different social effects.

Each economic unit concentrates on the production of a final use-value. The division of labour within the economic unit is a division of labour in detail, its product being a single use-value. The participants in this division of labour are interested in this use-value being (a) socially necessary, i.e. it should find someone who needs it; (b) exchangeable, i.e. acceptable to the customer in terms of its price; and (c) that its production costs should be as low as possible while the price obtained for it should be as high as possible. In the conditions of market equilibrium, the difference between the production costs and the price depends on the economic unit's productivity of labour.

Thus, the specific interest of the economic unit is expressed as follows. The economic unit as the producer of certain use-values depends on their realisation (sale). This interest of the economic unit is entirely different from the interest of all other economic units and cannot be identified with them. True, there are different groups of people working within the economic unit with different (and even conflicting) individual or group interests but, however different their particular interests may be, the interest in the prosperity of the economic unit is common to all these individuals and groups. Moreover, none of them can assert or satisfy his particular interest in any other way than through the interest of the economic unit. As long as he is an employee of the economic unit, most of his material goals can be achieved only through the realisation of the enterprise's interest.

Even if one abolishes the market and establishes the nation-wide factory with economic units as its workshops, each workshop remains an organisationally differentiated and technologically separate unit *whose specific interest remains the same*: to obtain an equivalent for its products. If this interest is disturbed or abolished, the economic unit loses interest in producing, its output will decline, the quality of its work will deteriorate and the economic unit will cease to prosper along with its employees.

Why, then, was it believed that as soon as economic units are nationalised and become workshops of a single nation-wide factory, a universal harmony of interests would be created? This belief was based on the following logical construction: since all economic units would be in the hands of a single owner, and directed according to a single plan, they would not have to engage in a competitive struggle; therefore, a unity of interests similar to that within an enterprise would prevail within the 'society-wide' plant. This error was caused, above all, by the fact that differences in interests were being deduced solely from the *forms* of ownership of property rather than from the position of people (and economic units) in the social division of labour. Within nationalised property there are many types of conflicts of interests, stemming not only from the different specialisation of people and from their position on the social ladder, but also from their age, sex, place of residence and dozens of other factors. Where such conflicts of interest exist within an economic unit they may be overcome by the *specific enterprise interest*. Conversely, the common material interest of society is unable to offset these conflicts since the state cannot simultaneously give a preferential treatment to all branches or to all the enterprises within a branch. This results in a sharp struggle of interests among enterprises (workshops of the nation-wide plant) and branches for investment, wage and bonus fund allocation, for priority deliveries of raw materials, for assignments of new machinery, for lower plan targets, for a more advantageous assortment plan, etc.

The second difference between the division of labour within society and within an economic unit is this: the quantitative proportions which are subject to intra-enterprise planning are conditioned mostly by technology and by the organisation of labour while the quantitative proportions of the society-wide planning are conditioned by the changing interests and needs of people, by the structure of their demand, by their individual and group preferences and dozens of other factors. While the intra-enterprise plan dealing with products is a matter of arithmetic, the social plan dealing with people is also a matter of politics, psychology and sociology. While enterprise planning is an instrument of production, social planning should be a means of satisfying human needs. The principles of direct intra-enterprise management and planning cannot be successfully applied to the whole of society.

To sum up, neither a legal measure (e.g. nationalisation) nor the concept of a nation-wide plant can eliminate the division of labour in general and in particular. No legal, political or organisational change is able to abolish the social division of labour or to turn the division of labour within society into that within the enterprise. As long as the *social* division of labour and scarcity prevail, it would scarcely be possible to eliminate exchange of products in accordance with the principle of equivalence and, therefore, it would also scarcely be possible to overcome man's objective dependence on exchange-value.

2.3. CONFLICTS BETWEEN SOCIAL CAPITAL AND LABOUR

If the non-market concept is applied consistently, then the only alternative source of information for the economic units must be the central plan. It should provide the economic units at least with the following set of information:

1. What they are required to produce.
2. What should be the quality, quantity and the assortment of their prescribed output.
3. What should be the maximum tolerated costs of their production, including wages and salaries.
4. What is the minimum acceptable level of the productivity of labour in every economic unit.
5. By whom the unit will be supplied and what will be the terms of its co-operation with the suppliers.
6. To whom, and for what price, the unit's output will be sold.

The very nature of this minimum information suggests that the social plan has to be worked out in *one centre* and its targets must be *binding* on all economic units. This also suggests that centralism is an inevitable price which must always be paid for the abolition of the market without the prior eradication of its preconditions.

The inevitability of centralism in the non-market socialist system seriously challenges the Marxian proposition that after the expropriators have been expropriated, contradictions and conflicts between labour and capital would disappear. What kind of conflicts did Marx have in mind?

In terms of the value-composition of a commodity, Marx distinguishes between (1) constant capital (c) which represents the value of the means of production, (2) variable capital (v) which represents the value of the labour power, and (3) surplus-value (s) which is produced exclusively by v and fully appropriated by capitalists. Since the value of a commodity consists of $c + v + s$, then, *ceteris paribus*, the larger the v the smaller the s, and vice versa. Thus, the interest of labour in the maximisation of v (wages) and the interest of capital in the maximisation of s (profits) are mutually exclusive. If the proletariat gains, the bourgeoisie loses. If capital gains, labour must lose.

While the fund of wages (v) is spent by the workers for consumer goods and services, the fund of surplus-value (s) is divided into two parts (for the sake of simplicity, I leave aside the division of surplus-value into profit, interest and ground-rent): the first part is consumed by the capitalists as revenue, the second part is used as capital, i.e. it is accumulated. *Ceteris paribus*, the larger one of these parts is, the smaller is the other. If capital as property and capital as a productive function are represented by the same person, the conflict between revenue and accumulation would be resolved by a deliberate act of every individual capitalist. If the two functions of capital are separated from each other (e.g. in joint-stock companies), the picture might change. Those who personify the title to income (shareholders) could be primarily interested in revenue while those who personify the functioning capital (corporate executives) are primarily concerned with accumulation. Under the circumstances, the interest of the *owners* of capital in revenue may conflict with the interest of the *administrators* of capital in accumulation.

While the conflict between v and s reflects the cleavage between the vital economic interests of wage labour and capital, the conflict between revenue and accumulation reflects the separation of capital as a property from capital as a productive function. Each of these two distinct conflicts is modified in the non-market socialist system.

To begin with, nationalisation of the means of production abolishes capital as private property and, consequently, as a title to private revenue. On the one hand, it disentitles the former owners of the means of production to their unearned income, but it does not entitle either individual toilers or the whole of associated producers to any unearned income. On the other hand, the expropriation of private property cannot abolish capital as a productive function. While capital disappears as a title to the appropriation of ground-rent, interest and profit, it does not disappear as a sum total of the social means of production employed in the process of social production. Since social capital has to serve economic growth, innovation and modernisation, a part of the social surplus-product has to be regularly accumulated and invested.

Unlike in capitalist society, the producers as a whole are now also owners of the social capital. Being both producers and owners, they are supposed to be interested in the simultaneous maximisation of v and s. Since this is impossible (*ceteris paribus*, the larger one of these parts of national income ($v + s$) is, the smaller is the other), they cannot avoid a permanent conflict of interests stemming from their twofold socio-economic position. If they pursue their current individual consumption, they decide for a higher share of the social fund of wages (v) in the national income ($v + s$). If they pursue current collective consumption, they decide for the allocation of a higher share of s to public and social services at the expense of accumulation or individual consumption. And finally, if they pursue a *future* consumption, they decide for a reduction in their current living standards by increasing the share of s in $v + s$ and/or by allocating a higher share of s to the social fund of accumulation at the expense of public and social services.

But is it really the producers who make these decisions? As far as non-market socialist systems are concerned, their centralised structure requires that all basic economic decisions be made at the top of the social hierarchy. Because the producers are dispersed, of technological necessity, in economic units without direct access to the top decision-making, the basic division of labour between those who rule, control, plan and manage, and between those who are ruled, controlled, planned and managed, cannot but remain in existence despite the nationalisation of the means of production. From the functional point of view, it is irrelevant who has a formal title to property; *what is relevant is who disposes of it, who decides on it, who manipulates it, in whose interest one makes decisions and in whose interest controlling functions are exercised.* Since property as a title has been *de facto* abolished so that everybody is formally both an owner and non-owner of the means of production, the interests stemming from the property title are negligible while the interests stemming from the social division of labour are dominant. Which of them are formulated, defended and promoted by the ruling group? Those which correspond to its position in the social division of labour, those which bolster and perpetuate that position. Since the power elite exercises solely the *controlling* functions, it is naturally in its interest to consolidate that monopoly position which, in other societies, is a position of the propertied class. In a society based on hierarchical command economic rule (if the economic structure is reflected by the political superstructure, the same command rule prevails also in politics), the ruling class cannot be the workers reduced, as they are by the social division of labour, to carry out *directed* functions. As the ruling class, the workers must be substituted for by a group of administrators, managers and planners, in short by bureaucrats.

Being deprived of *direct* decision-making, the workers (producers) remain interested merely in good working conditions and maximum wages. Since their interest in maximum wages (individual consumption) or in maximum fringe benefits and social services (collective social consumption) is contrary to the interest in maximum accumulation represented by the ruling group, the basic conflict between v and s does not disappear.

Why is it that the administrators of the social capital are keenly interested in accumulation? The very fact that they are administrators of accumulated labour (capital) gives them social power. Since their power is directly proportionate to the magnitude of social capital, their interest in extended accumulation is equal to their interest in extended power.

However, economic power is tied to political power; they cannot be separated – particularly not on the highest (central) level. Since the economy is part of the state, political power is a prerequisite of economic power. Since political organs simultaneously exercise the function of supreme economic management, economic power has merged with political power. Since economic power is exercised by state organs, top economic managers hold at the same time top political positions. In a non-market system, cause and effect behave exactly according to the Hegelian precept: they constantly change places with each other.

One may conclude that a non-market socialist system, based on centralised economic management and state control of the means of production, can eliminate neither economic conflicts between (social) labour and (social) capital, nor can it eliminate political conflicts between the respective representatives of consumption and accumulation.

2.4. NON-MARKET SOCIALIST SYSTEM AND ALIENATION

According to Marx, the externalisation and alienation of labour stemming from market relations is due to the fact that the producer is not interested in the use-value but only in the exchange-value of his product. How much can this situation change in the conditions of the non-market system with the central plan whose information (targets, indicators) is binding on economic units?

Even in the non-market system, the producers continue to be interested in the amount of their wages, i.e. in exchange-value. Though their material interest does not depend on whether their product finds a customer who will buy it on the market for the satisfaction of his needs, it does depend on their fulfilling the plan targets. If, in a market society, the producers' interest in the exchange-value was mediated through the use-value, now their interest in the exchange-value is mediated through the plan targets. The producers do not work directly in order to produce use-values, but they work for entirely abstract and, in themselves, irrational plan targets. If Marx saw alienation of man from his work in the substitution of concrete labour by an abstract wage-earning activity, how would he view a situation in which the substitution of abstract activity for concrete labour persists and, on top of that, another intermediary has been interposed in the form of plan targets? In fact, nothing has changed for the better. The worker still works under the pressure of external necessity. He continues to be a *detail worker*. His labour continues to have a meaning for him only as an abstract wage-earning activity. If, in the capitalist market system, his wage (exchange-value of his essential needs) was directly tied to the exchange-value of his product; now it is tied to it through several plan targets. If, in the previous system, his work was alienated from him because he produced not directly for consumption but for the market, it is now alienated from him because he produces not directly for consumption but for the plan. A *factual* overcoming of the externalisation and alienation of labour is out of the question because, except for the fact that the plan was interposed between production and consumption, the essence of alienation has remained the same. While the mediation between production and consumption has been preserved, one intermediary (the market) has been replaced by another (the plan). The difference, then, is purely formal. But from the practical point of view, and thus also from the point of view of the producer's personal feelings, this new intermediary is less perfect. In a market economy, the producers are guided by the effective demand which expresses the needs of the consumers; in a non-market economy, they are guided by the plan targets which express consumers' needs only very roughly and inaccurately. This is caused by the fact that the direct feedback between production and consumption (market) has been abolished. Under the circumstances, the central planning board should obtain all relevant information concerning the real consumer demand by a roundabout way. This information does not go directly to the producers. It goes to the planning board and, after having been summarised, it is sent to the producers in the form of plan targets. Because this information is not direct but mediated, it cannot reach the producers on time. Because this information assumes the artificial form of targets, it fails to supply the producers with such subtleties as quality, fashion, taste, measures and assortment of the needed consumer goods.

This deficiency of the plan has one important effect which has been dealt with in detail elsewhere.[13] Since every working man is simultaneously both a producer and a consumer, his economic essence is split in two parts; as a producer he reacts through his material interest in the targets of the plan, while as a consumer he tries to satisfy his material needs and interests through his effective demand. He obtains his wages for meeting the plan targets and he wants to exchange his labour income for the use-values he needs. For the reasons mentioned above, his demand for the desired use-values cannot be entirely identical with the sum of the fulfilled plan targets. Therefore, a part of his effective demand remains temporarily or permanently unsatisfied. Whether abolished or existing only formally, the market ceases to be a source of relevant information for the producers. That is why any consumer's attempt to promote his needs through effective demand is as irrational as Don Quixote's tilting against windmills. The situation is totally absurd: man works, fulfils the plan targets, gets his wages, but is unable to use a part of his earned income to get what he needs. Owing to the logic of the non-market system, he is forced to behave as a schizophrenic: his material interest as a producer is tied to the plan targets. His interest as a consumer can be spelled out only through effective demand. If, as a producer, he meets the effective demand expressed by himself as a consumer, he would behave against his interest as a producer. If, as a producer, he does not meet the effective demand expressed by himself as a consumer, he would behave against his interest as a consumer and live in permanent frustration. Under the circumstances there is no way out. The market alienation of his labour not only has not been overcome or even lessened but, on the contrary, it has been augmented by another specific alienation created by the non-market system, *the alienation of man from his wages.*

Since the real structure of society (social division of labour and scarcity) differs from its organisation and institutional forms (direct allocation and distribution), the blind natural law of value finds its way of operating spontaneously in the form of a black market. The black market is always present in any society which has prevented the official market from performing its active function of regulating proportions and replaced it by non-economic priorities which are either contrary to, or at least not in accord with, the structure of the effective demand. In such a situation, a kind of imbalance between production and consumption is inevitable. The Soviet economist Lev Kritsman dealt with this problem as early as 1924 in his then famous book *The Heroic Period of the Great Russian Revolution.*[14] Himself an advocate of a non-market model of socialism, Kritsman admits that the planned economy in kind contains some elements of anarchy as long as it is made up of separate technological and production units and as long as there is scarcity. The separateness of economic units creates different and often conflicting producers' interests and preferences which are at variance with the interests, priorities and preferences of those who centrally allocate resources. Unless the central planning board simulates the market by setting parametric prices which reflect relations between demand and supply, the demand is unlimited while the supply is rather limited. As a result, economic units can never obtain all that they need in required proportions, qualities and quantities. This fact, argues Kritsman, must necessarily lead to a shortage of products.

Kritsman compares socialist central planning in kind with capitalist market economy and concludes that while capitalism suffers from over-production, non-market socialism has to suffer from under-production. In capitalism, surpluses are accumulated in the hands of producers who cannot find buyers. In non-market socialism, the surpluses are accumulated in the hands of those who are supposed to use final products. If the user obtains everything he needs, except one single component, he cannot either start production or use the final product. It is the past labour embodied in such unused products which remains idle and unemployed in non-market socialism as compared with the idle live labour in capitalism. While capitalist crises are caused by over-production, says Kritsman, socialist crises are caused by short supply.

Kritsman's theory holds only in a strict non-market model. Once the regular market is deliberately abolished, a peculiar black market develops within the sphere of production. This black market assumes such specific forms as personal political influence of the managers of economic units who use their connections to get all they need on a priority basis at the expense of other applicants. Another form of this black market is doing unplanned favours for one another. If a manager is able to arrange the delivery of some short-supply items in exchange for the delivery of other short-supply items, he can obtain everything he needs. Another weapon of this black market is bribery. While it is officially impossible to pay a higher price for an item in short supply, it is possible to bribe those officials who are able to deliver, on a priority basis, the materials or products on which the fulfilment of the plan, and thus also the level of wages and bonuses for employees, depends.

When the demand for consumer goods and services exceeds the supply, the employees of the state trade outlets hold back the goods which are in short supply and sell them only to those customers who are willing to offer them either a bribe or a favour in return. In the first instance, the black market creates an informally fixed scale of illegal surcharges on top of the official prices which are paid to the salesperson or to the store manager; in the second instance, society reverts to the ancient times of total or expanded form of value (barter) when goods were exchanged for other goods (money did not yet exist) with all the difficulties which this form of exchange carries with it. If the customer is interested in a use-value which is in short supply, he must offer the seller another use-value which is in equally short supply. This use-value need not be a product, it may be a service: arranging for the seller's child to be admitted to a university, speeding up the processing of his application at a government office, etc. In such cases, money plays only a secondary role; it is taken for granted as the purchase price of the product or service which is in short supply but it means very little compared to the extra favour which becomes a part of the deal.

Only the ruling group may be spared everyday worries caused by a short supply of goods and services. Within this rather narrow circle of people, both the market and scarcity have already been overcome. This provides high officials with a feeling of satisfaction over the state of affairs and confirms the theoretical dogma that market and money alienation could be easily defeated by central command planning. The rank-and-file producers are, of necessity, in a different position. They are not thinking about overcoming the alienation of market and money. They are thinking about how to overcome privately the difficulties placed in their way by the social command planning. There is an obvious solution in the form of the black market and of moonlighting. The goods and services which cannot be obtained through the official institutions of socialist economy, set up for that purpose, can be obtained through the employees of these institutions at their own profit and by their individual action. Either directly during business hours, or after hours, these employees provide short-supply goods or services for a special reward to those who need them. Mass bribery, pilfering, stealing from one another and moonlighting are inevitably present in non-market economies and create, under the cover of the official institutions, an entirely different but very real parallel structure.

The economic consequences of this reality are extremely far-reaching. Bribery, pilfering, stealing and moonlighting result in a redistribution of the national income and in a thorough change of the planned structure of the effective demand. The process goes on stealthily, behind the back of the official planning, and the organs of the state have no control over it. The unplanned redistribution of incomes through the black market creates an entirely different structure of effective demand which cannot be estimated *ex ante* by the planners operating with official, state-controlled scales of wages and salaries, retirement payments or social security benefits. This is why each subsequent plan contains, in its targets, new disproportions which are then overcome by a further expansion of the black market, moonlighting, bribery, and a further wave of unofficial redistribution of the national income.

Another aspect of this redistribution of the national income concerns the material balances. The services provided outside of the official plan depend on the materials and spare parts which must be made available to the moonlighters. The only source of these materials and parts are the store-rooms of the socialist enterprises from which these material values flow through dozens of invisible channels into the black market of services. The actual material balances of socialist enterprises thus differ markedly from the planned material balances, since in addition to their being distributed according to the plan, they are also distributed according to the 'natural' law of value, i.e. of the (black) market. The disproportions in the actual material balances prevent the fulfilment of the actual planned tasks which causes new disproportions in the subsequent planned period.

The third characteristic feature of these spontaneous processes is the change in the reproduction of the labour power. If unplanned services are provided during business hours, which is possible particularly in the maintenance enterprises of the housing and communal economy, the presumed fund of working hours provided for in the plan obviously differs from the actual fund of working hours which is determined in some industries by the black market. But even if these services are provided after hours or on weekends, the actual fund of working hours decreases contrary to the plan. If workers or craftsmen spend several hours a day (or a dozen hours over the weekend) on private orders, in addition to their regular working time, their output in their official employment must necessarily decline.

All these changes proceeding behind the backs of the planning bodies undermine the credibility of the plan targets and push the plan to an irrational level. If the non-market system behaves consistently to its doctrine, it would have to react to all these essentially *economic* phenomena by *non-economic* measures: by further efforts at centralisation, by expanding the control apparatus, by strengthening the plan and by trying to eliminate the black market by administrative means. All these measures are inadequate since they are aimed at suppressing the *effects* rather than eliminating their *causes*. Such a practice is very dangerous. If the state aims its campaigns against all that weakens the discipline of the plan, against all that is aimed at satisfying the unplanned human needs and interests by labelling them as anti-social or even anti-socialist, then the producers would naturally ask who is at fault: is it they, or is it the non-market system? Since no one is likely to find anything wrong in his effort to satisfy his own needs, one must begin to look for the faults in the very system. Thus, the producers gradually become alienated from the non-market system as a whole.

It may be objected that, in such a system, the producers are at least no longer alienated from their product which now belongs not to the capitalists but to the entire society. Formally, it should be so. But the producers, owing to the centralised nature of the non-market system, are deprived of the disposal of their product. Since they are deprived of direct participation in economic decision-making they have no say either in decisions about the social fund of consumption or the social fund of accumulation or about their structure. Under the circumstances, they cannot but feel alienated from their product which is under the control of the administrators of social capital. While all the old forms of worker's alienation from his labour and from his product have not disappeared, new specific forms of alienation of the worker from his wage, from the plan and from the entire system have been brought about by the non-market concept of socialism.

2.5. LIMITS OF COMMAND PLANNING

The essence of command planning and direct control of a non-market economy from one centre consists in a planning board which conveys all necessary information to the directed units in the form of a mandatory directive whereby it deprives the subordinated units of independent decision-making. If the central decisions are to be correct and their implementation speedy and purposeful, the directing centre must first obtain a considerable amount of information from all prospective consumers (a summary of needs) as well as from all producers (a summary of productive capacities), process it and, having made a specific decision concerning priorities, send a part of the information in the form of binding targets to the subordinated unit which is then expected to implement the decision.

If one assumes (and that is the case of the intra-enterprise management) that direct control would not be disturbed by outside influences and therefore operates in a more or less an ideal manner, it could be efficient and effective. It would proceed approximately as follows. The directing centre receives the necessary amount of unbiased and reliable data. It processes the data and makes an evaluation which results in the optimum decision. It then conveys its decision to the directed unit in the form of a directive accompanied by an explanation as to the manner in which it is desired that the directive be implemented.

However, what is valid for intra-enterprise management may not necessarily be valid for the control of society. Disturbing influences are at work here, particularly the already mentioned conflict between the interests of the directing centre and those of the subordinated unit. For if the interests of the directed unit are not identical with those of the centre, the directed unit tries to communicate to the centre only such data as will influence the central decision in the direction of the unit's particular interests (e.g. to obtain a lower, less demanding plan, new investments, new workers, etc.). It may distort some of the data or present them in a different context. Thus the directing centre receives either insufficient data to make the optimum decision or incorrect data preventing it from making its decision with a full knowledge of the actual state of affairs.

When the centre has made its decision, it conveys the pertinent information to the subordinated unit in the form of a directive. If the directive is to be implemented according to the intent of the directing centre, it must be formulated quite unequivocally, and the explanation accompanying it must not allow for any deviation from the intent of the decision-making body. It can be assumed that the directed unit will try, in interpreting the directive, to assert its own interest and to interpret the meaning of the directive in a manner which it finds most suitable. It can also be assumed that the directed units will try to foist on the centre the data which will influence the solution to their advantage while the centre will try to convey to the directed units directives which unequivocally express only the interest of the centre.

If the central directive is not identical with, or if it is even contrary to, the interests of the directed unit, the latter (and this is confirmed by the practice of all the countries in which the command system of economic planning prevails) will do all it can either not to implement the directive or to interpret it in its own way, in its own interests. The centre tries to prevent this possibility by providing every directive with accompanying sanctions. If the sanctions are to be effective, they must be very harsh: as long as the negative consequences of the non-fulfilment of the directive do not outweight the positive result gained by the directed unit from disobeying the directive, the orders will not be implemented. But if the directives are not implemented, direct control loses its meaning. There are, hence, only two realistic alternatives: either the atmosphere of harsh sanctions and of fear is created, or the imperative control not accompanied by drastic sanctions is ineffective.

Though theoretically conceivable, the third alternative suggested by romantic revolutionaries is scarcely realistic. It consists of an assumption that the directed units will disregard their particular interests owing to a high degree of class revolutionary consciousness of their managers and employees. A long and complex history of command socialist planning in various countries does not offer any single evidence that such an assumption holds under normal peacetime circumstances. It may hold only in time of emergency (e.g. during a war) when an outside threat sets internal conflicts of interests aside.

In 1920 a Viennese economist, Ludwig von Mises, published his famous article[15] which launched an international discussion on economic calculation in socialist economic systems. Von Mises suggested that economic calculation was impossible in a system which had abolished the market. Since there is no capital market, Mises argued, there is no way to express the monetary value of the means of production (prices) in the sense of exchange ratios and, therefore, there is no index of alternatives available in the sphere of capital goods. Since an objective price structure providing for an impartial criterion is a *sine qua non* for any rational economic decision-making, a non-market economic system cannot behave rationally. While von Mises doubted the very theoretical possibility of economic calculation in the non-market economic system, other economists[16] were more cautious. They did not deny the theoretical possibility of a rational allocation of resources in a socialist economy but doubted its practical applicability. In a strictly formal manner, a solution of the problem had been offered by Enrico Barone[17] as early as 1908. Barone suggested that economic equilibrium might be solved in a socialist system by the same method of trial and error as in a capitalist system, but he failed to show how it could be arranged. It was only F. M. Taylor[18] who first indicated how the problem (i.e. who uses the trial-and-error method and how) could be solved, and Oscar Lange[19] who elaborated on Taylor's suggestion and made of it an economic theory of socialism. Lange based his theory on two assumptions: if there is (1) a competitive market of consumers' goods and (2) free choice of occupation and work-place, the central planning board can set so-called parametric prices by the trial-and-error method.[20]

Even without the real market of capital goods, the planners can determine the 'right' accounting prices in a similar manner as the 'right' market prices are determined by virtue of competition under capitalism. The planners will simply watch the quantities demanded and the quantities supplied and raise prices whenever there is an excess of demand over supply as well as lowering prices whenever the reverse is the case until, by trial and error, the price is found at which demand and supply are in balance.

Without going into a detailed examination of the discussion, I would wish to make two remarks. First, all the participants of the discussion accepted a rather dubious assumption that socialism cannot but abolish the market of capital goods. Second, the suggested solution of the problem is a quasi-market solution: the planning board simulates the market rather than behaving according to the logic of the non-market system. True, Lange has admitted that the procedure of trial and error is applicable also to a socialist system which *does not* meet his two assumptions (a competitive market of consumer goods and free choice of occupation), i.e. even if the central planning board arbitrarily decides which use-values are to be produced and in what quantities, how consumers' goods are to be rationed and how various occupations are to be filled by assignment, but he did not fail to add:

> By demonstrating the economic consistency and workability of a socialist economy with free choice neither in consumption nor in occupation, but directed rather by a preference scale imposed by the bureaucrats in the Central Planning Board, we do not mean, of course, to recommend such a system. Mr Lerner has sufficiently shown the undemocratic character of such a system and its incompatibility with the ideals of the socialist movement. Such a system would scarcely be tolerated by any civilised people.[21]

Of course, command non-market socialism *is* possible both in theory and in practice. In a strictly theoretical sense, it can even be rational *if* the preferences of the central planners coincided with the preferences of the producers, of the consumers and of the productive units. But even if such a coincidence were possible, the command market system would be, by definition, undemocratic and therefore unacceptable for any democratic socialist theory.

If as Lange has shown, the non-market system cannot be democratic and efficient without the central planning board simulating the market, one relevant question arises: why suppress the market mechanism just to replace it by a substitute? Being fully aware that no analogy is perfect, I cannot resist the temptation to offer the following one. To keep the temperature stable in a huge building, two basic alternatives are possible. The first would use thermostats installed in every room which keep the temperature at the desired level. The second would employ hundreds of people watching thermometers in every room and maintaining a stable temperature by opening and closing windows. The first alternative is more efficient and more economical; it also frees people from performing tedious functions which could be trusted to a mechanical device. Indeed, there is no rational reason for simulating a self-regulating mechanism by a less perfect performance by human beings.

If I compare one self-regulating mechanism (the thermostat) with another (the market), I can see no substantial difference provided that the market (a regulator) is not *laissez-faire* but is in turn regulated by the plan. Even if I assumed that the central planning board succeeded in eliminating all possible conflicts between the interests of the directed units and those of the society, absorbed all data and simulated the non-existing market perfectly, the following situation would occur. The directed unit conveys to the centre all available data, truthful, objective and accurate. The directing centre makes an optimum decision, transmits a clear and unequivocal directive to the directed unit, and the latter implements the directive willingly, accurately and speedily, since it is in its own interest to do so. If this postulated situation were realised, would it not be simpler for the directed unit to make decisions itself? Its interest would be identical with that of the directing centre, the same data would be available to it, and the unit should be ready and willing to do whatever the central body was doing in its stead. Why, then, the needless transmission of data from the bottom to the top, and vice versa?

The objection is sufficiently logical to form a basis for suggesting a system of *indirect central control*. The essence of such a system is that the directing centre does not determine either what the directed units have to do or what they must not do, but adjusts the conditions of their activity so that they make decisions independently, in their own interest and in a manner which is also in the eminent interest of society. One instrument of indirect control would be generally binding rules which must be adhered to by the directed units but within which the units are free to make their decisions. Indirect control assumes that the behaviour of the directed units is purposeful (goal-oriented).

But how to establish the rules for the activity of the directed units in a manner that makes it possible for the centre to regulate their behaviour indirectly? Generally speaking, the centre must acquaint itself with the basic interests of the directed units and establish the rules for their decision-making so that any decision aimed at satisfying the particular interests of the directed units is in accord with the overall aim of society. The result will be a 'strengthening of control', i.e. the directed units will act of their own will and in their own interest in a manner required by the directing centre.

If one conceives of a national economy as a goal-oriented (cybernetic) system, it should have not only its own self-regulator (the market). Since a national economy is a unity of production, distribution, exchange and consumption, it should also have feedback between its basic components, i.e. between production and consumption. If one agrees with Marx that production is (productive) consumption, that consumption is the (re)production (of man), and that exchange consists not merely of exchange of commodities but also of exchange of economic activities, then there has to be a feedback providing for a steady flow of information between production and consumption as well as within each of these two big components of social economy.

Although it would be foolish not to agree with Marx's suggestion that the market, as an *exclusive* regulator of economic processes, fails to maintain equilibrium and stimulate steady economic growth, it has been shown that, if the market is wholly eliminated and replaced in all its functions by the central plan, there is scarcely a *practical* possibility of rational economic calculation. Consequently, the mere abolition of the market is not a sufficient precondition for a more efficient functioning of socialist economic systems as compared with capitalist ones. That is why the traditional Marxian concept of direct allocation and distribution as the *exclusive* and *obligatory* socialist alternative to the market cannot be accepted. The plan may and should be used as a political tool for promoting preferential social values, for interfering with the objective-less, spontaneous and impersonal market mechanism, for controlling, regulating and taming it, for shaping the market according to societal priorities and for eliminating it from non-economic sectors, but never for replacing the market as *the* economic self-regulator. While the plan could and should be powerful and superior to the market, it should not become omnipotent; while it should serve as the means to an end, it should not become the end itself.

2.6. REAL OR FORMAL ECONOMIC LIBERATION OF MAN?

If my analysis in this chapter is correct, why then was Marx so preoccupied with the abolition of commodity production, the market and the law of value immediately after the socialist revolution? In addition to his moral prejudice towards the market as well as his philosophic and economic condemnation of the market, the answer lies in Marx's concept of freedom in the economic sphere. On many occasions both Marx and Engels indicated that as long as man is an *economic* being, he cannot be freed at all. The most authoritative statement concerning this concept was made on the last pages of the third volume of Marx's key work, *Das Kapital*:

> In fact, the realm of freedom actually begins only where labour which is determined by necessity and mundane considerations ceases; thus in the very nature of things it lies beyond the sphere of actual material production. Just as the savage must wrestle with Nature to satisfy his wants, to maintain and reproduce life, so must civilised man, and he must do so in all social formations and under all possible modes of production. With his development this realm of physical necessity expands as a result of his wants; but at the same time, the forces of production which satisfy these wants also increase. Freedom in this field can only consist in socialised man, the associated producers, rationally regulating their interchange with Nature, bringing it under their common control instead of being ruled by it as by the blind forces of Nature; and achieving this with the least expenditure of energy and under conditions most favourable to, and worthy of, their human nature. But it nonetheless still remains a realm of necessity. Beyond it begins the development of human energy which is an end itself, the true realm of freedom which, however, can blossom forth only with the realm of necessity as its basis. The shortening of the working day is its basic prerequisite.[22]

This somewhat pessimistic conclusion might be avoided if one interprets the common control of man's interchange with Nature not as mere social planning but in a different manner. The possibility of a new interpretation is indicated first of all in the above-quoted paragraph. Common control of production processes 'most favourable to, and worthy of, human nature' might simply mean that the society is able to introduce automation of the entire industrial production by 'a technological application of science'.[23] If so, then the old industrial division of labour would actually disappear and men would be freed from labour as an objectified activity. The realm of necessity (material production) would still remain the basis for the realm of freedom without using people as detail labourers by employing them mainly in the capacity of social planners and controllers of the production process. Although this work might still be called 'objectified' labour, it could be proportionally distributed among all the associated producers and the working day, week, month, year could be shortened to an insignificant minimum.

The key to this interpretation rests on the twofold meaning of the term 'appropriation'. Appropriation may be simply understood as mere aquisitiveness; it may also be understood, however, as the opposite to alienation.* Let me compare the term as used by Marx in its two different meanings:

> All the preceding classes that got the upper hand, sought to fortify their already acquired status by subjecting society at large to their conditions of *appropriation*. The proletarians cannot become masters of the productive forces of society, except by abolishing their own previous mode of *appropriation*, and thereby, also every other previous mode of *appropriation*.[24]

This mere appropriation of the means of production by the proletariat is but the first, easiest step towards communism. It is but a *legal* negation of private property, an 'expropriation of expropriators' rather than the *real appropriation*[25] of the totality of productive forces by the proletariat. A mere nationalisation (appropriation of the means of production by all in an acquisitive or expropriative sense) may introduce nothing more than a crude communism which is a negation of the bourgeois society rather than its positive overcoming. It is a rather strange communism, however:

> It [communism] wishes to eliminate talent, etc., by force. Immediate physical possession seems to it the unique goal of life and existence. The role of *worker* is not abolished but extended to all men. The relation of private property remains the relation of the community to the world of things . . . . This communism, which negates the *personality* of man in every sphere, is only the logical expression of

---

*To make this distinction more clear, the following analogy may be used. One may appropriate a painting simply by purchasing it in order to possess it. This kind of appropriation will not help one to understand the painting, to enjoy the creativeness of the artist, to become enriched by taking in the unique qualities of the piece of art and to improve one's receptiveness to creative art. One possesses the painting without having actually appropriated it. On the other hand, in order to appropriate the painting in the latter interpretation of the term, one need not possess it, one may simply enjoy its beauty through sensitively perceiving it, understanding it, and thus generally appropriating it.

private property which is this negation. Universal *envy* setting itself up as a power is only a camouflaged form of cupidity which re-establishes itself and satisfies itself in a different way. The thoughts of every individual private property owner are *at least* directed against any *wealthier* private property owner, in the form of envy and the desire to reduce everything to a common level; so that this envy and levelling in fact constitute the essence of competition. Crude communism is only the culmination of such envy and levelling-down on the basis of a *preconceived* minimum. How little this abolition of private property represents a genuine appropriation is shown by the abstract negation of the whole world of culture and civilisation, and the regression to the *unnatural* simplicity of the poor and wantless individual who has not only not surpassed private property but has not yet even attained to it.[26]

Thus, the mere negation of private property, and the mere abolition of the market without overcoming scarcity and social division of labour, introduces crude communism which is far from 'the real *appropriation of human* nature through and for man'.[27] The crudeness of this kind of communism stems from its immature conditions. Scarcity requires a restrictive distribution of wealth not only in terms of material consumption but particularly in terms of letting people freely develop their talents and faculties. The history of medieval social utopias has shown that any communist idea based on scarcity must necessarily lead, both in theory and in practice, to a barrack egalitarianism, as well as to the dominance of an 'average' interest of an 'average' man. Scarcity further requires that resources be allocated according to a few priorities which always means that some interests of some social groups have to be left unsatisfied. The restrictive allocation cannot be carried out without a suppression of minority interests. (One may add 'at best'; at the worst, even the majority interests may be suppressed.) Such a communism must, of necessity, make an individual wholly subservient to the society, deprive him of a choice and put collective priorities above his particular ones.

Moreover, the social division of labour based on both technical specialisation and social distinctions between those who control and those who are controlled would last until men appropriate and master their own general productive force and until there is no need for using coercion in order to make people conform with the given state of affairs. Since this crude communism can hardly be efficient enough to develop general productive forces to the extent sufficient for supersession of scarcity as well as abolition of the old division of labour, the two basic preconditions of the market would be perpetuated rather than gradually overcome by a dynamic and innovative development.

It might be argued that, despite its drawbacks and limitations, crude communism is a necessary and unavoidable transitory stage between capitalism and communism. If accepted, this argument would suggest that people have no alternative for creating a post-capitalist system in which they are to work and live, that they are predestined by a fatal necessity (or by Marx's aversion for the market). I have already noted that Marx, while proposing the abolition of the market without overcoming its material causes, indicated some if not all of the negative effects of the non-market solution, namely that the social power of money must be given to persons to be exercised over persons. To make this point more clear, let me return to Marx's condemnation of money.

In the *Third Paris Manuscript*, Marx makes a distinction between effective demand supported by money, and ineffective demand not supported by money. He sees the difference as that between *being* and *thought*. 'If I have no money for travel I have no *need* – that is, no real and realisable need – to travel', says Marx.[28] Would this situation change if the market were eliminated *without* the supersession of scarcity? It would not and could not. Even in a socialist non-market system based on scarcity, travelling would be out of the question for those who cannot afford this expensive kind of human activity. Since incomes are now determined by the planners, only those who were found meritorious enough would be allowed to have the real need for travel. Moreover, since they have lost – as producers – their formerly autonomous position, not only the level of their income but also the structure of their consumption would now depend on those who decide, on behalf of the society as a whole, which personal needs coincide with the social priorities. The position of an individual would become even worse: in addition to money, he would even have to get permission to travel. As long as society is subject to all kinds of restrictions dictated by scarcity, there is no escape from people's dependence on money. Because this dependence is now accompanied by the loss of personal independence, the individual does not gain anything while having been deprived of a choice.

In the same *Third Manuscript* Marx writes, 'The extent of the power of money is the extent of my power.' Alternatively, one may suggest that, under a different set of circumstances, the terms office, rank position, etc., may substitute for money: the extent of the power of my office is the extent of my power. When Marx says, 'I am bad, dishonest, unscrupulous, stupid; but money is honoured, and hence its possessor' one may alternatively say: I am bad, dishonest, unscrupulous, stupid; but the office is honoured and hence its possessor. When Marx says, 'I am *brainless* but money is the *real* brain of all things and how then should its possessor be brainless?' one may say alternatively: I am brainless but the office is the real brain of all things and how then should its possessor be brainless?[29] etc., etc.

Office (position, rank, etc.) may be substituted for money, and vice versa. At one point, as I have already noted, Marx admits it: 'Rob the thing of this social power and you must give it to persons to exercise over persons.'[30] It turns out that, under certain social conditions, money and direct power stemming from office, position, etc., are not only mutually substitutive but also complement each other. On the one hand, those who possess money may also use it to get the power of office. On the other hand, those who hold the power of office may also use it to get money. Hence, it is possible to combine indirect power of money with direct power of office. However, if one analyses indirect power of money and direct power of office as alternative systemic arrangements, there is a great difference between them. To begin with, the power of money would appear as horizontal, as a chain of exchanges. Certainly, I can buy for my money whatever I desire *provided* there is a seller who would be willing to accept my terms of the contract. Conversely, the direct power of office would appear as vertical (hierarchical), as a chain of orders going from the top down. I may get whatever I wish because I am able to enforce my will whenever my orders are not respected. Hence, while the power of money is not enforceable, the power of office is enforceable.

Secondly, even people dominated by the social power of money may preserve a degree of choice. If I need a job to make my living I must sell my labour power. But I have a choice to whom I sell it, under which terms, in which region or country, for which period of time, etc. However, if I am compelled to work by an extra-economic coercion resting upon the power which gives to an authority a chance to force me to work at its pleasure, my choice vanishes. Then I become a mere object of an external domination and manipulation stemming from the loss of personal independence. Needless to say, my position would be qualitatively different within the two sets of circumstances.

Thirdly, one has to distinguish clearly between two kinds of the power of money. If money is used as mere money, it gives to its holder *personal* power; if money is used as capital, it gives to its holder *social* power over other people's labour and product. Money which cannot be used as capital by individuals – and this is the case of socialist market systems – cannot give individuals any social power either. Hence, if every individual obtains from the socialist society a monetary equivalent for his contribution to labour output, he disposes of a certain amount of money which is freely exchangeable for various products and services. Since people have different tastes and needs,[31] their incomes would be spent in a different manner. For instance, those who prefer travel to fashion would save on clothing while those preferring fashion to travel would save on travel. If consumer goods and services are distributed through the market exchange, a choice for each individual would be preserved. In a strictly non-market economy, a preference scale of the planners would be imposed upon individuals. While scarce goods and services are distributed by virtue of prices in the market system, they would have to be distributed by virtue of privilege in a non-market system. The free consumption choice would vanish.

Both money and office represent a privilege. In saying this, however, one has to be aware of a difference between the two privileges. The privilege of money is more democratic than the privilege of office provided that (i) the sum of money at one's disposal is determined by the principle of equal pay for equal work, and (ii) all unearned incomes have been eliminated. Limited though your amount of money may be, as the possessor of a given sum of money you are equal to all who possess the same sum of money irrespective of whether or not they hold office. Unlike the office-holders, the individuals possessing more money than you have no social power over you. In these circumstances, there is no rational socialist argument against the use of money for distribution of scarce goods and services. If you have at your disposal a certain sum of money you are not necessarily either less privileged than, or dependent on, someone having at his disposal a bigger sum of money.

I may conclude that it is scarcity which gives power to money, and that it is scarcity and the division of labour which give power to offices. If one is freed from the power of money and put under the power of office instead, then, obviously, one's unfreedom has not been superseded. At best, one type of domination has been substituted for another. Thus, Marx's concept of the economic liberation of man offers only a formal rather than a real solution. What is more, of the two kinds of domination, the power of money – in view of the above restricting assumptions applied to the market model of socialism – is more conducive to man's economic freedom than the power of office.

This conclusion brings me back to the old problem: is it ever possible

to free men from any economic domination? Marx says that such a
possibility exists, provided:

> The worker no longer inserts transformed natural objects as in-
> termediaries between the material and himself; he now inserts the
> natural process that he has transformed into an industrial one
> between himself and inorganic nature, over which *he has achieved*
> *mastery*. He is no longer the principal agent of the production
> process: *he exists alongside it.* In this transformation, what appears as
> the mainstay of production and wealth is neither the immediate
> labour performed by the worker, nor the time that he works – but *the*
> *appropriation by man of his own general productive force, his under-*
> *standing of nature and the mastery of it; in a word, the development of*
> *the social individual.*[32]

It is at this point that Marx uses the term 'appropriation' as the
opposite of 'alienation', i.e. not in the sense of economics but in the
strictly philosophical sense. Only if men exist *alongside* material
production could they become immediately and directly social individuals and, therefore, any mediation of money or office would be
superfluous and unnecessary. It is at this point only that both the market
(economic unfreedom) and the state (political unfreedom) should and
could wither away, die out, since their very foundation has definitely
been undermined: neither scarcity nor social division of labour exists
anymore.

Marx's picture of the communist society is quite different from that of
crude communism:

> As soon as labour, in its direct form, has ceased to be the main source
> of wealth, then labour time ceases, and must cease, to be its standard
> measurement, and thus exchange value must cease to be the
> measurement of use value. The surplus labour of the masses has
> ceased to be a condition for the development of wealth in general; in
> the same way the non-labour of the few has ceased to be a condition
> for the development of the general powers of the human mind.
> Production based on exchange value, therefore, falls apart, and the
> immediate process of material production finds itself stripped of its
> impoverished, antagonistic form. Individuals are then in a position to
> develop freely. It is no longer a question of reducing the necessary
> labour time in order to create surplus labour, but of reducing the
> necessary labour of society to a minimum. The counterpart of this

reduction is that all members of society can develop their education in
the arts, sciences, etc., thanks to the free time and means available to
all.[33]

It is, however, a long way from crude communism to *the* communism.
If Marx's perception of *the* communist society is to be something more
than a utopian dream, then communism should be both historically and
logically derived from a more democratic and efficient socialist structure
than that which was critically discussed above. Prior to offering an
alternative to Marx's model of socialism, however, I have first to
analyse Marx's *political* concept of a post-capitalist system.

3 Marx's Concept of Political Liberation of Man

3.1. THE THEORY OF THE STATE

Contrary to the widespread belief that Marx's political theory is just a reflection of his economic theory, it combines at least three basic approaches to politics: economic, sociological and political. Marx's *economic* approach to politics consists in his famous concept of base and superstructure, the base being the economic structure of society and the superstructure being an ensemble of politics, law, ideology, culture, etc. Marx's *sociological* approach to politics is based on his concept of the social division of labour and of classes. And finally, Marx's *political* approach to politics stems from his concept of politics as the *power* reflecting and regulating conflicts in civil society.

Without discussing Marx's (and Engels') political theory in detail, I must briefly examine their theory of the state before I can turn to those aspects of Marxian political teaching most relevant to the political liberation of man. Marx's concept of the state consists of four basic components:

1. The state is a *coercive* organisation, or an organised coercion, used by the ruling class for the oppression of another (exploited) class.
2. The state is a *political* organisation of society, a class rule, a result of irreconcilable class conflicts.
3. The state is a mechanism of *social co-operation* in which both the rulers and the ruled have some common interests.
4. The state means the *government machine*, a special organism separated from the civil society through the social division of labour.

According to Marx and Engels, every state has its (class) content and its (government) form. In terms of the content, every state is *the dictatorship of the ruling class*. Should bourgeois state be a democratic republic, a fascist tyranny or a constitutional monarchy, it makes no difference from the point of view of its class content. While particular governmental forms do matter for all practical purposes, they do not matter at all for those concerned merely with the essence of the state.

To be a member of the ruling class does not mean that one has to hold a governmental position. It is enough that the personal power of individual class members is, at the same time, also their social power. With private ownership of the estate, a medieval nobleman acquired power over his serfs; with private ownership of capital, a capitalist acquires power over his employees. A manufacturer or a banker are members of the *ruling* class not because they hold legislative or executive positions in the bourgeois state, but because they make decisions which have a social impact on the lives of hundreds and thousands of people. They participate, in their capacity as capitalists, in the economic control of society. Since the economic power of the ruling class is a precondition for its political power, every member of the ruling class takes part in the total power exercised by the class as a whole.

Second, the state is a political organisation of society.[1] As such, it rests on class rule. (If there were no need for class political rule, there would be no need for the existence of the state.)[2] Political power as the essence of politics meant for Marx, interchangeably, either the expression of class conflicts within bourgeois society (*The Poverty of Philosophy*), or of class antagonism in civil society (ibid.), or of class oppression (*The Communist Manifesto*). Consequently, politics is applied to civil society only. Marx did not accentuate enough the fact that political conflicts may reflect not only (antagonistic) class conflicts, but also conflicts *within* a social class or, yet more important, within a *classless* society. For instance, there may be a conflict between industry, agriculture and services, between various industrial branches, etc. There may also be conflicts concerning ethical values (e.g. abortion, capital punishment, etc.). These conflicts have little to do with class structure and class oppression: they may occur in any society. Marx's and Engels' perception of politics was too schematic, too narrow and too class-oriented. For one thing, politics reflects not only class conflicts but all the conflicts of interest between major social groups. Second, politics reflects not only the conflicts which stem from economics but also those stemming from politics itself (e.g. competition for influence or power between different segments of the ruling class or between different social classes and groups), from conflicting ethical values or ideological concepts. Contrary to Marx's and Engels' belief, it is therefore very unlikely that 'the public power will lose its political character'[3] even after the supersession of class distinctions.

Third, the state is always a kind of social co-operation. People living on the same territory and performing different social functions are mutually interdependent. Whether divided into antagonistic (or co-operative) social classes or not, in so far as they live in a given state, they are interested in its smooth functioning. For that matter, the state is a goal-oriented entity with the general interest confronted with thousands of particular and individual interests produced by civil society. It is not as Marx believed an *imaginary* general interest only. Even if it is formulated by the ruling class, it ought to be acceptable, or at least tolerable, for the oppressed class. Irrespective of whether the general interest is shared by the antagonistic classes equally or unequally, neither of them could satisfy its particular interests outside the co-operation. Consequently, if the state fails to satisfy the basic needs of the oppressed classes, or does not respond to their basic interests, it could not properly function and, eventually, would cease to satisfy even the interests of the ruling class. This is why no ruling class can ignore, without a possible punishment of revolution, the basic needs and interests of the oppressed classes, why it cannot afford not to incorporate them, at least partly, in the general interest represented by the state. People's mutual interdependence cannot but create their common interest in the stability of the co-operation. Any oppressed class has rather limited alternatives: either it destroys the existing social order and frees itself from oppression, or it tries to get better treatment within the old system. If there is no chance for revolutionary change, the oppressed class should be interested in the stability of the old society. This is why the ruling class has to present its specific class interest as the general interest and its specific class ideology as the universal ideology.[4]

It is in this connection that the state has to be represented, on an increasing scale, by a special group of people who have chosen the administration of public affairs as their life profession. This group consists of professional politicians and bureaucrats. In democratic societies the professional politicians represent not only the ruling class but also the oppressed classes. The representatives of the oppressed classes have the choice: either they aim at the revolutionary change which would make the hitherto oppressed class a ruling class, or they try to improve the lot of their class-brothers within the old society. In some cases they may combine both alternatives. The representatives of the ruling class also have the choice: either they yield to the demands of the oppressed classes by introducing social, economic and political reforms, or they defend the *status quo*. If they decide on the former alternative, they serve the long-term interest of their class. If they decide on the latter, they unknowingly expedite the coming of social revolution.

Provided there is a balance of power between the rulers and the ruled, the state could become relatively independent from the competing classes and strengthen the autonomy of the government machinery. Says Engels: 'By way of exception . . . periods occur in which the warring classes balance each other so nearly that the state power, as ostensible mediator, acquires for the moment, a certain degree of independence of both.'[5] What Engels sees as an exception is becoming more and more a rule. It would be in accord with Marx's own methodology if one draws an analogy from the economic sphere. 'All labour in which many individuals co-operate requires a commanding will to co-ordinate and unify the process.'[6] This is a function of economic management, supervision and planning. Under certain circumstances, this function is performed by those who own the means of production, e.g. by the capitalists. Under a different set of circumstances, capital as a function may be separated from its ownership. If so, one could reasonably expect that the owners of capital retain control over the managers. But if capital is dispersed in stock companies, the shareholders may lose their control over the board of directors and corporate executives. As the owners are primarily interested in their dividends (in their short-term class interest), the executives should be and ought to be interested in the long-term prosperity of the corporation. If one substitutes professional politicians for the boards of directors, bureacracy for the corporate executives and the ruling class for the shareholders, the relations between the ruling class and the bourgeois state would become much more transparent.

One must not forget that Marx and Engels had lived in England during its liberal but still pre-democratic era. Marx was quite right in saying that the working class was not a part of civil society. Without universal suffrage there was no chance for a balance between the political influence of the bourgeoisie and that of the proletariat. Marx and Engels even suggested that the proletariat had no country. Before the proletariat won its battle to become incorporated into civil society, this could have been so. However, this has changed with the gradual democratisation of liberal systems.* In his essay *On the Jewish Question*, Marx admits that while political emancipation 'is not the final form of human emancipation in general . . . it is the final form of human emancipation *within* the hitherto world order'.[7] Marx was also aware of some other implications of universal suffrage. He agreed with Thomas Hamilton that universal suffrage meant the *political* supersession of private property: 'Is not private property abolished in idea if the non-property owner has become the legislator for the property owner? The *property qualification* for the suffrage is the last *political* form of giving recognition to private property.'[8]

It may be argued that my interpretation of the Marxian theory of the state does not follow the letter of Marxism. Some may even doubt if it reflects the spirit of Marxism. I do not hide my intention to revise some of Marx's and Engels' propositions and to adjust them to the needs of democratic socialism. It will be seen later that Marx's theory suffers much more from its author's methodological inconsistencies than from imaginary cleavages between the young and the old Marx. It was not only Lenin who changed the spirit of Marxism: some elements of Leninism are present in the original Marxist theory. It is not by chance that prevailing contemporary interpretations of Marx's teaching stress his class concept of the state rather than his concept of the state as a co-operative social organisation. The latter, containing the notion of the state as 'an organisation which tried to hold in equilibrium the economic inequalities', has had a long tradition among the Marxists which goes back to Antonio Labriola.[9] It is likely that the machinery of the bourgeois state would balance economic inequalities along the lines of the capitalistic social structure. After all, the bourgeois state is a product of bourgeois society whose stability and durability are equally dear both to the bourgeoisie and the government machinery. Unlike the bourgeoisie, however, the professional bourgeois politicians and the bureaucrats approach the state of public affairs more impartially: they value balanced powers and political stability much more than short-term economic gains. The bureaucrats are aware of their specific interests which conflict, both in the short and the long term, with those of the bourgeoisie. What is more, 'The bureaucracy has the state, the spiritual essence of society, in its possession, as its *private property*.'[10]

---

*When the French and German social democratic parties voted for the war credits in their respective parliaments in 1914, Lenin blamed them for having betrayed their international duties. He overlooked, however, that at the time both the French and German proletariat had become part of the French and German civil societies respectively.

Under certain circumstances (state capitalism), the bourgeoisie as a ruling class may be survived by the bourgeois state. It is not difficult to imagine the state run by the corporate technocracy and the state bureaucracy, each of them strongly devoted to their respective hierarchies and closed organisations. Certainly, the bureaucracy has lived and will live as a *functional* ruling class much longer than any propertied ruling class, the bourgeoisie included. This is why the bureaucracy is not eager to identify absolutely with any class provided that the power of the two basic social classes (e.g. capital and labour) is balanced. The process of the growing independence of the state machinery from the ruling class goes hand in hand with the growing independence of the corporate technocracy from the formal owners of capital. Thus, the state is being gradually transformed into a relatively independent machinery alienated and separated from the civil society. In other words, the state is becoming what it has always pretended to be.

But how to apply Marx's theory of the state to a post-capitalist society? What will happen to the state after victorious socialist revolutions? (I continue with a theoretical examination of Marx's and Engels' concept and not with an analysis of the existing post-capitalist states.) The answer seems to be readily found in the concepts of the dictatorship of the proletariat and that of the withering away of the state. Everyone who merely follows the letter of Marxism might suggest that these two concepts are rather clear and consistent: After the seizure of political power, the proletariat establishes its class dictatorship whose basic aim is to build a classless society. With this task accomplished, the state begins to die out, to wither away. Eventually it will be substituted by a community in which political power is dissolved in economics and power over people has been replaced by the administration of things. However, the picture is not as clear as Marx and Engels would have liked to believe.

The first difficulty rests with the very term 'the dictatorship of the proletariat'. To my knowledge, it was used by Marx no more than five times: in 1850 in *The Class Struggles in France* ('. . . the class dictatorship of the proletariat as the inevitable transit point to the abolition of class differences generally . . .');[11] in Marx's famous letter to J. Weydemeyer of 5 March 1852 ('. . . that the class struggle leads to the dictatorship of the proletariat . . .');[12] in 1875 in *The Critique of the Gotha Program*, which was published only in 1890–1 ('Between capitalist and communist society lies the period of the revolutionary transformation of the one into the other. Corresponding to this is also a political transition period in which the state can be nothing but the *revolutionary dictatorship* of the proletariat.');[13] in a declaration signed by K. Marx, F. Engels, G. Julian Henry, August Willich and Adam J. Vidill;[14] and in the speech on the Seventh Anniversary of the International on 25 September 1871 in London.[15]

Of the terms used on the five different occasions, I prefer the first one, namely 'the *class* dictatorship of the proletariat'. For one thing, Marx and Engels conceived of every state as the dictatorship of the ruling *class* and not as the dictatorship of the government. (Incidentally, Marx and Engels were never preoccupied with government *forms*.) At this point I should recall that in *The Communist Manifesto* Marx and Engels said that 'the first step in the revolution by the working class is to raise the proletariat to the position of ruling class, to win the battle for democracy'.[16] This would correspond to the hypothesis that the authors of the *Manifesto* were concerned primarily with the *content* rather than with the *form* of a post-revolution state.[17] Consequently, one knows at least one thing for sure: whatever the form of the immediate post-revolution state, its rule should have a strict class character.

But what about the form? One ought not to be mistaken by the ending of the quotation from the *Communist Manifesto*, i.e. *to win the battle for democracy*. Democracy, as Marx might very well have known, meant no more or no less than rule by the majority, by the many (as compared to aristocracy as rule by the few, and to monarchy as rule by the one). Since Marx and Engels were certain that, at the time of socialist revolution, the proletariat would be in the majority, this very notion of democracy merely suggests that the dictatorship of the proletariat is to be rule *of* the majority, *by* the majority and *for* the majority.

Although I do not know any explicit statement by Marx on what the dictatorship of the proletariat ought to be in terms of the government form, I may try to reconstruct an approximate picture of a post-socialist revolution state in the context of his other ideas.

It is known that Marx positively assessed political emancipation of man, universal suffrage and the right to representation and association. Knowing that these three principles are simultaneously basic articles of the liberal faith, one may speculate that Marx would not reject them. Incidentally, in the mid-nineteenth century, only the most conservative and reactionary people were against liberal freedoms. It would therefore have been very unlikely if a socialist, indeed the socialist aiming at the liberation of man from any kind of unfreedom, preferred the dictatorship of the government to a kind of democratic system. This hypothesis seems to be in accord with an optimistic Engels' assertion that 'each step forward in civilisation was a step towards free-

dom . . .',[18] with both the historical setting and the humanistic
background of Marx's 'scientific socialism' as well as with Engels'
explicit statement in his comments on the draft of the Erfurt Programme
in 1891: 'If one thing is certain it is that our Party and the working class
can only come to power under the form of the democratic republic. This
is even the specific form for the dictatorship of the proletariat, as the
great French revolution has already shown . . . .'[19]

Karl Kautsky, a recognised authority on the Second International,
shared Engels' view in his book *The Dictatorship of the Proletariat*
(1918) by conceiving of the dictatorship of the proletariat as a system in
which broad masses of people participate in the political process
through universal suffrage as well as through such civil liberties as
freedom of speech and freedom of association. Rosa Luxemburg, a
representative of a revolutionary and yet democratic wing of European
Marxism, was always the foremost advocate of a democratic interpretation of the ambiguous Marxian concept of the dictatorship of
the proletariat: 'Yes, dictatorship! But this dictatorship consists in the
manner of applying democracy, not in its elimination . . . .'[20] She really
meant what she said. For her, the dictatorship of the proletariat was by
definition 'a dictatorship of the class, not of a party or of a clique –
dictatorship of the class, that means in the broadest public form on the
basis of the most active, unlimited participation of the mass of the
people, of unlimited democracy'.[21] She even went as far as any liberal
would go: 'Freedom only for the supporters of the government, only for
the members of one party – however numerous they may be – is no
freedom at all. Freedom is always and exclusively freedom for the one
who thinks differently.'[22]

It was only Lenin who quite explicitly rejected the traditional
incorporation of basic (liberal) political freedoms in the Marxist
concept of the dictatorship of the proletariat (Lenin's revision is
discussed in the next chapter), and it was Stalin who praised him for it:

The Marxist-Leninist theory is not dogma but a guide to action.
Before the second Russian revolution (February 1917), the Marxists
of all countries assumed that the parliamentary democratic republic
was the most suitable form of society in the period of transition from
capitalism to Socialism. It is true that in the seventies Marx stated
that the most suitable form for the dictatorship of the proletariat was
a political organisation of the type of the Paris Commune, and not the
Parliamentary republic. But, unfortunately, Marx did not develop
this proposition any further in his writings and it was committed to

oblivion. Moreover, Engels' authoritative statement . . . [cf. note 19] . . . later became a guiding principle for all Marxists . . . . As a result of a study of the experience of the two Russian revolutions, Lenin, on the basis of the theory of Marxism, arrived at the conclusion that the best political form for the dictatorship of the proletariat was not a parliamentary democratic republic, but a republic of Soviets . . . . The opportunists of all countries clung to the parliamentary republic and accused Lenin of departing from Marxism and destroying democracy. But it was Lenin, of course, who was the real Marxist who had mastered the theory of Marxism, and not the opportunists, for Lenin was advancing the Marxist theory by enriching it with new experience, whereas the opportunists were dragging it back and transforming one of its propositions into a dogma.[23]

Despite the authoritative form of his statement, Stalin was wrong. First, he ascribed to Engels what Engels never said. While Engels was talking about a *democratic* republic, Stalin quoted him as if he had said *parliamentary* republic. Second, Stalin ascribed to Marx what had been actually said by Engels. Marx never equated the Paris Commune with the dictatorship of the proletariat; it was Engels who did: 'Well and good, gentlemen, do you want to know what this dictatorship looks like? Look at the Paris Commune! That was the Dictatorship of the Proletariat.'[24] But Stalin was wrong yet for another reason. It *was* Lenin and not Kautsky or Luxemburg who revised 'the old proposition' of Marxism. Lenin's revision does not lack a certain logic, however. The original Marxism was a product of the same cultural heritage as western liberalism: that of ancient Greek and Roman philosophy, law and political thought; that of Judaism and Christianity. Unlike Western and Central Europe, Russia had accepted Christianity in its Byzantine form. Therefore, it never went through such milestones of European civilisation as reformation, renaissance, rationalism and enlightenment. What is more, Russia never wholly accepted the spiritual roots either of the classical or of the modern European political culture based on humanism and individualism. Instead of this, some elements of Asiatic political culture with some Asiatic institutions, values and customs were incorporated in the Russian semi-European, semi-Asiatic civilisation. There was no reason why Marx and Engels should not have shared the (liberal) belief that man had the right to individual freedoms. As a matter of fact, the liberal freedoms were not enough for them: they demanded the *total* liberation of man which would extend rather than negate the freedoms already enjoyed by some western nations. This was clearly indicated by Marx in his evaluation of the Paris Commune which was based on universal suffrage, on the full accountability of all elected officials to the electorate, on the principle that all officials were subject to recall by their constituencies, etc.[25] However distinct from liberal democracy the Paris Commune might have been, it certainly was not a dictatorial form of government.

Moreover, Lenin was attacked by the social democrats not for the soviet *form* of the post-revolution Russian state, but for its lack of democratic content. The soviets, which had initially emerged quite spontaneously in the 1905 and (February) 1917 revolutions, were actually deprived of their real power after the Kronstadt uprising and later even degraded to one of the many 'transmission belts' of the elitist, vanguard party. It is not the soviet form which distinguishes Leninism from Marxism; it was and is the concept of the Party and that of its leading role which cannot but lead to the type of dictatorship characterised by Rosa Luxemburg in her critique of Leninism quoted in note 22.

I am reminded, however, of Engels' dictum taken from his letter (of 18–28 March 1875) to A. Bebel: 'As, therefore, the state is only a transitional institution which is used in the struggle, in the revolution, to hold down one's adversaries by force, it is pure nonsense to talk of a free people's state: so long as the proletariat still *uses* the state, it does not use it in the interests of freedom but in order to hold down its adversaries, and as soon as it becomes possible to speak of freedom the state as such ceases to exist.'[26] If interpreted literally, Engels' idea is very simple: the proletariat uses the state only during the revolution to hold down adversaries. Once the revolution is won, the state is no longer necessary and, therefore, the dictatorship of the proletariat is not necessary either. Consequently, there cannot be any dictatorial form of government in a socialist state.

Engels' suggestion that 'where is the state there is no freedom' could be accepted in its general, philosophical meaning only. In the same quoted letter Engels emphasised 'the first condition of all freedom: that all officials should be responsible for all their official acts to every citizen before the ordinary courts and according to common law'.[27] Consequently, if there were a state in which all officials were subject to such responsibility, one could speak about freedom compatible with the existence of the state, even if it were only freedom in the political sense. Because political theory as well as political movements are primarily interested in the political rather than the philosophical meaning of freedom, I may for a moment dismiss Engels' idea of incompatibility of freedom with the state as irrelevant to the discussion about government forms of the dictatorship of the proletariat (I shall return briefly to this problem in the next chapter).

But what to do with the more practical-political aspect of Engels' suggestion, namely that the proletariat uses the state in order to hold down its adversaries? Well, as I have already noted, the proletarian state should have a class content. But to draw one's attention to the class content of the proletarian state ('to hold down its adversaries') is not tantamount to dictatorship as the government form. What is the main task of the proletarian state? To abolish classes through the expropriation of the means of production from the bourgeoisie. The elimination of the bourgeoisie *as a class* is by no means identical with a physical liquidation of the capitalists. It simply means that the bourgeoisie would be deprived of its privilege to private property and put on an equal footing with the proletariat. This measure, directed only against *one* of the many liberal freedoms, the freedom of private property, might be carried out, as one may easily imagine, in a civilised way, with the approval of the majority and, therefore, in quite a democratic manner.[28] Neither Marx nor Engels ever fought the bourgeoisie as persons; they did so always in class terms. Hence, after the expropriation of the expropriators, there is no need for any further oppression of the former ruling class. As Engels put it:

The first act by virtue of which the state really constitutes itself the representative of the whole society – the taking possession of the means of production in the name of society – this is, at the same time, its last independent act as a state. State interference in social relations becomes, in one domain after another, superfluous, and then dies out of itself; the government of persons is replaced by the administration of things, and by the conduct of processes of production. The state is not 'abolished'. It dies out.[29]

Elsewhere Engels is even more specific:

Society, which will re-organise production on the basis of a free and equal association of the producers, will put the whole machinery of state where it will then belong: into a museum of antiquities, by the side of the spinning-wheel and the bronze axe.[30]

The concept of 'withering away' or 'dying out' of the state, which

Marx shared with Engels, could be consistent with the concept of the dictatorship of the proletariat *only* if the latter was conceived as the *class* dictatorship and not as the dictatorial *form* of government. If the main reason for the class dictatorship of the proletariat is the abolition of classes, there would be no need for any class dictatorship, and hence for any state, after the bourgeoisie *as a class* has been abolished. However, if it were dictatorship as the government form, it might be directed not only against the bourgeois class but against any individual, or against any group of individuals that, for whatever reason, disagrees with the government. Had such a dictatorship in the strict sense been established – and the only reason for its establishment could be the intention to oppress everyone who thinks or acts otherwise than the dictators – when, one may ask, would it start to wither away? Practically never, for there will be always some people who will think and act differently from the government.

While there is no single indication that Marx or Engels ever conceived of the dictatorship of the proletariat as dictatorship in the strict sense, there *are* their explicit suggestions that it should be the *class* dictatorship of the proletariat (Marx) acquiring the form of the democratic republic (Engels). In addition to this, the whole historical setting of Marxism, the concept of the 'withering away' of the state as well as the unanimously democratic interpretation of the term 'the dictatorship of the proletariat' by all Marxists prior to Lenin, give strong support to my conclusion.

A good intention, i.e. the democratic interpretation of the term 'the dictatorship of the proletariat', is laudable. The good intention, however, is not enough. There should be a real chance to materialise it in political practice. To find out whether this is possible or not, I should address myself to yet another relevant question: how can the proletariat *as a class* become the *ruling class*?

Except for Asiatic theocracies, all previous ruling classes (slaveholders, feudal lords, capitalists) had ruled (or still rule) due to private property. Each individual member of any hitherto known possessing class derived his *social* power from his *individual* power embodied in private control of the means of production, be it slaves, land or capital. The proletariat is the first non-possessing class which is to come to power. In terms of the social division of labour, the proletariat has been condemned to perform ordained and directed functions, to implement orders coming from the management. Owing to the very nature of both the social and the technical division of labour, the proletariat operates at the bottom of the economic organisation of society. This state of affairs cannot be changed by a mere nationalisation of private property which does not mean anything more than that the means of production would pass from the hands of the bourgeoisie into the hands of the state: 'The proletariat seizes political power and turns the means of production into state property.'[31] Or: 'The proletariat will use its political supremacy to wrest, by degrees, all capital from the bourgeoisie, to centralise all instruments of production in the hands of the state, i.e. of the proletariat organised as the ruling class . . . .'[32] From these two suggestions one cannot but conclude that, first, the means of production are to be administered by the state in a *centralised* manner and, second, that the state itself becomes just another expression for the proletariat organised as the ruling class.

Strictly speaking, if the means of production are 'centralised in the hands of the state', then the proletariat, dispersed in thousands of economic units, would have no direct access to the central decision-making. Since no member of the proletariat can turn his personal power into his social power, it is out of the question for any individual proletarian to rule. As an individual (unlike an individual slaveholder, feudal lord or capitalist), the proletarian cannot rule over other people. *Even as a class, the proletariat cannot exercise its economic power except in the system of economic self-management.* In any *centralised* economic system, however, economic power has to be executed *on behalf* of the proletariat (rather than *by* the proletariat) by a special group of people. Even if this special group of people consisted of the proletarians, these *ruling* proletarians could be at best the *former* proletarians while the actual subordinate position of their class would remain unchanged. The number of people who can actually rule in any centralised system is rather limited. By no means may it include the proletariat as a whole, the entire *class* of the proletariat. The proletarians who would be going on with their productive functions at the bottom of the economic organisation of society cannot rule: their position within both the social and technical division of labour does not allow for it. In this respect, the proletariat is distinct from all previous ruling classes whose managerial and supervisory functions have been derived from private property or social division of labour.

Thus, given the centralisation of all means of production in the hands of the state *and* the concept of *one nation, one factory*, any *economic class* rule of the proletariat is, by definition, impossible. But what about a *political class* rule?

We are told that 'the state is the proletariat organised as the ruling class'. But is it ever possible? Yes, it seems possible *provided* the

proletariat acts simultaneously as a producing class, as an administrative class, as an army (probably as the armed working people), as a
public militia substituting for the police, and so on. In this case, and only
in this case, would it be possible to make the proletariat the ruling class.
This case, however, is the exclusive case of the most direct popular
democracy and of the most direct self-government.

At this point, I may expect quite a logical objection: Well, but why do
you demand for the *class* rule of the proletariat such an exclusive and
rather extreme type of government while, in the case of the *class* rule of
the previous classes, you have allowed for a more realistic governmental
form? But I do not demand it. It was Marx and Engels who demanded it
in *The Communist Manifesto* ('the state is the proletarit organised as the
ruling class'). In three previous social systems (slavery, feudalism,
capitalism) both social and political power were based on *private* rather
than on public property. This is why the propertied classes ruled. What
is more, the rule was and is a function of mental rather than of physical
labour, and since the propertied classes used to get an exclusive
education, they more or less automatically occupied both private and
public decision-making positions. But if social and political power is
being derived exclusively from public property, *all should rule*. And all
may rule only provided there is a *direct popular democracy*.

However, one may still object that at least the bourgeois class did not
rule and does not necessarily rule directly in the political sphere, that it
always used to be (and still is) represented by professional politicians
and bureaucrats who *govern*. This is true. There is and there will always
be a distinction between governing and ruling. That is why the Marxist
theory does not speak about the governing classes; it speaks about the
ruling classes. Though the bourgeoisie does rule as a class, it *does not
govern as a class*. A certain group of people always governs either on its
behalf or parallel with its class rule. But what is important, as long as the
bourgeosie holds economic power, it is neither wholly subordinated to,
nor wholly dependent on, the government. *Because of its economic
power*, the bourgeosie as a class can hire and fire (through elections, viz.
contributions to electoral campaigns, the use of private mass media,
etc.) its political representatives. Conversely, if there were exclusive
state property in a socialist state, the proletariat would be left property-
less, with no direct economic power, with no economic base for its class
rule. In this case, those who govern would have to be at the same time
both the representatives *and* the employers of the ruling class. However,
such a situation would obviously be absurd.

Hence there is no reason to believe that the principle of the bourgeois *class* rule may be applied to the *class* rule of the proletariat. In this respect, Marx and Engels were quite consistent when they declared that the post-capitalist state should be the proletariat organised as the ruling class. This is the only way any class deriving its social and political power from social rather than from private property can actually rule. There is even at least one *explicit* indication that this was the state of affairs Marx had in mind. Says Marx in his political pamphlet *The Civil War in France*: 'The communal *regime* once established in Paris and secondary centres, the old *centralised* government would in provinces, too, give way to the *self-government of the producers*.'[33]

According to the logic of the concept of the class dictatorship of the proletariat, self-government of direct producers is the only viable model for the class democratic rule of the working class. But this is not all. Once the bourgeoisie has been abolished as a class through expropriation of the means of production and class distinctions have disappeared, there is no need for any organised class coercion and, consequently, for any class rule either. The state as a coercive class organisation dies out in the first instance.

If the socialist state is really the proletariat organised as the ruling class in its first short revolutionary stage and the working people freely associated on the basis of self-government in its second stage, then, consequently, there is no need for maintaining a special government machinery separated and alienated from society. Hence the state as the special apparatus of the hierarchically organised bureaucracy should die out simultaneously with the strengthening of self-government. This process could be facilitated if the proletariat, after the seizure of political power, destroys the bourgeois state machinery without creating a new one.

Third, if politics is just the official expression of the antagonisms in the civil society, then, logically, politics should wither away simultaneously with the state. Though this process starts immediately after the abolition of classes, it can be completed only when the associated producers have reached the point of their total human emancipation:

Only when the real, individual man re-absorbs in himself the abstract citizen, and as an individual human being has become a *species-being* in his everyday life, in his particular work, and in his particular situation, only when man has recognised and organised his '*forces propres*' as *social* forces, and consequently no longer separates social power from himself in the shape of *political* power, only then will human emancipation be accomplished.[34]

In short, according to Marx's concept, the three characteristics of the state as an organised coercion, a specific government machinery and a political organisation of society, as only transient moments in the course of social history, will wither away in the above order. However, the remaining Marxist characteristic of the state (as well as of any other social organisation, e.g. tribal, communal, etc.) cannot die out with the state proper. It is that of (the state as) the social co-operation based on a common (general) interest of all its members.

Whether or not the social co-operation is based on division of labour, it always requires a kind of management and co-ordination. In pre-class (tribal) society the managerial functions had been performed either by the senior members of the community, or by the ablest or the strongest – to use the contemporary language, by the leaders. In class societies, those functions have usually been performed by the proprietors (corporate capitalism may serve as an exception to the rule). Who should and who could perform the managerial functions in the post-capitalist classless societies? I have already argued that the proletariat could perform the managerial functions only if organised as the ruling class through self-management and self-government. But even in the strictly self-managed and self-governed communities, there are some functions which cannot be performed directly by the workers. Certain functions may be performed only by people with special training, knowledge, experience and abilities. This reality of life suggests that, even in an ideal classless and stateless communist co-operation, some people have to organise, co-ordinate, plan and manage the work of their fellow-citizens. In short, some people have to govern. Does it mean, however, that such positions would have to endow the incumbents with a special power? Marx replies in the negative. His categorical *no* has been derived from the famous concept of an orchestra conductor. Let me look at this concept more closely. Says Marx:

> All combined labour on a large scale requires, more or less, a directing authority, in order to secure the harmonious working of the individual activities, and to perform the general functions that have their origin in the action of the combined organism, as distinguished from the action of its separate organs. A single violin player is his own conductor; an orchestra requires a separate one.[35] . . . An orchestra conductor need not own the instruments of his orchestra, nor is it within the scope of his duties as conductor to have anything to do with the 'wages' of the other musicians.[36]

Marx conceived of the stateless communist society as the complex co-operation of men. In the economic sphere, this co-operation is *centralised* according to his concept of one nation, one factory; in this lies the basic distinction between the anarchist and Marxist perception of the stateless society. The direct central planning calls for compulsion and excludes the direct self-management of work units by the producers. In the decentralised political sphere, however, there should be no compulsion whatsoever: mere administration of things will be combined with the broadest possible self-government. Hence the cleavage in the concept (centralised economy vs. decentralised politics) seems quite visible. Could this cleavage be reconciled? Marx replies in the affirmative. The management, planning, co-ordination and control, says Marx, are quite conceivable without any compulsion either in the economic or the political sphere. Look at the orchestra! Its conductor plans, manages, organises and co-ordinates the activity of the players, but he conducts rather than rules, performing a technical rather than a political function. All members of the orchestra, each of them performing a distinct role by playing a different part, aim at a common end in which every participant of the co-operation is equally interested. Instead of compulsion, a voluntary co-operation; instead of rule, a self-disciplined participation. Despite the division of labour there is a perfect unity of interests. The orchestra model is the *general* model for the co-operation in the classless community of free associates: the combined labour and all combined social activities would not require rulers but just 'conductors' who will co-ordinate individual workers involved in team jobs.

With the concept of the orchestra Marx makes the same mistake as he did with his concept of *one nation, one factory*, namely that he confuses a micro-system with a macro-system. The orchestra is a typical micro-system while society is not. The division of labour within an orchestra is that in detail while the division of labour within society is that in particular and in general. Moreover, an orchestra as such is hardly a political body. Its members are put together for just one reason – to perform music. They may belong to different races, ideologies, nationalities, social classes, churches and political parties: all these distinctions are irrelevant to their job. The individual players are even not comparable to detail workers. Each of the players has mastered his instrument in full; hence he might also perform as a soloist or a music teacher on his own. They do co-operate just for a purpose.

But even in an orchestra it is necessary to decide about the repertoire. Besides the question of *what* will be played, the question *how* the orchestra interprets symphonies or concertos is also to be decided. The latter concerns the conception of how the compositions are to be performed which depends on the artistic tastes and values of the musicians involved. From time to time it would be necessary to decide who is eligible for filling an opening, or which player is to be fired. At least three alternative models are available for decision-making: either the conductor, or the orchestra as a whole, or an outside committee would decide. But who would hire and fire the conductor? In which way is he to be appointed? By selection? By a public competition? And in either case, who would select him?

As one can see, the general model of an orchestra may be materialised in alternative managerial and organisational systems. While the technical and goal-oriented activity of the orchestra would be more or less the same (the conductor conducts, the players play), in one case it could be quite a democratic self-management of all musicians involved, in another case it could be a rather despotic rule of the conductor, and in still another case the orchestra could be manipulated from the outside by a committee or a board of trustees.

I may go even further. *So long as scarcity prevails*, someone actually has to decide about the wages, about the ownership of the instruments, about the financing of both the orchestra and the concert hall. Someone has to decide whether the orchestra is to be a profit-oriented or a non-profitable organisation. If the latter model were accepted, someone would have to decide about the subsidies, and so on. There is no way of avoiding all these and other questions.

If applied to society as a whole, these questions are, unlike the *technical* essence of the orchestra's inner structure, of a political nature. And since the orchestra may be subject to at least the three above-mentioned systemic arrangements, the very orchestral model as the pattern for a non-compulsive complex co-operation of men fails to offer any guaranteed protection from coercive rule.[37] Whether class or classless, compulsion *is* implicitly present in Marx's concept of one nation, one factory and therefore cannot be absent in his metaphor of the *social* orchestra. This conclusion follows from the iron logic of Marx's materialistic concept of history whose core lies in the theory of base and superstructure.

3.2. BASE AND SUPERSTRUCTURE

In the social production of their life, men enter into definite relations that are indispensable and independent of their will, relations of production which correspond to a definite stage of development of their material productive forces. The sum total of these relations of production constitutes the economic structure of society, the real foundation, on which rises a legal and political superstructure and to which correspond definite forms of social consciousness. The mode of production of material life conditions the social, political and intellectual life process in general. It is not the consciousness of men that determines their being but, on the contrary, their social being which determines their consciousness. . . . With the change of the economic foundation, the entire immense superstructure is more or less rapidly transformed . . .[38]

In this classical concise paragraph the entire essence of Marx's materialistic approach to social history has been most precisely formulated. If there is anything which unequivocally expresses the basic principles of Marx's methodology, it could be found in this conceptual proposition. And yet this paragraph has often been misinterpreted, or the whole concept of the base and superstructure has been ignored by many contemporary students of Marxism.

It seems abundantly clear that at least two conclusions may be derived from this formulation: (1) that it is the *economic structure* of society which conditions the political superstructure; (2) that the economic base *and* the political superstructure must not be, in the long run, mutually contradictory or, what is just another expression of the same idea, they ought to be in structural accord. Not only in the sense that it is impossible to have a *feudal* economic base and a *capitalist* political superstructure, but also in the sense that it is equally impossible to have a vertically (hierarchically) organised economic base and a horizontally organised political superstructure.

Even if there could be arguments (and, indeed, there have been many) about the interrelations and interactions between the base and the superstructure, the very existence of the concept can hardly be denied. For instance, one may or may not agree with Engels, that the production and reproduction of real life is only 'the *ultimately* determining element in history'[39] and that the superstructure, be it politics, religion, law, ideology or a constitution, does play an active part in social life and influence the base. One may argue about whether the economic foundation *determines* or merely *conditions* the political superstructure (I would agree with the latter) and whether, under certain circumstances (e.g. during and immediately after a social revolution), the superstructure (politics) may or may not be primary and the base (economics) secondary (I would say that the base and the superstructure may change places). One may strongly disagree with Engels' suggestion that the economic base includes the '*entire technique of production and transport*'[40] as well as with Marx's short-cut between the level of technology and the mode of production ('The windmill gives you society with the feudal lord; the steam mill, society with the industrial capitalist'),[41] for this proposition does not make much sense: the windmill *might* also give you society with small commodity producers, and the steam mill might also give you society with socialist co-operative industries. All these and other inconsistencies (incidentally, heavy volumes of selected writings of Marx and Engels are full of such inconsistencies) bring down Marx's and Engels' scholarship and should be critically examined in many still unwritten doctoral dissertations. In the whole body of Marxism, however, there is no single inconsistency as to the validity of the base–superstructure concept.[42] According to Marx, the economic base *is* the sum total of relations of production which, in the context of *A Contribution to the Critique of Political Economy*, is conceived in the broad sense as a unity of the process of production, distribution, exchange and consumption. Hence, by definition, the social division of labour, property forms, forms of social intercourse, the exchange of commodities *and* activities have been incorporated in the economic base by Marx himself. On the other hand, Marx never included productive forces in the economic base. Productive forces consist of means of production and producers themselves. The same level of productive forces may serve as a technological and human foundation for different *economic* bases, e.g. ancient and feudal, capitalist and socialist. Between the productive forces and the economic base a similar relation exists as that between the base and superstructure: if the productive forces are in accord with the relations of production (the economic base), they develop smoothly and steadily. If they are not in accord with the economic base, then, eventually, the conflict is to be resolved in favour of the productive forces: an obsolete economic base gives way to a new set of relations of production which would more properly reflect the level of productive forces. Thus, it is a *three*-tier schema: productive forces, economic base and superstructure. While, *in the last instance*, productive forces condition the economic base, and the economic base conditions the superstructure, the latter, in turn, influences the economic base and the economic base influences the development of productive forces. Here, too, cause and effect mutually change place.

On the one hand, Marx believed that the most revolutionary element of this three-tier schema were productive forces; on the other hand, he did recognise (like Adam Smith) that the social division of labour (an element of the base) was a productive force; and finally, he was aware that an element of the superstructure (e.g. Protestant puritanism) was instrumental for the whole period of industrialisation in England when it accelerated the process of accumulation of capital. The simplicity of the schema is not able to reflect all the complex and complicated interrelations between the three tiers: it is only *in the last instance* that the economic factor (both in terms of productive forces and production relations) conditions the superstructure. There is never an absolute accord among those three tiers or elements of the schema; nevertheless, there is an objective tendency leading to an accord between the productive forces and the production relations on the one hand and between the economic base and the superstructure on the other. An intricate interdependence of the three tiers could be observed throughout social history which has evolved from lower and simpler structures to higher and more complex ones.

It seems almost impossible to eradicate the *base–superstructure* concept from Marxist theory. It is known that Marx occasionally vulgarised this concept; that there have been indications that he would have liked to see a more direct and simpler *cause-and-effect* relation between technological changes and political events, or between the level of economic development and the level of revolutionary class consciousness of the proletariat.[43] In one of his key works Marx even dehumanised man by saying that 'the human essence is no abstraction inherent in each single individual. In its reality, it is the ensemble of the social relations.[44] If one realises that the production relations conditioned by the level of productive forces form the economic base, one has to admit that there are some grounds for accusing Marx of being an economic determinist. But even the most non-deterministic and humanistic interpretation of the base–superstructure concept would not allow for a simultaneous application of Marx's perception of the economic and political liberation of man.

We are told by Marx that 'with the change of economic foundation, the entire superstructure is more or less rapidly transformed', i.e. transformed along the lines of the restructured economic base. Even if one faces the political (sub)system structured differently from, or contrary to, the economic (sub)system, the former would have to be put in accord with the latter, or the latter would have to be adjusted to the former. But it is impossible to maintain structurally opposite or substantially diverse subsystems (base and superstructure) of the social

system for a longer period of time. In other words, whoever wants to
analyse a political system must not isolate it from its economic
foundation. No Marxist may legitimately construct a social system
whose political superstructure would differ structurally from its economic base. This is Marx's own methodological proposition or, if you
wish, Marx's own methodological dogma. Because it was he who
formulated and declared it, one is entitled to ask him to comply with his
own rule.

Let me look again at Marx's perception of the post-socialist
revolution economic sysytem. It is structured as one huge nation-wide
factory with individual enterprises being merely its workshops. It is
organised in a strictly centralised manner with the means of production
controlled by the state. Central planning consists of direct (non-
mediated) allocation of resources in physical units. The market has
been abolished simultaneously with the autonomy of economic units
and with the personal independence of producers. But division of
labour has not yet been superseded. Neither is scarcity overcome.[45] A
hierarchical industrial organisation with a strong authority of managers, planners and supervisors is maintained ('Wanting to abolish
authority in large-scale industry is tantamount to wanting to abolish
industry itself, to destroy the power loom in order to return to the
spinning wheel')[46] and, of necessity, extended from a workshop (a
factory) to society as a whole. Could one have, in the circumstances, a
self-managed, self-governed, participatory and popular class democratic political system? Could one have a chain of self-managed political
units extended to 'even the smallest country hamlet'?[47] Could one have
the communes which administer 'their common affairs by an assembly
of delegations'?[48] Would it be possible to have a system in which 'the
few but important functions still remaining for a central government
were to be discharged by Communal and therefore strictly responsible
agents'?[49] The system 'which begins with the self-government and the
commune'?[50]

If one accepts Marx's concept of base and superstructure, a
centralised, hierarchically organised economic subsystem *cannot* coexist
with a pluralistic, horizontally organised self-governed political subsystem. In a society with one huge nation-wide factory there is no room
either for self-managed economic units or for self-governed communes.
In a society with command central planning there is no room for
autonomous policy-making in the provinces, cities and villages. Because
the majority of decisions – according to Marx's and Engels' prediction – should be concerned with the administration of things (i.e.

with economics), the cleavage between the two concepts is quite obvious. What is more, in any centralised economic system the working class *as a whole* cannot control public economy. But without controlling public economy, according to Marx, it is impossible to control politics. In the long run, no class can exercise control over politics without being in control of economics.

In his comments on Bakunin, Marx accepted that the people making decisions on behalf of society as a whole would be elected by universal suffrage, and went on: 'and as soon as the functions have ceased to be political, then there exists (1) no governmental function; (2) the distribution of general functions has become a business matter which does not afford any room for domination; (3) the election has none of its present political character.'[51] But when could such functions cease to be political? I suggest that only after the supersession of social division of labour and scarcity. As long as there is social division of labour and scarcity, there must be a hierarchy of bodies deciding about conflicting priorities and, consequently, about conflicts of interests. The decisions would have to be binding for the people – without this the *one society, one factory* system would collapse. In other words, elected bodies would have to perform governmental functions.

Marx's suggestion that there will be no room for domination is not adequately substantiated. For a long period of time in which social division of labour and scarcity will prevail, all persons elected to general functions will administer not only things but also people. And whoever administers people, or decides about people, is in a dominant position vis-à-vis those who are the objects of his decisions.

Marx's weak point has been demonstrated in the following argument:

Bakunin: Result: rule of the great majority of the people by a privileged minority. But, the Marxists say, this minority will consist of workers. Yes, indeed, but of ex-workers, who, once they become only representatives or rulers of the people, cease to be workers.

Marx: No more than a manufacturer today ceases to be a capitalist when he becomes a member of the municipal council.[52]

Well, Marx could have been right in the case of a *municipal* councillor in a small town. But *his* future society would have to have a *central* government with many offices including a central planning board, many agencies involved in income distribution, in allocation of investment, in regulation of foreign affairs, etc. These jobs cannot be done either on a part-time basis or in one's leisure time. If such positions were held by manufacturers or bankers, the incumbents would not cease to be manufacturers or bankers. They would simply hire managers to run their businesses. A worker would cease to be the worker, however. He would become a government official without retaining his business.* It would be analogous to other previous ruling classes: had a feudal lord become a king's minister, he would not have ceased to be a feudal lord; had a slaveowner become a Roman senator, he would not have ceased to be a slaveowner. But hypothetically, had a serf (slave) become a king's minister (a Roman senator), he certainly could not have done it without a change in his class (caste, estate) status.

In his argument with Bakunin, Marx also suggested that 'if Mr Bakunin were in the know, if only with the position of a manager in a workers' co-operative, he would send all his nightmares about authority to the devil'.[53] Here, Marx did not give enough attention to the fact that:

1. In a *laissez-faire* capitalist society, any workers' co-operative is an independent and autonomous commodity-producing unit subject to no other outside authority than that of the market (i.e. the manager is *not* responsible to any central planning board or to any higher (supra-enterprise) authority.
2. The manager of Marx's hypothetical workers' co-operative was an elected administrator of a *group* property and therefore responsible exclusively to the co-operative's owners, i.e. to his fellow-workers, while an administrator of the *state*-owned factory is primarily responsible to central planning and supervising authorities.
3. His hypothetical workers' co-operative as a micro-system was a part of a decentralised and horizontally organised market macro-system with an infinite number of autonomous economic units and by no means a part of the nation-wide centrally organised factory.

If I may use an analogy from the political sphere, then Marx's hypothetical workers' co-operative was a *community* while his suggested nation-wide factory was a *society*. Let me discuss these two different concepts in a more detailed manner.

---

* An analogy may be offered here. If the manufacturer became a manager of his own factory, he would not cease to be a manufacturer. If a worker became a manager of a factory, he would cease to be a worker and become an executive.

3.3. MARX'S CONCEPT OF COMMUNITY

Both civil society and the state are based on the division of labour and classes. This is why man has to play several different social roles. On the one hand, man is an independent *individual*, i.e. a member of the civil society, and a *citizen*, i.e. a subject of the state. On the other hand, man is a *worker* (producer). Third, he is a *consumer*. As a *homo oeconomicus* he behaves according to economic stimulators (e.g. to the market); he is also *homo faber* who performs specialised functions within the social division of labour. As a social being, he is a *member of a social class*; in the illusory community of the state, he also becomes a *homo politicus* whose private life is separated from his public life and whose private interest is separated from a common interest (the general will). In the civil society based on the universal market, man becomes an *exchanger* whose relations to other men are market relations and, therefore, quite impersonal: men behave to each other not as human beings but as agents of the market-exchange, as *sellers* and *buyers*. In their economic life, men are ruled by the law of value; in their political life, men are ruled by laws. In these circumstances, man cannot be free. He cannot be freed from religion; at best, he receives religious freedom. He cannot be freed from property; at best, he receives freedom to own property.[54] He cannot be freed from labour; at best he receives free labour.[55] Instead of being freed from the state, he receives political emancipation within the state.[56]

Although the liberal state guarantees religious freedom, free labour, freedom to own property and political emancipation to the working class it is not enough. Marx's concept of freedom is absolute: man ought to be freed from all kinds of alienation, oppression, exploitation, estrangement and domination. What is more, he should be freed also from his illusions about his position in the civil society (i.e. from ideology). This concept of human freedom might be accepted as philosophical and, within the framework of philosophy, normative. However, it is hardly acceptable as a *political* concept. Unlike philosophy, politics does not deal with what 'ought to be'; it may deal only with what 'might be'. Therefore, the maximum freedom which one may reasonably pursue in politics is the *freedom of choice in given circumstances*. Since the circumstances make men, the choice is limited. Since men make circumstances,[57] their freedom of choice is much greater than a determinist would appreciate. In short, wherever Marx's normative philosophical concept either of liberation of man, or that of freedom, is applied to economics and politics, it inevitably turns into a sort of religion or, at best, into an ideological myth or utopia.

In economic terms this utopia consists in 'the realm of freedom' with labour abolished, with no scarcity and with an unlimited free creativeness of men. In political terms this utopia consists in the concept of community. Although Marx has failed to define clearly what the term actually means, one may trace some of its characteristics in his critique of civil society. According to Marx, man is, in essence, a social being. Because his *own* essence, his *human* essence, is his *communal* essence, he may become the social being only in the community and through the community.[58] As compared to civil society, the community is to be based on popular participation rather than on rule ('When a man rules himself, he does not rule himself; since he is only himself and no one else').[59] Since there is no rule in the community, there are no formal (legal) procedures either: no clearly defined and binding rights and duties, no clearly defined and binding claims and obligations; in short, where there is no outside power over people, there cannot be a separation of powers either. There is not even a general will of the people: 'Under collective property, the so-called will of the people disappears in order to make way for the real will of the co-operative.'[60] According to Marx, the community is not a political organisation: it is a mere social entity whose organisation is essentially economic;[61] and where there is no politics, there is no political democracy either. With labour abolished, the economic organisation is based on the 'complete and no longer restricted self-activity'[62] of men. In all previous illusory communities the individuals participated in their communal relations only as average members of their class. 'With the community of revolutionary proletarians . . . who take their conditions of existence and those of all members of society under their control, it is just the reverse; it is as individuals that the individuals participate in it.'[63] The communist community 'is opposed to right, both political and private, as also in its most general form as the rights of man',[64] for the rights of man, according to Marx, are privileges. And consequently, in the community without politics, without rule and without law, there is no guarantee for man's personal independence either. Instead of guarantees, there will be *the* freedom:

The transformation through the division of labour of personal powers (relationships) into material powers, cannot be dispelled by dismissing the general idea of it from one's mind, but can only be abolished by the individuals again subjecting these material powers to themselves and abolishing the division of labour. This is not possible without the community. Only in the community [with others] has each individual the means of cultivating his gifts in all directions; only in the community, therefore, is personal freedom possible. In the previous substitutes for the community, in the state, etc., personal freedom has existed only for the individuals who developed within the relationship of the ruling class, and only insofar as they were individuals of this class. The illusory community, in which individuals have up until now combined, always took on an independent existence in relation to them, and was at the same time, since it was the combination of one class against another, not only a completely illusory community, but a new fetter as well. In the real community the individuals obtain their freedom in and through their association.[65]

This concept of community is based on Marx's strength of logical abstraction. Marx was not only preoccupied, but even obsessed, with a search for synthesis: from both personal and objective dependence, through personal independence based on objective dependence, to a total independence (freedom) of man. But man's freedom cannot consist in his total independence. Man cannot be independent either in social or in natural terms. He is a prisoner of nature for he is mortal. He is a social being for he cannot preserve his human characteristics outside a human community. But a community of men (if it be the human community) should always rely on certain persistent patterns of behaviour, rules, beliefs and values which, in turn, follow from a definite economic and social structure. If Marx's ultimate goal was a free, unlimited development of emancipated men, then one would expect Marx to have cared about a set of principles applying to his ideal community. Without such a set of principles, men would be turned back to the state of Nature of the social-contract political philosophers or to Ovid's Golden Age. Since it goes without saying that *this* could not have been Marx's intention, I should examine his concept of community in my own way. I intend to discuss the concept of community under the conditions of social division of labour and scarcity which, as one may reasonably expect, will prevail in any foreseeable future and therefore ought to be taken into consideration by any Marxist theoretician or politician. This qualification could help me to clarify Marx's vague and unsystematic remarks concerning the 'genuine community' as opposed to the 'illusory community' of both the civil society and the state. The first characteristic of community is a fellowship stemming from common sentiments, interests, intentions, ideas and values. However, the community still dominated by social division of labour and scarcity would hardly be capable of harmonising all interests of its members on macro, e.g. provincial or national, levels. Such a global community is conceivable merely in terms of general ideas and values shared by the majority of its associates, but certainly not in terms of their particular interests, priorities and preferences. This is why the community concept can be applied basically to micro-systems, i.e. to local or work entities in which people feel they fully belong, are concerned about their common affairs and involved in a kind of self-government or self-management. To be concerned and involved the associates have to know each other or, at least, to know quite intimately their common interests. What is more, they ought to feel that all matters of their communal concern are, at the same time, also the matters of their personal concern, that there is no separation between their public (communal) and private (individual) lives. In this sense, Marx's genuine community is incompatible with private property and social classes.

The second characteristic of community is its co-operative spirit. Co-operation rather than competition is instrumental for any kind of communal arrangements. By saying this, however, I should immediately make a qualification: some competition would be necessary in any community concerned about performance, productivity and dynamic development of its productive forces.

The third characteristic of community consists in that power transforms into authority. If a bearer of power exercises it to the benefit of a recipient who voluntarily accepts it, such power is called authority.[66] In an ideal community, e.g. one without division of labour and scarcity, with a high degree of socialisation, etc., it might be merely the authority of knowledge rather than the authority of force which will prevail. In a realistic community still based on division of labour and scarcity it could also be authority based on force. Incidentally, it would be in accord with Marx's and Engels' suggestion that 'the public power will lose its political character.'[67] This phrase indicates that there *is* still public power. If such public power were exercised to the benefit of its recipients and not to the benefit of its bearers, it could legitimately be called authority.

The fourth characteristic of community rests on mutual aid, assistance and solidarity rather than on equivalent exchange. While this could hardly be a universal pattern for relations following the distributive principle 'according to work', it might be a supplementary pattern for distribution 'according to need' in education, medicine, etc., as well as an assistance to the handicapped or disabled.

And finally, the fifth characteristic of community consists in self-government and/or self-management. A kind of participatory democracy is conceivable both in political and work communities. However, communal self-government and/or self-management presupposes an autonomy of the communities which ought to be subject to no *direct* outside power. The communal power (authority) rests exclusively with its members. Vis-à-vis other micro-systems (communities) this does not create any great problem. If each community were autonomous, then, obviously, its relations to all other communities would be based on reciprocal equality and equivalence. The very fact that the communities are separated from each other makes their mutual *horizontal* relations a necessity. Incidentally, even in hierarchical structures, interrelationships among the units at the bottom of each given pyramid are horizontal: the council of village A cannot decide about internal matters of village B, and the management of work unit C cannot interfere with internal matters of work unit D.

Real problems begin with a micro-system's (community's) relation to its macro-system, i.e. to the society as a whole. To survive as a community, a work (local) unit must preserve its autonomy from higher tiers of government and/or management. Since Marx perceived his post-socialist revolution *economy* as one nation-wide factory whose basic work units (enterprises) are not autonomous and independent communities but mere workshops of the centralised economic organisation, his concept of community cannot apply to the economic sphere. The very concept of direct social planning in which central commands substitute for a self-regulating mechanism is incompatible with communal arrangements (e.g. self-management) in the work units. In the political sphere, however, Marx subscribed to the community concept. His communes or communities are to be autonomous and to decide, in a decentralised way, about almost everything. Those few things which the (former) central government would be left to deal with could be decided upon by an assembly of communities' delegates. Apart from the obvious cleavage between the centralised structure of the economic base (nation-wide factory) and the decentralised political superstructure (self-governed communities), Marx's synthesis suffers from yet another inconsistency. According to Marx's own proposition, the community is not a political organisation but a mere social entity whose organisation is essentially economic. If the economy were organised as one nation-wide factory subject to direct central planning, then the (social) communities could not become 'essentially economic' organisations and 'essentially economic' work units could not become communities.

At this point, one may expect the following question: Why is it not possible to run the entire nation-wide factory as a self-managed community? It is impossible because the nation-wide factory is just another expression for the national economy as a whole with such great divisions as agriculture, forestry, industry, trade, transport, communication, construction and services, with branches (e.g. heavy and light industry) divided into numerous sub-branches (e.g. textile industry, further subdivided into wool, cotton, synthetic, etc., production) located in geographically, technologically and organisationally separate units. Those who work in one specific economic unit can participate *directly* only in the management of their working place, not of all working places. Their *managerial* participation could be extended to all working places or, for that matter, to the national economy as a whole, only (a) indirectly and (b) provided there was a steady unity of interests. In the conditions of scarcity, the unity of interests is conceivable only in exceptional (emergency) situations, but is otherwise quite unrealistic given the particular interests of each work collective. As for indirect participation, it would be simply representation and not self-management. What is more, the direct producers (workers) could be represented in the top (central) planning and managerial bodies to a limited extent only. The central planning and managerial board ought to employ a large number of skilled specialists familiar with planning techniques and managerial functions. Engels' belief that 'people will be able to manage everything very simply'[68] has not been confirmed by praxis. Those specialists (bureaucrats, technocrats) could be controlled by elected representatives of the workers only formally.

If so, the question might be re-formulated: Why not run the workshops (economic units) of the nation-wide factory as self-managed work communities? This would hardly be possible for the following reasons:

(i) As mere workshops of the nation-wide factory, the economic units have lost their former autonomy. Therefore, they are subject to central planning and, consequently, to central management. Central management and self-management are mutually exclusive.

(ii) Even if I assumed that each economic unit would be run by a self-management body rather than by a manager appointed by a higher authority, the former would have to comply with the orders of the central planning board instead of making autonomous decisions. The form (self-management) would be deprived of its content (autonomous decision-making).

Thus, Marx's community concept for the political sphere clashes with his nation-wide factory concept for the economic sphere. Since economic base and superstructure are to be in structural accord, one is facing a dilemma: either to accept and introduce Marx's centralised society-type organised economy and to revise Marx's concept of the decentralised community-type polity, or to accept and introduce the decentralised community-type polity and to revise Marx's concept of the centralised society-type organised economy. In either case, a substantial revision of Marxism is unavoidable if the theory is to be applied to post-capitalist societies.

Part Two

Marx's Concept of Economic and Political Liberation of Man: A Revision

4 A Traditional Revision

4.1. THREE QUASI-REVISIONS

There have been only two major revisions concerning the intrinsic cleavage between Marx's economic and political perception of socialist society. These revisions consisted in adjusting Marx's political concept to the economic structure of the post-capitalist system by Lenin and in formulating the concept of a market-type self-managed socialist economy by the Yugoslavs. Prior to analysing these two major revisions, I have to discuss briefly also three conventional revisionisms.

(a) MARX AND ENGELS

It is customary for Marxist political parties to call revisionistic either a rejection of Marxist revolutionary ideas, or a deviation from the revolutionary way to socialism. If one accepts this stand, one would have to label Marx and Engels themselves revisionists. It is generally known that their strong belief in violent revolution as the only means through which the proletariat can seize political power, particularly strongly formulated in their writings between 1848 (*The Communist Manifesto*) and 1850 (*Address of the Central Committee to the Communist League*), was modified during the last period of their lives in some of their letters, speeches or remarks. In a speech in The Hague on 8 October 1872, Marx added The Netherlands to the United States and England as countries where socialism, in his opinion, could come into effect by peaceful means, and explicitly suggested that in North America 'barricades are unnecessary' because if the proletariat wants to win, it 'can win victory at the polls'.[1] It was also in this speech that Marx, usually concerned with social structures rather than with political cultures, paid surprisingly high attention to 'the institutions, the customs and the traditions of the various countries [which] must be taken into account'.[2] In 1891 Engels also put France on Marx's list of the countries ready for a peaceful road to socialism. In the introduction to Marx's *Class Struggles in France* written just five months before his death, Engels admitted that 'the time of surprise attacks, of revolutions carried through small conscious minorities at the head of unconscious masses, is past';[3] that with universal suffrage, 'rebellion in the old style, the street fight with barricades, which up to 1848 gave everywhere the final decision, was to a considerable extent obsolete';[4] that 'the bourgeoisie and the government came to be much more afraid of the legal than of the illegal action of the workers' party, of the results of elections than of those of rebellion';[5] that 'even in France the Socialists are realising more and more that no lasting victory is possible for them unless they first win the great mass of people, i.e. in this case, the peasants. Slow propaganda work and parliamentary activity are being recognised here, too, as the most immediate task of the Party.'[6] Finally, in the same highly controversial introduction Engels also said this:

> The irony of world history turns everything upside down. We, the 'revolutionists', the 'overthrowers' – we are thriving far better on legal methods than on illegal methods and overthrow. The parties of Order, as they call themselves, are perishing under the legal conditions created by themselves. They cry despairingly with Odilon Barrot: *la légalité nous tue*, legality is the death of us; whereas we, under this legality, get firm muscles and rosy cheeks and look like life eternal. And as *we* are not so crazy as to let ourselves be driven to street fighting in order to please them, then in the end there is nothing left for them to do but themselves break through fatal legality.[7]

To prove that Engels' ideas were not accidental, Wolfe quotes from Engels' article written for the *Almanac* of the French Parti Ouvrier in 1892:

> . . . legality works so splendidly for us that we would be fools to break it . . .. We can afford to let them break their own laws. In the meantime (we politely say to them): 'Be so good as to shoot first, *meine Herren Bourgeois*!'[8]

These few selected remarks may serve as an indication that, in the last period of their lives, Marx and Engels became more concerned with the systemic (socialist) change than with its violent (revolutionary) form. There is even explicit evidence that Marx saw the socialist revolution as a failure to resolve class and social contradictions by political and evolutionary (reformist) means: 'If the unavoidable evolution turns into a revolution, it not only would be the fault of the ruling classes, but also of the working class.'[9]

To be sure, Marx still believed that an evolutionary way was applicable *only* in the countries which had already won their battle for liberal democracy and, certainly, the Germany of 1880 had to be excluded from that group. Even as far as England was concerned, Marx had some doubts whether the theoretical possibility of an evolutionary socialist change could become a historical fact. But he wished to see the peaceful transformation materialise.[10] He repeatedly told Engels that the best thing would be 'if we could buy out the whole lot of them' (i.e. the big land proprietors).[11] Be it before or after the proletariat's victory,[12] it nevertheless testifies to the fact that an idea about a peaceful transition to socialism was not, in principle, contrary to the taste of the founding fathers of Marxism. Although there have been some arguments about the circumstances under which Engels had written and published his last introduction to Marx's *Class Struggles in France*,[13] one thing remains undisputed: the above-quoted ideas are at variance with the militant principles that Marx and Engels had expressed in the *Address of the Central Committee to the Communist League* (March 1850) from which Lenin, later on, borrowed many of his strategic and tactical concepts. If one asks the question what could have caused such a change in Marx's and Engels' minds, only one likely answer might be offered: they took into account some positive fruits of the democratisation of liberal capitalism which they could have observed during the last third of the ninteenth century. By saying this I must add, however, that neither Marx nor Engels have ever offered any *consistent* revision of their theory even if they might have seen that the real development of capitalism did not follow exactly their economic laws, tendencies and predictions. It was only Eduard Bernstein who dared openly to challenge both the theoretical principles and the revolutionary spirit of Marxism.

(b) EDUARD BERNSTEIN

Bernstein did basically two things.[14] First, he refused to accept Marx's general law of capitalist accumulation with its prediction of an inevitable growth of relative and absolute misery of the working class as well as the inevitable class polarisation of capitalist society. Second, he challenged Marx's belief that socialist revolution and the dictatorship of the proletariat were either necessary or desirable. On the first point, Bernstein offered a lot of statistical data to prove his case. On the second, he maintained that Marx had underestimated the capacity of liberalism to evolve into liberal *democracy*. This *political* development, argued Bernstein, had changed both the structure of capitalist economy and that of the hitherto class-dominated capitalist state.

One may or may not agree with Bernstein's propositions. But even those who disagree with his revision are likely to admit that his counter-concept has reflected not only some important structural changes in the capitalist system but also a new mood of a significant segment of the working class in Western European countries. The fact that liberal capitalism had yielded, owing to the irrepressible and irresistible political democratisation, to the pressures of economically and politically organised labour, led Bernstein to resurrect, within the socialist movement, the liberal concept of freedom philosophically condemned by Hegel and normatively superseded by Marx. It was the Kantian concept of freedom whose basic principle is 'that no one can force me (insofar as he considers another person's welfare) to be happy in his way, but *each must seek his own happiness* in the way that suits him best provided that he permits *another the freedom* to pursue a similar goal; it is therefore possible to *formulate* a universal law for the *freedom of all* which does not interfere with the freedom of each'.[15] One must agree with Fetscher who sees the obvious limits of this concept in that it refers only negatively to one's fellow-man as the barrier to one's individual freedom. But one must not overlook the fact that Marx's concept of freedom, based on the supersession of competitive exchange ('The only force that brings them together and puts them in relation with each other, is the selfishness, the gain and the private interest of each'),[16] is impossible without the supersession of commodity relations, the market and material incentives. This Marxian concept of freedom pursuing the *total* emancipation of man as the communal, co-operative being was a very distant end which meant nothing for Bernstein, while the social democratic movement, able to democratise liberalism and extend freedom from the bourgeoisie to the working class first in the political and then also through a less and less class-dominated state in the economic sphere, meant for him everything. This movement had already represented the former rightless poor who were not becoming poorer but better off and who were gaining basic civil freedoms and rights. Those who have been naught did not want to become all – at least as Bernstein saw it. They wanted to become something, and since they were already becoming something they feared that they might lose a bit more than just their chains. It was the famous liberal *reasonability* that had penetrated the working class, which instinctively felt that its increasing well-being could be better secured by strong trade unions and reformist social democratic parties than by a militant revolutionary movement pursuing remote and utopian ends. Wrong or right, Bernstein had reflected with his slogan 'Back to Kant' the tendency which later on prevailed in all western and central European countries: the transformation of Marxian revolutionary communism into a reformistic social democratism.

If one compares Bernstein's sober and reasonable concept of everydayness, relying on uninspiring ideas as well as small unheroic deeds, with Marx's social theory, one may clearly see the former's internal limits. Whereas Marx wanted to change the world, Bernstein wanted merely to improve it and make the lot of the working man more bearable. He lacked Marx's ingenious strength of both the abstract analysis and vision. His counter-concept could not have appealed to those who wanted 'to storm the Heaven', i.e. to abolish the 'prehistoric' (class) system and to change the very nature of man. It did appeal, however, to those socialists who had subscribed to the maxim that best things should never be allowed to kill good things or to the paraphrased aphorism of Jefferson that no more good must be attempted than the class can bear. Instead of behaving as an impatient intellectual who demands the implementation of an abstract and only philosophically defined Utopia by virtue of revolutionary struggle, Bernstein insisted on everyday efforts to preserve what has already been achieved as well as on an extension of the foundation without which the working class could not proceed towards its gradual emancipation, namely the extension of political democracy. He realised that the proletariat could achieve its ends only within the democratic system of guaranteed freedoms and rights. His realism consisted not in demanding the ideal but in demanding the possible. He was honest enough to admit that he was a revisionist, that he was a reformist leader who deliberately stripped the Marxist doctrine of its ethical holiness by rejecting the labour theory of value. He did not believe in the withering away of the state and politics and was rather sceptical about the disappearance of man *qua homo oeconomicus*. Democracy as the protected freedom of the class of wage-earning and salaried working people meant for him much more than centralisation of the means of production in the hands of the state for the sake of a strong central planning. He believed that political democracy and liberal freedoms extended to the working class are much more important than a militant class struggle which, in his opinion, could bring about only a crude communism, and that socialism without the Kantian freedom would lose its legitimacy. In short, while he did not want to keep liberalism for ever, neither did he want to negate it prematurely.

(c) KARL KAUTSKY

In contradistinction to Bernstein, Karl Kautsky was in 1898 still sitting on the letter of Marxism which he had accepted as the holy doctrine.[17] It was he who systematically put together and elaborated on Marx's notions concerning the economic organisation of socialist society. His efforts resulted in the first *explicit* formulation of the one nation, one factory concept. While Marx had been rather general in his occasional comments on the future proletarian national economy, Kautsky was more specific. As the main theoretician of the biggest Marxist political party he felt obliged to concretise what his master had just abstractly indicated. Like Marx and Engels, Kautsky was absolutely convinced that socialism and the market were mutually exclusive. In order practically to eliminate both the production for sale and circulation of commodities, he developed Marx's notion about the society best organised for the production of wealth as that which had only a single entrepreneur in charge, apportioning the work to the various members of the community in accordance with a predetermined rule,[18] into the concept equating the socialist society with a 'single gigantic industrial concern in which the same principles would have to prevail as in any large industrial establishment'.[19] Moreover, Kautsky strongly believed that the substitution of production for sale by production for use would require a degree of national self-sufficiency and autarky. Once the market exchange has been eliminated within a national economy, argued Kautsky, it ought not to dominate economic relations among states. This statement, which later served as a point of departure for Lenin's monopoly of foreign trade as well as Stalin's autarkic economic policy, was in accord with both Marx's perception of post-capitalist economic organisation and that of economic relations among socialist nations: aid and co-operation were to substitute for international trade. However strange and naïve this suggestion could have seemed, it did not lack its merits. If one sees the supersession of the market as a *sine qua non* for the society in which one's efforts should no longer be dependent on one's greediness but on the needs of others, and in which, by definition, the exchange of strict equivalents would perpetuate the existence of man *qua homo oeconomicus* who sees his fellow-men as mere exchangers of equal values, then, consequently, an extension of this concept to the sphere of international economic relations would have to aim at maximum restriction of foreign trade which is but the exchange shaped according to the principle of comparative advantage. Because the market as a criterion of comparative advantage has been abolished, there would be no way to measure the latter which, once unmeasurable, loses its meaning. Therefore, Kautsky's emphasis on a maximum possible degree of self-sufficiency of individual nations appears to be the most logical, though the least economic, solution of the dilemma facing the non-market national economies.

Kautsky freely admitted that his society, organised along the lines of the nation-wide factory, would have to bring freedom of labour to an end:

> It is true that in one respect the working-man does enjoy freedom under the capitalist system. If the work does not suit him in one factory, he is free to seek work in another; he can change his employer. In a socialist community, where all the means of production are in a single hand, there is but one employer; to change is impossible.[20]

Unlike Bernstein, for whom freedom of labour was one of the greatest achievements in the historical process of gradual liberation of working men, Kautsky in 1891 did not pay too much attention to the abolition of this mere 'formal' and 'liberal' freedom. He drily suggested that 'it is true that socialist production is irreconcilable with the full freedom of labour, that is, with the freedom of the labourer to work when, where and how he wills'.[21] Though he knew much better than Marx that, once the authoritative discipline of the plan was established, the very idea of the labourer wandering freely and spontaneously from factory to factory and from one job to another would become just a utopian dream, Kautsky the author of the *Erfurt Program* had nothing to say against the boring discipline of the unfree (in the Kantian liberal terms) labour in his one nation, one factory socialist system. It was only Kautsky the reformer, Kautsky 'the renegade' (Lenin) who bitterly revised, after his one nation, one factory system had been established in Russia, the old Marxian concept:

> Without money only two kinds of economy are possible: First of all the primitive economy (already mentioned). Adapted to modern dimensions, this would mean that the whole of productive activity of the State would form a single factory, under one central control, which would assign its tasks to each single business, collect the

products of the entire population, and assign to each business its means of production and to each consumer his means of consumption in kind. The ideal of such a condition is the prison or the barracks.[22]

Some quarter of a century after Bernstein, *the* guardian of the Marxian dogmatic faith Karl Kautsky has also completed the full circle: he realised that, in the circumstances which require a kind of market, one cannot have both of the best worlds at the same time, i.e. production for use *and* free labour.

Kautsky also realised something else, however. He strictly distinguished two different types of market exchange: that which takes place between capital and labour, and that which takes place either among enterprises for the purpose of productive consumption or between enterprises and households for the purpose of personal consumption. The former represents capital relation and may be abolished without the simultaneous abolition of the latter. While the market exchange between labour and capital cannot exist without the market exchange among enterprises and/or between the enterprises and consumers, the latter can be maintained without the former and yet not violate the basic socialist principle that labour becomes an exclusive source of income for each associated producer.[23]

While Bernstein rejected Marxism both in its revolutionary spirit and economic theories, while Kautsky, after having defended for decades every single sentence of Marx, eventually gave up Marxism as well, Lenin was the first Marxist who tried to restore the theoretical integrity and cohesion of Marx's teaching by revising Marx's theory of socialist revolution and that of the post-revolutionary political structure of socialist society.

4.2. LENINISM

Unlike Marx who has always maintained that 'the emancipation of the working class must be done by the working class itself'[24] and that the working class as the class *for itself* must become the ruling class, Lenin has taken the most elitist stand by suggesting that the proletariat is unable to reach anything more than a trade union level of class consciousness; that the working class has to be led by its revolutionary vanguard party whose core consists of professional revolutionaries; that the party is organised strongly along the principles of hierarchy and iron discipline; that it relies on centralism rather than on autonomism, on bureaucracy rather than on democracy;[25] that all other organisations of the working class have to be led and supervised by the party; that after the victorious socialist revolution, the same principle applies also to other organisations, be it the state or associations of peasants, intelligentsia, youth, women, etc.; that within the party, the higher bodies are superior to lower bodies; that all decisions of the high bodies are binding on subordinated party organs, etc.

Though Marx and Engels did not develop any consistent concept of the proletarian party, they referred occasionally to certain principles to which the communist movement should adhere. It follows from Section II of *The Communist Manifesto* that 'the Communists do not form a *separate* party opposed to other working-class parties; they have no interests separate and apart from those of the proletariat as a whole; they do not set up any sectarian principles of their own by which to shape and mould the proletarian movement.[26] In this respect, Engels was usually more specific than Marx. In his letter to Johann Philip Becker (1 April 1880) Engels suggested that 'the looser the organisation [of the party], the firmer it is in reality'.[27] In his article 'On the History of the Communist League' Engels noted that 'the organisation itself was thoroughly democratic, with elective and always removable boards. This alone barred all hankering after conspiracy, which requires dictatorship, and the League was converted – for ordinary peace times at least – into a pure propaganda society. These new Rules were submitted to the communities for discussion – so democratic was the procedure now followed – then once again debated at the Second Congress and finally adopted by the latter on December 8, 1874'.[28] In a letter to Karl Kautsky, Engels made it quite clear that the party officials should be the servants rather than the bosses of the party members,[29] and in a letter to August Bebel he went so far as to compare the party leaders' manners with those of the Prussian police minister Puttkammer.[30] Finally, it suffices to look at the rules of the Communist League (1847) and the International Working Men's Association (1864) to realise that Marx's and Engels' political party was organised contrary to Lenin's principles. Although the Communist League was, like Lenin's party, a conspiratorial underground organisation, its structure was rather loose. The highest body of the League was the Congress whose legislative decisions had to be submitted to the communities (i.e. lower bodies) for acceptance or rejection. The members of the executive body of the League (Central Authority) were responsible to the Congress; therefore, they had a seat in it but *no deciding vote*. The members of the League had the right to recall their officers at any time should they not be satisfied with their conduct of their office.[31]

It has been emphasised in the General Rules of the International Working Men's Association that 'the economic emancipation of the working classes is . . . the great end to which every political movement ought to be subordinate as a means'; that 'all societies and individuals adhering to [the Association] will acknowledge truth, justice and morality as the basis of their conduct toward each other and toward all men . . .'; that 'it acknowledges no rights without duties, no duties without rights'; that 'everybody who acknowledges and defends the principles of the Association is eligible to become a member . . .',[32] etc. Rosa Luxemburg also preferred a loose party organization. In her article 'Organisational Questions of Russian Social Democracy', she wrote: 'The "discipline" which Lenin has in mind is implanted in the proletariat not only by the factory but also by the barracks, by modern bureaucratism – in short, the whole mechanism of the centralised bourgeois state.'[33]

It is only natural that any political party adhering to a doctrine leans towards centralisation – one ought not to forget that it was Kautsky's social democratic party which Engels compared to the Prussian police minister. And yet Lenin called the same Kautsky's party 'opportunistic and autonomistic'. There have been many explanations why Lenin conceptualised his over-centralised vanguard party: Russian backwardness, the Tsarist police system (in a sense, Lenin's party was a negative copy of the Tsarist *okhranka* or, to put it more charitably, of the Tsarist bureaucracy), lack of the industrial proletariat in the agricultural Russian empire, etc. However, these explanations are not enough. Even if the Russian specifics could have initially contributed to Lenin's concept of the ultracentralistic vanguard party, why then did Lenin extend this unique concept through the Third International to the world communist movement as a whole? Why then did Lenin impose the organisational patterns of his own party, through the twenty-one conditions for joining the Third International, even on the communist parties in the highly industrially developed liberal democracies of central and western Europe? Why then did Lenin preserve these patterns not only during the Civil War but also after the introduction of his New Economic Policy?

I would like to suggest yet another explanation. Objectively, Lenin's concept of the party and, consequently, his concept of the dictatorship of the proletariat in which the vanguard party was supposed to play the leading role, does represent a revision of Marx's political concept of socialism and its adjustment to the concept of one factory, one nation.

Let me look at Lenin's revision in a more detailed manner.

If Kautsky's was too absolute a formulation of the social-wide factory concept, then Lenin's statement concerning the concept was absurd: 'The whole society will have become a single office and a single factory with equality of labour and pay . . .. *All* citizens are transferred into hired employees of the state which consists of the armed workers. All citizens become employees and workers of a *single* country-wide state syndicate.'[34]

The absurdity of the statement follows from the fact that in order to transfer *all* citizens into hired employees of the state, a previous full-scale socialisation of productive forces would be required. No doubt, at the time Lenin wrote this categorical statement he subscribed to the general Marxist belief that nationalisation of the means of production and their centralisation in the hands of the state would make labour not only immediately social labour, but also immediately socially necessary labour. Lenin also believed – as Hilferding did before him – that commodity production had been undermined and had already started to wither away in the monopoly stage of capitalism.[35] If this was true for large capitalist syndicates, why should this not be true for a single, nation-wide syndicate representing a national socialist economy as a whole? Contrary to Hilferding and Lenin, however, commodity production had *not* been undermined by the emergence of big capitalist corporations. The only thing which had really happened was that the kind of commodity and market relations known to Marx had been replaced by another kind of commodity and market relations. The capitalist commodity production known to Ricardo and Marx was much more similar to the pre-capitalist small-commodity production than to that of the highly developed capitalism of the twentieth century. While the difference between the market of small-commodity production and the *laissez-faire* market of Marx's *Das Kapital* was primarily quantitative, the difference between the *laissez-faire* capitalist market and the oligopolistic market is primarily qualitative. In the former commodity productions the enterprises worked for unknown markets and made decisions without having an *ex ante* knowledge of social demand and supply. The entire difference between the small-commodity and the *laissez-faire* production was that of scale. To be sure, there is also a difference of scale between *laissez-faire* capitalism and monopoly capitalism. In the latter, however, large corporations also *do* control social demand and supply; in other words, the market of the *consumer* has been replaced by the market of the *producer*. Notwithstanding the fact that the big firms know *ex ante* to whom and for what prices they will sell their production, their products retain the commodity form.

It was only *after* the October Revolution that Lenin became more sceptical about the *genuine* socialisation of labour. He realised that a change in the nature of labour does not depend on the nationalisation of the means of production alone, but above all, on the immensely developed productive forces which he had already seen *in* the world's largest international corporations. He emphasised that 'even the greatest possible "determination" in the world is not enough to pass *from* nationalisation and confiscation *to* socialisation'.[36] This was particularly true for Russia with its sea of small-commodity agricultural production and with its as yet weak and diverse industry. This was why Lenin preferred state capitalism to anarchic small-peasant commodity production, why he called state capitalism 'more progressive' than the pre-capitalistic economic forms still prevailing in Russia and why he saw a capitalist monopoly as *the* pattern for socialist economy:

> To make things even clearer, let us first of all take the most concrete example of state capitalism. Everybody knows what this example is. It is Germany. Here we have the 'last word' in modern-scale capitalist engineering and planned organisation, subordinated to *Junker-bourgeois imperialism.* Cross out the words in italics, and in place of the militarist, Junker, bourgeois, imperialist *state* put *also a state,* but of different social type, of a different social content – a Soviet state, that is, a proletarian state, and you will have the *sum total* of the conditions necessary for socialism.[37]

At this stage, Lenin's general concept formulated in *The State and Revolution*, was given a more concrete form. State capitalism was to be replaced by state socialism; the German war economy with its strict semi-bureaucratic, semi-military central planning and control was chosen as a model for the socialistically organised economic systems. Instead of private corporations subordinated to the temporary war command planning of a capitalist state, one would have nationalised enterprises subordinated to a permanent command planning of a socialist state. Such command planning would rely on '*unquestioning subordination* to a single will [which] is absolutely necessary for the success of processes organised on the pattern of large-scale machine industry'.[38] On the one hand, socialism 'is unconceivable without planned state organisation which keeps tens of millions of people to the strictest observance of a united standard in production and distribution, [on the other hand] socialism is inconceivable unless the proletariat is the ruler of the state'.[39] But the proletariat cannot become directly the ruling class of the state whose national economy is run from one centre. It may become 'the ruler of the state' only through the vanguard party which is *also* run from one centre. Only this vanguard could provide for 'a single will', be it the Central Committee or an individual dictator.[40]

As a result, there are two *similar* structures, one for the economic, another for the political sphere: the single country-wide state syndicate with a factory discipline and hierarchy extended to the whole of society,[41] and the single party with the same authoritative discipline and hierarchy. No self-management or self-government, no industrial democracy within economic units,[42] no workers' control, no free associated labour deciding about the socialised means of production, but one nation-wide super-monopoly with united economic and political power in the hands of a few party leaders or, sometimes, in the hands of one dictator. It is nothing else but an absolute statism.

Of course, Lenin never suggested that such an organisation would last for ever, nor did he say that it was his ideal.[43] Sometime in the future, after the division of labour and scarcity have been superseded and the state has died out, there will be no reason for the factory discipline to be extended to the society as a whole. But was it reasonable to expect that such a system might ever overcome scarcity, the social division of labour and bureaucracy? The concentration of all power in a few central state and party bodies, the '*unquestioning subordination* [of the people] to a single will' – this reminds one of a prison or the barracks rather than of the 'free association of free individuals' as demanded by Karl Marx. The latter was just a dream which Lenin, quite realistically, brought back to earth. Anyone who wants to organise the whole of society as one single factory must pay for it the price consisting in the loss of freedom and democracy.

Lenin never admired freedom in the Kantian formulation or democracy as understood by the liberals. He was aware of a connection between commodity production on the one hand and freedom, equality and democracy on the other.[44] He expected that with the supersession of commodity relations, *liberal* freedom, equality and democracy would disappear. Any attempt to incorporate these concepts in the dictatorship of the proletariat is, according to Lenin, tantamount to accepting bourgeois ideology. Lenin was concerned with a negation of liberal freedom rather than with its positive overcoming through the total emancipation of man as suggested by Marx.

At this point I have to stress the fact that Lenin could not have known the unpublished manuscripts of the young Marx, and was hardly intimate with such works as the *German Ideology*. Not only Lenin but, for that matter, all his contemporaries were acquainted mainly with Marx's mature economic and political writings and with Engels' theoretical and polemical works. Moreover, Lenin failed to understand properly Marx's famous passage in the third volume of *Das Kapital* dealing with the realm of necessity and the realm of freedom as well as Engels' notion in *Anti-Dühring* concerning the kingdom of necessity and the kingdom of freedom. Since the realm of freedom 'can only consist in socialised men, the associated producers, rationally regulating their interchange with Nature, bringing it under common control',[45] and the kingdom of freedom can only consist in that 'the whole sphere of the conditions of life which environ man, and which have hitherto ruled man, now comes under the dominion and control of man',[46] freedom in this broader philosophical sense presupposes the end of the state as an organisation superimposed upon the society. But it is true only for *this* kind of freedom, not for freedom in the political sense. Therefore, when Lenin repeated Engels' dictum 'while the state exists there can be no freedom', and 'when there is freedom, there will be no state',[47] he confused two absolutely different concepts of freedom. So did Malaparte who repeated the latter quotation in his *Technique of the Coup d'Etat*. Gramsci rightly criticised Malaparte for this mistake: 'In the latter proposition, the term "freedom" cannot be taken in its ordinary meaning of "political freedom, freedom of the press, etc.", but was counterposed to "necessity" . . .. Malaparte has not caught even the faintest whiff of the significance of the proposition.'[48] One may only add that Lenin has not caught the significance of Marx's and Engels' propositions either.

It is Lenin's *The State and Revolution* which is usually cited as *the* example that Lenin *was* a faithful executor of Marx's and Engels' concept of the dictatorship of the proletariat. I have already argued that there was no meaningful concept of the dictatorship of the proletariat in Marx's writings, and that there were democratic interpretations of the concept by Engels, Kautsky and Rosa Luxemburg. Now I may add that there were also different interpretations of the concept in various writings of Lenin. As early as 1906 Lenin offered a 'scholarly' definition of dictatorship in his essay 'The Victory of the Cadets and the Tasks of the Workers' Party': 'The scientific term "dictatorship" means nothing more nor less than authority untrammelled by any laws, absolutely unrestricted by any rules whatever, and based directly on force. The term "dictatorship" *has no other meaning than this . . ..*'[49]

Basic elements of this early definition have been incorporated in Lenin's classical definition of the dictatorship of the proletariat which appeared in his polemics against Karl Kautsky's concept of the dictatorship of the proletariat. Said Lenin in 1918: 'Dictatorship is the rule based directly upon force and unrestricted by any laws. The revolutionary dictatorship of the proletariat is rule won and maintained by the use of violence of the proletariat against bourgeoisie, rule that is unrestricted by any laws.'[50]

However, one must not take this statement of Lenin concerning the rule of the proletariat too literally. Two years later, on 30 December 1920, in his polemics against Trotsky and Bukharin, Lenin made it absolutely clear that the dictatorship can be exercised neither by the proletarian class as a whole, nor by a mass proletarian organisation (trade unions), because the proletariat is divided, degraded and corrupted. The proletariat as a whole is 'like an arrangement of cogwheels'; it is only its vanguard – the party – that has absorbed the revolutionary energy of the class and that is the only proper force which can exercise this dictatorship on behalf of the proletariat. But even this dictatorship through the vanguard could not work 'without a number of "transmission belts" running from the vanguard to the mass of the advanced class, and from the latter to the mass of the working people'.[51]

This was a horrible picture indeed. Whatever Marx and Engels could have conceived of the term 'the dictatorship of the proletariat', they certainly would have been surprised at what Lenin had to offer under the label of Marxism: the 'divided, degraded[52] and corrupted' proletariat as 'an arrangement of cogwheels' governed by its vanguard by virtue of 'transmission belts' (note that Lenin's terminology had nothing in common with Marx's humanistic language) was still called 'the advanced class' as compared to the mass of the working people. But neither Marx nor Engels would have any right to complain. It was they who suggested the concept of one social factory without thinking too much about its real meaning and practical implications. In a huge social factory the proletarians never become the ruling class; at best, they may play the part of 'cogwheels' and 'transmission belts'. Any society organised along the principles of a factory has to rely on the machinery of power (the party) which cannot but use the working class as a mere mechanism for transmitting the power from the top downward.

Of course, there were also other definitions of the dictatorship of the proletariat offered by Lenin. For instance, on 29 May 1919, Lenin shifted the emphasis from the use of force to the organisational tasks of the building of socialism. In his *Greetings to the Hungarian Workers* he pointed out that 'the essence of proletarian dictatorship is not in force alone, or even mainly in force', and in *A Great Beginning*, written in July 1919, he repeated almost verbatim the same for the Russian workers.[53] It did not mean, however, that his previous definitions of the dictatorship of the proletariat lost their validity. Between 1906 and 1924 Lenin defined and re-defined the dictatorship of the proletariat on various occasions in so many different ways that it would require a special book just to discuss all the subtleties of his sophistics. In its practice, however, the Bolshevik party has followed and still follows mainly the concept which Lenin so bluntly formulated in his polemics against Trotsky on 30 December 1920.

In the light of all that has been just said, I have to answer the question of how to interpret *The State and Revolution*. Even if I admit that it was this pamphlet in which Lenin conceived of dictatorship of the proletariat as the most consistent direct popular participation of the working masses in political and economic decision-making, one must not forget that *The State and Revolution* has to be read with the knowledge of Lenin's concept of the party as seen through his *What Is To Be Done?* and *One Step Forward, Two Steps Backward*. Because Lenin never departed from the principles expressed in these two basic works; because he made us know how the ideas of *The State and Revolution* were to be interpreted for practical political use after the October Revolution;[54] and finally, because his conception of the dictatorship of the proletariat in *The State and Revolution* is based on the one nation, one factory concept which, in the context of Lenin's earlier and later works already mentioned, represents the barracks socialism *par excellence*, no reference to *The State and Revolution* could hide the fact that Lenin did revise Marx's political perception of the first phase of communist society.

However, some people ascribe to Lenin yet another revision of Marx. After a short experience with war communism Lenin realised that his over-centralised non-market system could not work. One must give him credit for his frank admission of the mistake. Said Lenin:

Borne along on the crest of the wave of enthusiasm, rousing first the political enthusiasm and then the military enthusiasm of the people, we expected to accomplish economic tasks just as great as the political and military tasks we had accomplished by relying directly on this enthusiasm. We expected – or perhaps it would be truer to say we presumed without having given it adequate consideration – to be able to organise the state production and the state distribution of products

on communist lines in a small-peasant country directly as ordered by
the proletarian state. Experience has proved that we were wrong.[55]

This self-criticism, as well as the switch from war communism
through tax in kind to the New Economic Policy, was caused by the fact
that in 1920 Russia had been a country with prevailing small-
commodity peasant production. Lenin made it clear on several occasions that NEP was a temporary retreat for one or two decades. He
suggested that the party 'shall not retreat too far', that there 'are signs
that we shall be able to stop this retreat in the not too distant future'.[56]
On the one hand, he was aware that the temporary reintroduction of
commodity production, money, credit and the market was contrary to
the Marxist perception of socialism.[57] He exclaimed: 'Communism and
trade? It sounds strange. The two seem to be unconnected, incongruous,
poles apart. But if we study it from the point of view of *economics*, we
shall find that the one is no more remote from the other than
communism is from small-peasant, patriarchal farming.'[58] On the other
hand, Marxist communism is also incompatible with patriarchal
farming. Hence it was the Russian backwardness which led Lenin to the
introduction of NEP: one cannot abolish commodity production and
trade in a country with prevailing small-peasant agriculture. What is
more, trade was the only possible *economic* link between the scores of
millions of small farmers and large-scale industry.[59] In other words,
Lenin's New Economic Policy was caused by lack of Russian industrial
development, by lack of machinery and electricity needed for a large-
scale agriculture which, if it had existed, could easily have been included
in the centrally planned and centrally managed nation-wide factory.[60]
There is nowhere in the heavy volumes of Lenin's collected works a
single statement which would repudiate, *in principle*, the old Marxian
thesis concerning the incompatability of the market with socialism. The
temporary revival of the market in the early 1920s was, according to
Lenin, just a retreat, certainly a retreat for a few decades rather than for a
few years, but by no means a fundamental revision of Marx's concept of
market-free socialist economy.

Lenin's New Economic Policy has for decades been subject to
different interpretations. Firstly, it actually lasted only a few years,
though Lenin conceived it as a long-term method for the building of
socialism in Russia. It consisted, among other things, in concessions to
foreign capitalists which, according to Lenin, would eventually be
turned back into the hands of the Soviet state. Secondly, NEP was
caused by lack of Russian industrial development, by lack of large-scale

agriculture equipped with modern machinery. Lenin realised that Russia would first have to go through a period of fast industrialisation because 'socialism is inconceivable without large-scale capitalist engineering based on the latest discoveries of modern science'.[61] He also realised that Russia was not mature enough for *direct* transformation to socialism, that she did not meet standard Marxian conditions for the lower phase of communism. Therefore, the Russian national economy could not have been immediately turned into one huge nation-wide factory which always had been and remained as Lenin's model of socialist society.

Three basic interpretations of NEP have been offered to date. The first was suggested by Stalin in his address to the Central Committee of the Party in July 1928. Stalin defined war communism as an extraordinary measure caused by civil war and foreign intervention and maintained that, had it not been for these two reasons, there would have been no war communism in Russia at all, that the Soviet Party and Government would have started the dictatorship of the proletariat with NEP already in 1918.[62] This interpretation ignores the fact that during the period immediately following the October Revolution no leader of the Bolshevik party dared to challenge the generally recognised Marxian principle of the incompatibility of commodity, money and market relations with socialism.[63] Their belief in direct allocation of resources in physical terms was at the time still unshakable. Stalin's interpretation was just an *ex post* attempt to prove that war communism had been imposed upon the party by circumstances and that Lenin was never naïve enough to believe genuinely in its merits. In other words, Stalin wanted to prove that the party had not erred.

The second interpretation is a revision of that of Stalin. Not war communism, but the New Economic Policy was imposed upon the party by circumstances, namely by the fact that Russia was not mature enough for the market-free centralised economic system and, on top of that, because she was economically exhausted by long fighting in both the First World War and the Civil War. As soon as Russia had recovered, NEP was abandoned and the policy of industrialisation was carried out along the principles of a non-market economic system with the assistance of commercial accounting (*khozrashchot*). This, it could be argued, was perfectly consistent with Lenin's concept of NEP as that of a retreat, with Lenin's demand to use commercial *methods* without changing the nature of command planning,[64] with Marx's and Lenin's suggestions that bookkeeping and commercial accounting were indispensable in any socialist economy.[65]

The third interpretation of NEP suggests that it was Lenin who first revised the dogma of the 'incompatibility of commodity production with the building of socialism'.[66] It has appeared and reappeared in writings of those eastern European and Soviet economists who have been in favour of market-oriented reforms and who wanted to exploit some of Lenin's ideas concerning NEP to add more legitimacy to their proposals aiming at marketisation of socialist economies. They have appreciated, however, that Lenin always used to talk not of the developed socialist economies but of the concrete Russians economy in the early 1920s and that Lenin died before he might have formulated his principles of NEP in a more general fashion.

Be that as it may, it *was* Lenin who introduced NEP, and it was NEP which undermined the strong central economic control that had prevailed during the period of war communism. Significantly enough, the same Lenin never gave the slightest consideration to the undermining of political centralism. On the contrary, the introduction of NEP had been preceded, on Lenin's suggestion, by the ban on factions within the Party. Thus, the economic retreat was not to be followed by any political retreat, and the revival of economic pluralism by no means meant either a revival of political pluralism or an introduction of industrial democracy. At the Tenth Congress of the Party, the so-called workers' opposition was defeated, and its motion that the workers should run industrial enterprises was rejected. Lenin the author of NEP never agreed either with self-government or with self-management.[67] Lenin's insistence on the preservation of the hierarchical structure of the Party indicates that it is the second of the above interpretations of NEP which seems to reflect most accurately his real intentions.

Everyone who accepts my analysis ought to accept also its logical consequences, namely that the concept of market-free, commodity-free and money-free socialist economy organised along the principles of one nation, one factory and subject to command social planning, leads inevitably to the Leninist dictatorship of the proletariat exercised by the party structured according to the principles first suggested by Lenin.

4.3. THE YUGOSLAV REVISION

According to the Yugoslav conception of socialism, the social development following a victorious socialist revolution requires a short transitory period (the dictatorship of the proletariat) in which 'the proletariat will use its political supremacy to wrest, by degrees, all capital from the bourgeoisie . . . . In the beginning, this cannot be effected except by the means of despotic inroads on the rights of property, and on the conditions of bourgeois production . . . .[68] There is no reason, however, to maintain the dictatorship of the proletariat during the entire lower phase of communism. According to Marx, the proletariat 'can apply only the economic means that will abolish its own character as *salariat*, and hence as a class; with its complete victory, therefore, its rule comes to an end, because its class character has disappeared'.[69] What, then, would replace the dictatorship of the proletariat? The Yugoslavs have found the answer in the same work of Marx: 'When class rule has disappeared, there will be no state in the present political sense.'[70] What does it mean? If one consults Marx again, the answer would be quite unequivocal: 'The matter begins with the self-government by the community.'[71]

Hence, in terms of politics, the state is still preserved, but it is no longer the state in the present (i.e. coercive) political sense. The state is no longer 'superimposed upon society'; on the contrary, it becomes 'completely subordinated to it'.[72] The society now consists of self-governed communities which are able to administer public affairs with the working people (rather than the working class) being the sole holders of power and of government of social affairs. As a theoretical concept, this arrangement is in full accord with classical Marxian thought. (This does not necessarily mean that the theoretical concept has been ideally reflected by the Yugoslav political praxis.)

The Yugoslav interpretation is the only one which introduces two stages into the Marxist theory of socialist revolution. The first centralistic and *étatist* period cannot be avoided: the dictatorship of the proletariat should use 'despotic inroads' on the rights of private property; it may use even dictatorial forms and methods of government. All this is but a short transitory period which has to be followed by democratic forms of self-government and self-management.

At this point, some new problems have to be solved. The first one concerns the form of the ownership of the means of production. Immediately after the revolution the means of production have to be nationalised and centralised in the hands of the state. According to both the Yugoslavs and the founding fathers of Marxism, this act is necessary though not sufficient for the building of socialism. Says Engels: 'State ownership of the productive forces is not the solution of the conflict, but concealed within it are the technical conditions that form the elements of that solution.'[73] Says Marx: '. . . the abolition of private property and communism are by no means identical . . . .'[74] And elsewhere:

'How little this annulment [a mere nationalisation] of private property is really an appropriation [of human essence] is in fact proved by the abstract negation of the entire world of culture and civilisation, the regression to the *unnatural* simplicity of the *poor* and crude man who has a few needs and who has not only failed to go beyond private property but has not yet even reached it.'[75]

The key to the Yugoslav interpretation of the abolition of private property may be found in *one* of Marx's concepts of capital, namely that 'capital is . . . the governing power over labour and its products'.[76] Be it the capitalist or the state, it is the *owner* of capital who dominates labour. In order to eliminate any external domination over labour, the workers themselves have to become owners of capital. And since the essence of the ownership of capital lies not in a title to property but in an effective power of command over labour and its products, the 'worker is free only when he is the owner of his instruments of labour – this can be the case either in individual or in collective form'.[77] To make it possible for a collective form, the form of social ownership rather than of state ownership of the means of production would be the solution for the means of production already socialised, and the form of individual ownership would be the solution for the means of production used by small peasants and artisans. (A co-operative form of property might be an alternative to individual ownership of individual means of production.) Consequently, the ownership of the means of production ought to be separated from the state and put under direct control of the employees by virtue of self-management. This does not necessarily mean that the social means of production would be *formally* owned by direct producers. Though they are still *owned* by the society as a whole, they are *controlled* by those who work with them. This arrangement is a precondition not only for the direct workers' control over their labour and products which represents a real rather than a formal abolition of capital relationships, but also for a gradual withering away of the state which, for the first time, may become subordinated to the society instead of being – as is the case of state socialism – superimposed upon the society.

So far so good: everything goes smoothly along the principles of Marxism. But since Marx's and Engels' rejection of the market is incompatible with the concept of a self-managed socialist economic system, the Yugoslavs had to revise Marx's non-market model of socialist economy which they did without having abandoned Marxism as a whole. In order to accomplish this task they had also to reinterpret a new Marx's notion of the dictatorship of the proletariat. To do this, the

Yugoslavs had to revise Lenin's revision of Marx's political perception of socialism in general and Lenin's concept of the party in particular. As to the latter, however, their efforts have been only partially successful.

It is my view that the Yugoslavs have been moved towards market self-managing socialism under the pressure of circumstances after having been expelled from the Soviet bloc and Cominform in the late 1940s. Prior to this event, Yugoslav communists had duly followed the Soviet model of state socialism under the leadership of the Communist Party of Yugoslavia which was organised according to Lenin's principles. After the first critical document had been issued by Cominform in 1948, Yugoslav leaders were behaving, for a period of time, more Stalinistically than Stalin himself. Only when they realised that such a response to the Soviet critique was futile did they change their mind and start to look for an alternative to the Soviet model of socialism. In order to win the support of the majority of the Yugoslav people, i.e. the peasantry, they abandoned collectivisation of agriculture and declared personal ownership of individual means of production fully compatible with socialism. In order to strengthen the ties between the workers and the party, they introduced their self-managing alternative to the Soviet-type state socialism. What is more, in order to demonstrate that theirs was quite a different party from all those associated with the Cominform, the Yugoslav communists changed its name from the Communist Party of Yugoslavia to the League of Communists of Yugoslavia. This change indicated that the Yugoslav communists wanted to turn back from Lenin to Marx. For one thing, the very term 'league' suggested that it was a loose political association rather than a strictly organised and disciplined party. For another, Marx's and Engels' party was also called the League of Communists, and its rules of 1847, as well as the rules of the International Working Men's Association of 1864, were formulated in a rather democratic manner.[78]

When the Yugoslavs realised that only a non-Leninist party was compatible with self-managing socialism, the Leninist principles and norms had been already deeply rooted in their party from top to bottom. The Yugoslav Communist Party used to hold the same monopoly of power, employ similar methods of coercion and exercise the same total control over the country as did any other Leninist party in power. Prior to the introduction of self-management, it fitted perfectly in the centralised structure of the Yugoslav economy. Only after the introduction of the self-managing system did the centralised structure of the party come into conflict with the new decentralised structure of the Yugoslav national economy.

While the Yugoslav revision of Marx's non-market concept of socialist economy was consistent and decisive, their revision of Lenin's concept of the party was half-hearted. No doubt the League of Communists of Yugoslavia has become less centralised than other ruling communist parties. Nevertheless, it still preserves its right to be the only leading organised force of the working class and working people, its guiding ideological role, its position of being the prime mover of the country's political activity and the protector of the country's socialist achievements. The inconsistency of the revision of Lenin's principles creates the most crucial problem of the unique Yugoslav self-managing socialism. This system suffers from the cleavage between the decentralised self-managed economy and the hierarchically organised communist party whose informal power contradicts formal arrangements of self-management in all political and economic institutions. If there is anything contrary to self-managing pluralism, self-managing democracy and self-managing horizontal relations, then it is democratic centralism. Its essence rests in that the superior organ makes decisions while the subordinate organ carries out orders. No self-managing enterprise ought to be directly and permanently subordinated to a superior organ, however. Obviously, the former's independence is limited by laws, central planning and social regulation, but it definitely must not be subject to any political or administrative body in the sense that it would have to carry out external orders. In the long run, democratism and pluralism in the economic sphere are incompatible with the authoritarian one-party system in the political sphere. Temporarily, these two principles can coexist provided that after a period of time one gives way to the other. If the pluralistic and democratic principle of self-management is to be preserved, then the authoritarian principle of the one-party system must be removed. If, however, the political monopoly of the party is to be preserved, then the principle of self-management would gradually be undermined. If the monopolistic political party is to have the right to an overall political control, it would intervene in the decision-making of self-managed units. It could impose its will either through the organs of state administration or indirectly through the activity of its members. According to the statutes of all Leninist parties their members are obliged to follow the party line wherever they happen to live or work. This creates the problem of split loyalty for each party member. On the one hand, he is expected to be loyal to his work unit and/or to his community. On the other hand, he is expected to be loyal to the party. (According to the doctrine of democratic centralism, the decisions of the ruling party are binding even

Marxism, Socialism, Freedom

for non-members.) If all interests represented by the party always coincided with all interests of all self-managed units, there would be no problem. Since, under the condition of social division of labour combined with scarcity, such unity of interests is scarcely possible, conflicts of interests make the split loyalty inevitable. If one's loyalty to the party prevails, the self-managing principles are upset. If one's loyalty to the self-managed community prevails, then the principle of democratic centralism is upset.

It may be suggested that the Leninist party may gradually evolve and change up to the point at which it would abandon the principles of democratic centralism and that of its leading role. Consequently, the party would, after a period of time, introduce freedom of factions, freedom of discussion and protection of minorities. If so, the party would become democratic enough to live with self-management. This would open its ranks to anyone, allow its members freedom of judgement and opinion and free them from the obligation to follow the party line in the self-managing organs. It is even possible to imagine an evolution of the monopolistic party towards an internal split resulting in the emergence of two or more political parties. But this is exactly what the Yugoslavs reject. They are afraid that such a development would lead to a *partyisation* of self-management and bring an associationist socialism to an end. They suspect that a multi-party system might shift the self-management to a traditional representative system and make the administration of microeconomic affairs a political battlefield. They argue that the principle of self-management does not rest in that one is the member of a political party but in that one has the right to participate in direct decision-making in his work-place as the producer. For this reason, they would like to see their associationist socialism evolving towards an integral self-management without any political party. The integral self-management calls for an extension of the participatory principle to regional, provincial and national levels of government. Even if one conceives of a self-managed *society* as a permanent congress of workers' and communal councils, or a federation of such councils, the self-management discussed so far merely as a system of horizontal relations would have to grow in the vertical direction. Self-managing bodies in work units would have to delegate their members to higher controlling organs which would carry out all the traditional functions of representative governments.

In this context, two questions arise. The first concerns the type of delegation, the second the mandate of the delegates. If the higher controlling bodies consisted of delegates from both economic and political communities, the democratic principle 'one man, one vote' would be violated. Those who for whatever reason were not economically active (housewives, pensioners, disabled) would be under-represented while the active producers would have the privilege of double-representation. Some people would be represented only as citizens, others as citizens *and* producers.

A special right of the associated producers to be separately represented in higher controlling bodies is at the very least problematic. Any kind of macroeconomic regulation including societal planning, distribution and redistribution of national income, equalisation of poor and rich regions, etc., is of a political nature and should be entrusted to *political* organs proportionally representing the people in their capacity as citizens. In this respect, the extension of the microeconomic self-management to the macropolitical level would be contrary to the principle of political equality.

The second question is of no less importance. If the delegates from self-managing units to higher controlling organs were allowed to represent merely the common local or particular interest of their constituencies, it would be rather difficult to reach consensus on conflicting priorities. Given the economy of scarcity, a preferential satisfaction of one particular (local) need would leave another particular (local) need unsatisfied. (Incidentally, even the most vital local needs cease to be vital when viewed from the national level.) If the delegates from self-managing units were given the mandate to deal autonomously with macropolitical issues in accordance with national (regional, provincial) preferences, the principle of delegation would vanish and the principle of representation would prevail.[79]

The complexity of this question may be demonstrated by quoting from Article 141 of the Yugoslav Constitution:

In taking stands on questions being decided in the assembly, the delegates shall act in conformity with the guidelines received from their self-managing organisations and communities and with the basic stands of the delegations or of socio-political organisations which have delegated them, and in conformity with the common and general social interests and needs; they shall be independent in their options and voting.[80]

Even if I leave aside the specific Yugoslav combination of the one-party system with self-management, the above-quoted article contains at least three mutually exclusive principles. The delegates shall act:

(1) in conformity with *the guidelines from their self-managing organi-sations and communities*;
(2) in conformity with *the common and general social interests and needs*;
(3) they shall be *independent* in their options and voting.

This clearly indicates that the problem has not been solved by the Yugoslavs, and one may add that it seems to be almost impossible to find its consistent solution *within the framework of self-management extended to the macroeconomic and macropolitical level.* (A solution for *micro*economic self-management combined with macropolitical repre-sentation is offered in Chapter 6.)

5 A General Democratic Revision

It is my intention to offer a general revision of Marxism which would make it possible to re-create, from Marx's intrinsically contradictory concept, a modern democratic theory of labour-managed systems leading to a rational, humanistic and above all realisable socialism. This theory can by no means bring about an ideal system. What it can do, however, is to propose the general structural arrangements for a democratic system 'combining the sober reasonableness of the liberal era with the care for the common social welfare'.[1]

5.1. MARX'S FINAL ENDS

The following statement, taken from Marx's and Engels' programmatic and most revolutionary political pamphlet, could be accepted by any democratic theory:

> In place of the old bourgeois society, with its classes and class antagonism, we shall have an association, in which the free development of each is the condition for the free development of all.[2]

If one tentatively analyses this concise statement, one could easily discover its logical meaning:

(a) It ought to be a *classless* society without private ownership of the means of production and, consequently, without any class control over labour and its products. An alternative to the former bourgeois control over capital could be a *social* control over capital. However, the social control must not be confused with state control. If it were the state which took over the control of the means of production from the bourgeoisie, one would have state capitalism instead of socialism.

(b) The society ought to be made up of working people, in which there will be no owners of capital nor any non-owners of capital. Therefore, there will be no unearned incomes from direct or indirect exploitation of others' labour.

(c) Marx and Engels have called such a society an *association*. This implies a democratic social structure with prevailing horizontal relations of equality. Such a structure cannot but rely on self-management in work-places and self-government in communities. All the necessary vertical relations could be based on a representative democratic system.

(d) We are told that the *free development of each is the condition for the free development of all*. However, there could be no free development of each without the unequivocal appreciation of individual freedoms and civil rights.

(e) While the guaranteed individual freedoms and civil rights are a necessary condition for the free development of each individual, they are not a sufficient condition. For Marx, the free development equals 'the development of human energy as an end in itself'.[3] In other words, each individual is entitled and encouraged to make the best of himself, to cultivate his talents and faculties either in universal or specialised ways to an optimum which would enable him to reach a degree of self-fulfilment and self-determination. Hence, in addition to the individual's freedom of choice and to the individual's right to decide about himself, a very high level of social productivity will be another necessary condition for the implementation of the concept. The development of productive forces has to be high enough to enable at least the distribution of the means of education and health according to one's needs.

It may be argued that there is nothing specifically communistic in this general proposition concerning the most salient characteristics of the society which was to replace, according to Marx and Engels, the old bourgeois system. The proposition might be readily accepted by any consistent socialist and, in my opinion, also by any consistent democrat. It does not bother me at the moment that the proposition would hardly be acceptable for the followers of Lenin and the New Left, or, for that matter, for old-fashioned liberals and conservatives. For those on the left side of the borderline, the proposition would seem too anarchistic, toothless and individualistic; for those on the right side it would seem (and rightly so) too radical because it excludes the right to unlimited appropriation of the means of production and private enterprise. What bothers me at the moment, however, is another question: could my interpretation of the proposition have been acceptable for Marx and Engels themselves? If I were allowed to make a speculation, I would have to say that for any Marxist in the nineteenth century, my interpretation would probably have seemed outrageous. But what about a Marxist who lives and thinks in the present-day world?

5.2. MARX'S REVOLUTIONARY MEANS

'Communism', wrote Marx and Engels in *The German Ideology*, 'is for us not a *state of affairs* which is to be established, an *ideal* to which reality [will] have to adjust itself. We call communism the *real* movement which abolishes *the present state of things*.'[4] The 'present state of things' obviously means the state of things in the 1840s and *not* the state of things in the 1970s. There is no need to describe the conditions of the working people in the rudimentary stages of western European industrialisation: it has been already done by quite a few authors including Engels' *The Condition of the Working-Class in England*. By contemporary standards it was a hell, and as we know today it was hell mainly for two reasons. First, capitalism had been going through the stage of extensive industrialisation in which everything was secondary except the accumulation of capital. It was virtually production for the sake of production, accumulation for the sake of accumulation: the surplus-value not only could have been, but it must have been, due to tough competition, spent mainly for investments. No wonder that the consumption of the working class was rather limited[5] and the degree of exploitation was without precedent. Second, the capitalist industrialisation took place in the conditions of a liberalism which was yet too distant from its later transformation into liberal democracy. The working class was weak and unorganised, without its own unions and political parties, not yet a part of civil society, not recognised as a political force by the liberal state. What is more, an analysis of all economic trends which could have been empirically tested and theoretically generalised was left to the economists only. The state, according to the famous doctrine formulated by Adam Smith, should have not interfered with a perfect job done by the invisible hand which, according to the then prevailing opinion, was able to harmonise conflicting interests of various exchangers. As an economist, Marx was just a critic of bourgeois political economy and a culminator of its classical school. On the one hand, he brought to perfection some classical concepts, notably the labour theory of value; on the other, he took over some inconsistences of his great predecessors, for instance Adam Smith's dual concept of productive labour. In some instances he performed below the

level of David Ricardo, as was the case with the model of growing
productivity of labour. Ricardo formulated a law according to which
any saving of labour decreases the value of commodities, be it the
saving of past labour (capital) or of present labour (wages). One may
construct at least five models of labour productivity growth.[6] The first
one is neutral, the second and the fourth have a negative effect on the
working class, while the third and the fifth have positive effects on
the working class. During Marx's lifetime the second and
fourth models prevailed. Marx generalised their negative effects in the
formulation of his general law of capitalist accumulation by project-
ing the observed trends into the future. What is more, he took
into consideration only economic factors and abstracted from politics.
No doubt, Marx's law of capitalist accumulation did reflect the
tendencies he could have empirically tested after having written *Das
Kapital*. The law might even have reflected the general tendency of the
capitalist system *if* politics had not changed the entire frame of reference
and *if* another two technological revolutions had not brought about an
integral growth of labour productivity. It can hardly be denied that the
growth of the organic composition of capital really locks out present
labour from the process of production and that, in the condition of
reproduction on an extended scale, every additional unit of capital
employs fewer workers than did the previous one. If there had been no
shortening of the working hours; if wages had been regulated exclusively by the law of supply and demand; if there had been no trade
unions, no socialist political parties, no labour legislation, no democratisation of liberal society and no state intervention in the anarchic
laissez-faire economy – in a word, if politics had not interfered with
private capitalism – then Marx's law would have been strongly felt by
the workers not only as a mere (and temporary) tendency but as a
determining force mercilessly perpetuating their then hopeless position
within the system. On top of it, there have been also important
technological and economic changes which did modify the law:
developed industries required new infrastructure and, consequently,
new jobs had to be created in the (tertiary) sphere of services (contrary
to Marx's assumption, capital gradually took over the sphere of services
and created mass leisure industries); compulsory primary and eventually also secondary schooling with a substantially extended higher
education have changed not only the structure of manpower but also its
needs, demands and gains; the concept of productive labour has been
drastically redefined, and the labour theory of value has become
obsolete; the changing structure of both economics and politics brought

about the consumer society and capitalism itself, previously identified
with the industrial system, has reached its post-industrial stage.

Was Marx wrong when he formulated this and other laws of the
motion of capitalist economy? As an economist, he was not too wrong.
Having taken into consideration economic factors only, he rightly concluded that, *if all other things remained equal*, capitalism would tend to
evolve according to his laws. But first, the other things did *not* remain
equal. And second, Marx might even not have admitted the discrepancy
between his theory and the reality of modern capitalism. He could argue
that nothing essential has changed, that the working class is still
exploited, that however much it may earn it is still dominated by capital,
money and the market as well as being alienated from its product and
from its labour. He might have argued further that what really matters is
not a redistribution of incomes and wealth but a redistribution of power
which, particularly in the economic sphere, remains concentrated in the
hands of corporate capital, technocracy and state bureaucracy. He
might have also argued that, in general, he had rightly predicted the
eventual class polarisation of capitalist societies in two camps, the first
incarnating labour (employees) and the second corporate capital
(employers). These arguments, repeatedly offered by many of Marx's
faithful followers, might be accepted if one allowed that social reality
ought to be compared with an ideal rather than with the past reality or,
for that matter, with the reality in the societies which have followed
Marx's advice and materialised his one nation, one factory concept.
Neither the nationalisation of capital nor the suppression of market
have brought Marx's ideals close to reality in the existing socialist states.
On the contrary, wherever Marx's economic perception of the socialist
system was put into practice, it has not matched the standards of social-
democratic welfare states.

Marx's and Engels' notions of socialism were at times rather
impatient and naïve. In 1848 they asserted that 'society can no longer
live under this bourgeoisie . . . [whose] existence is no longer compatible with society'; that 'it becomes evident that the bourgeoisie is
unfit any longer to be the ruling class in society . . . '.[7] This might have
been written only for propaganda reasons since Marx had been aware,
only a few months before he drafted the *Manifesto*, that 'the material
conditions have not been yet created which make necessary the
abolition of the bourgeois mode of production and therefore also the
definitive overthrow of the political rule of the bourgeoisie'.[8] Engels
admitted shortly before his death that both Marx and himself had been
over-optimistic as to the prospects for socialist revolution in 1848:

'[History] made it clear that the state of economic development on the Continent at that time was not by a long way ripe for the elimination of capitalist production.'[9]

How may one explain such inconsistencies? One of the possible answers to this question may lie in the discrepancy between the personal lifetime of the founding fathers of Marxism and the timing of history. Marx and Engels were quite confident that they had discovered the laws of motion of capitalist society and established, with a scientific precision, that capitalism would inevitably have to give way to a higher socio-economic system. However, the mere confidence that capitalism will eventually come to an end was not able to give them full satisfaction. They wanted to see the end of capitalism during their lives. But what to do if the time for the extinction of capitalism was not ripe enough? Obviously to accelerate history. And what could accelerate history if not a revolution?

Of course, Engels (and probably Marx also) knew only too well that 'all conspiracies are not only futile but even harmful . . . that re-volutions are not made deliberately and arbitrarily, but that everywhere and at all times they have been the necessary outcome of circumstances entirely independent of the will and the leadership of particular parties and classes'.[10] If so, then the only thing which a revolutionary could have done was to be over-optimistic, to see the situation in a better light than it actually was and could have been. Thus, for instance, the young radical Engels had asserted to his audience in the city of Elberfeld on 8 February 1845 that, in communist society, 'it will be easy to be informed about both production and consumption. Since we know how much, on the average, a person needs, it is easy to calculate how much is needed by a given number of individuals, and since production is no longer in the hands of private producers but in those of the community and its administrative bodies, it is a trifling matter *to regulate production according to needs*'.[11] He also romantically believed that 'it is vastly more easy to administer a communist community rather than a competitive one'.[12] Whereas one may reasonably doubt whether the most affluent contemporary society, the United States, is already rich enough to provide for the free development of all its members even if it introduced egalitarian distribution of wealth, Engels was sure in 1880 that 'the possibility of securing for every member of society, by means of socialised production, an existence not only fully sufficient materially, and becoming day by day fuller, but an existence guaranteeing to all the free development and exercise of their physical and mental faculties – this possibility is now for the first time here, but *it is* here'.[13]

I have already quoted (and could quote much more) from Marx's and Engels' suggestions that they would prefer peaceful socialist transformation to violent revolution *if* the bourgeoisie accepted the abolition of the 'present state of things' without too much of a fight. Such statements were too naïve to be taken for granted, however. As students of politics, class struggles and revolutions, Marx and Engels had to know that because the time for the abolition of capitalism was not ripe enough during their lifetime, it would be preposterous to expect that the ruling bourgeoisie would give up voluntarily what could not then have been taken from it even by violence. Marx knew this only too well: it was he who stated that 'no social order ever perishes before all the productive forces for which there is room in it have developed; and new, higher relations of production never appear before the material conditions of their existence have matured in the womb of the old society itself'.[14]

Let me assume that Marx's political party, be it the Communist League or the First International, had seized power in a European country at any time between 1848 and Marx's death in 1883. What could the party have done? Probably the same things the capitalists did:[15] going on with the accumulation, industrialisation and urbanisation, building infrastructure, extending schooling and shortening working hours. In a word, it would have done what capitalism did and does to date: building material preconditions for a higher socio-economic system which is supposed to overcome division of labour, commodity production and scarcity in order to 'organise society in such a way that every member of it can develop and use all his capabilities and powers in complete freedom and without thereby infringing the basic conditions of this society.'[16] The one difference would consist in that it would have been state capitalism rather than private capitalism. One may take the liberty of speculating that if the communists had seized power sometime in the middle of the nineteenth century, they would have tried, in accordance with Marx's perception of socialism, to centralise the means of production in the hands of the state, to abolish the market and to collectivise peasants and small producers. Since accumulation would have to remain the first priority in order to develop productive forces to the extent required for the achievement of communist ends, the state would not have died out but would have become very powerful instead: without the use of coercion it would have been impossible to implement all the socio-economic changes and carry out the priority of accumulation. What is more, the market is the only known mechanism of unauthoritative allocation of labour. Once abolished, freedom of labour would have to come to an end. If one assumes that the communist had won not in one European country only but on an international scale, one could conclude that liberalism would never have evolved into liberal democracy and that the inevitably crude communism would have hardly yielded a democratic and evolutionary alternative to the Marxian revolutionary socialism.

Some Marxists believe that even the worst revolution is still better than the best reform. Other Marxists believe that any revolution is caused by the failure to solve social cleavages by political means, i.e. by structural reforms relying on a compromise between the conflicting parties. In democratic systems where different groups and social classes enjoy freedom of association and the right to equal representation, socialist revolution is certainly not necessary: whoever wants to change the social nature of the system may do it at the polls provided he gets the majority of votes. This idea was entertained by Marx, as has been noted, in his letter to M. Hyndmann in 1880 and in his famous speech in The Hague in 1872 as well as by Engels in his introduction to Marx's *The Class Struggle in France, 1848–50*. But even if Marx and Engels had been against the (peaceful) political solution of the *capitalism–socialism* conflict, I would not be under any obligation to share their view. Any modern democracy is a very delicate and complex mechanism which can easily be broken but only very painfully re-created. The mechanism of all contemporary capitalist states creaks, stutters and works not as smoothly as many people would wish, but it is more expedient to improve it than to destroy it. One knows only too well that the destroyed mechanism would have to be replaced by another with a risk that the replacement would be worse than the original, and that it would not run perfectly anyhow – that is hardly conceivable. Just as the original, it would have to be improved from time to time, and reformed and adjusted to changing social conditions; a reform – permanent reform – is, indeed, the most inexpensive vehicle for social progress. What is more, a *systemic* reform remoulding social structures does the same job as a revolution. Unlike the violent revolution, the systemic reform has some advantages. First, it removes the fetters of social progress without removing the valuable elements of the old system. Second, it does not find itself an end that has to be defended, preserved and perpetuated, which is often the case with revolutions. It does find itself just one step forward which has to be followed by an infinite number of steps bringing society closer to final ends without pretending that the final ends could ever be accomplished. Third, any revolution, in order to defend the new regime, has to build strong agencies aimed at the suppression of its enemies. Once founded, these bodies start to live their own independent lives: they expand, stabilise and become an inseparable part of the new system. At the moment they are found no longer necessary, they already have been firmly established. If there are no more internal enemies, some will be found; if there are no more external enemies, some will be invented. The dialectics of means and ends is very tricky: it is the means rather than the ends which decide upon the nature of the system as well as about the everyday life of the people.

Revolution is justified only if it is aimed at the overthrow of dictatorial systems which cannot be changed by democratic means, or if the party defeated in democratic elections fails to leave office. Prior to the introduction of universal suffrage, governments could have ignored the will of the majority. Socialist political parties representing primarily the disfranchised masses could have claimed that revolution was the only realistic way that the underdogs could express their will. If a leftist political party fails to attract the electorate in modern liberal democracies, it should revise its programme rather than call for revolution. The Leninist argument that the masses are debased or unable to understand their own interests could be accepted only in underdeveloped countries where the illiterate masses of peasantry suffer not so much from capitalism as from the lack of capitalist development. Only here could the call for a vanguard revolutionary party be considered legitimate. In developed liberal democracies with educated, organised and cultured working masses, the same call for paternalistic vanguardism is absurd.

However, my argument against the revolutionary Marxist means consists in something more meaningful. To present the discussion in a logical manner, I have to start it with the liberal and Marxist concepts of freedom.

5.3. NEGATIVE AND POSITIVE FREEDOM

(a) NEGATIVE FREEDOM AND TWO MODELS OF CLASSLESS SOCIETY

I have already noted that Kant's concept of freedom has one obvious shortcoming: it refers only negatively to one's fellow-man as the barrier to one's individual freedom. This was probably the reason why Isaiah Berlin called it negative freedom, which simply means an absence of coercion.[17] Negative freedom may be interpreted either in a narrow political sense or in a broad philosophical sense. If one decides for the narrow interpretation, it would mean only an absence of political coercion used by an individual, a group, a social class, an institution or the state against another individual, group or class of people. If one decides for the broad interpretation, one would have to include in it any kind of coercion irrespective of its nature and concrete form.

As far as freedom in the narrow sense is concerned, it fully fits in the traditional liberal usage of the term. All people, even those who do not enjoy the right to vote,[18] are protected against an outside political coercion interfering with their right to pursue their own concept of happiness. Capitalism was the first socio-economic system which introduced, through its liberal concept of the state, this concept of freedom in a universal manner. Moreover, liberal capitalism was also the first socio-economic system which abolished extra-economic coercion to work. People have become personally free. They have to work only if they are forced to work by economic necessity. In this lies the basic Marxist objection against the liberal concept of freedom which distributes freedom unevenly and unequally: those who are not forced to work by economic necessity have more freedom than those who have to earn their livelihood. If a man is deprived of his own means of production and is forced by economic necessity to sell his labour power to, and work for, the owners of the means of production, he may still be free according to the narrow interpretation while unfree according to the broad interpretation of negative freedom. Indirect economic coercion to work is not only characteristic but also indispensable for capitalism: the very system could never have emerged and evolved if each individual had had his own means of production. On the one hand, the Marxists do appreciate that capitalism humanised the economic necessity by having made coercion to work indirect and less humiliating.[19] On the other hand, the Marxists do not ignore the fact that while the market is the only known unauthoritative allocator of labour guaranteeing each individual a choice to whom, and under which conditions, he sells his labour power, the *capitalist* market is unable – in peaceful times – to guarantee jobs for all those who want to work. Hence the proletariat does not suffer as much from (indirect) economic coercion to work as it does from lack of job security.

The limitation of liberal concepts of freedom to politics only has made the liberal distribution of negative freedom unequal. The class of the owners of the means of production has far more freedom from coercion in the broad sense than the proletariat. Moreover, the former has much more social power than the latter. The owners enjoy control over the labour and products of the non-owners. While formally equally free, the two main classes of capitalist society are in fact unequally free.

The inequality is caused not by politics but by economics. Therefore, the main task of the 'abolition of the present state of things' consists in an equalisation of economic freedom rather than in an abolition of universal political freedom. One must not forget that liberal capitalism protects the working class also from political coercion. Its basic shortcoming consists in that while it is able to give workers political security, it fails to give them economic security. A positive overcoming of the failure would require an extension of absence from coercion to the economic sphere. Is such an extension ever possible?

Let me assume that the private ownership of the means of production has been abolished. For the sake of simplicity let me further assume that all the means of production have already been socialised to such a degree that they could be owned in common by society as a whole. What would be the likely effect of such a radical social change? First, all unearned incomes would disappear with the abolition of private property. Nobody could any longer be entitled to an income from profit, rent, interest or dividend. Second, the only remaining source of income would be labour. From now on, all the members of the new classless society will have to work to make their living. Economic coercion to work will be extended to all. This coercion will stem from economic necessity and will be shared equally by all the productive population.

In the hypothetical circumstances, one may choose one of two alternative models of social relations in the new classless society:

(i) The means of production are centralised in the hands of the state with the market of capital, labour and consumer goods abolished, with the entire national economy run 'in accordance with an approved and authoritative plan'.[20] It will obviously be the planners who draft and execute the plan, who exercise control over social capital and, consequently, also over labour and its products, who allocate capital and labour according to the priorities of the plan. Instead of the former (market) freedom of labour, each individual will have to comply with the authoritative allocation of manpower carried out by the central planning board and its officials.

As the state has assumed responsibility for a direct authoritative allocation of labour, it has to assume also the responsibility for offering a job to each individual – not just the job one would wish but the job needed by the state.

Such an arrangement cannot reduce a degree of coercion in the economic sphere. Not because of the fact that coercion by economic necessity would be extended to all. Every society is forced by Nature to produce in order to live. It would be only just if this burden is shared equally by all. Incidentally, those who own their personal means of production are also forced to work by economic necessity, and yet no one could call their work forced labour as long as they retain control over it and its products. While people cannot avoid economic coercion to work, they may avoid both the authoritative form of the coercion and the coercive control over their labour and its products. In the above suggested arrangement, however, control over labour and its products is centralised in the hands of the state and hence separated from direct producers. Therefore, the allocation of labour inevitably assumes an authoritative form. While all are equally coerced into work by economic necessity, some are also privileged to coerce others into work by extra-economic means.

To sum up, coercion to work stemming from economic necessity has not been superseded. Its extension to all equalises freedom (or lack of it) by removing the privileges of the propertied class. However, the previous coercion in the broad sense (coercion by economic necessity) has assumed the form of coercion in the narrow sense (coercion by other men). While the former was 'independent of the arbitrary will of another person',[21] the latter is based upon the arbitrary power of one group of people over other people. Instead of being regulated by impersonal general rules of the market whose effect upon particular individuals (social groups) cannot be foreseen, it is regulated by personal specific rules of bureaucracy whose effect upon particular individuals (social groups) can be foreseen. An intensity of coercion by economic necessity has not diminished while an intensity of coercion by other men has substantially increased. The equalisation of coercion by economic necessity has not increased the aggregate negative freedom; on the contrary, the aggregate negative freedom has decreased.

What would happen, in this particular model of economic relations, to negative political freedom? Some may argue that no particular economic structure has any relevance for negative political liberty, that all political freedoms can be preserved if the government had a firm will to do so.[22] However, to rely on the goodwill of any government is hardly a fruitful method of scholarly investigation. Government's intentions apart, one should be rather concerned with structural and institutional guarantees of basic political freedoms.

In this hypothetical model, the government is an exclusive employer endowed with an authoritative power to allocate, without any market mediation, all productive factors, decide about conditions of employment, distribution of national income, rate of accumulation and structure of investments, rate of consumption and structure of consumer goods and services, etc. The same government is simultaneously a political representative of the society made up of employees of state institutions and enterprises, state pensioners and recipients of transfer payments. Hence, the government enjoys both economic and political power. The former is, of necessity, an authoritative power exercised in a centralised manner through commands, prohibitions and orders rather than through an indirect regulation of contractual relations among autonomous exchangers, be it economic units or individuals. In the circumstances, the latter cannot be too different from the former for it is not being applied to autonomous individuals, work collectives or social groups but to the employees of the state. Consequently, political power does not reflect primarily the relations between political representatives and citizens but those between the universal boss and his subordinates. Even if the government had a firm will to respect the political freedoms of its subjects, could it be simultaneously authoritative in its economic capacity and unauthoritative in its political capacity?

No government with a firm will to preserve political freedoms must insist on an introduction of the coercive economic system. One may hardly assume that rulers behaving as authoritarians when deciding about economic aspects of political matters would behave as libertarians when deciding about political aspects of economic matters. Neither may one assume that the rulers enjoying an arbitrary (economic) power over labour and its products would readily submit to a democratic political control exercised by their economic subordinates. *Without* a choice of employment, profession, movement, place of work and place of residence, and *with* a full material dependence on the monopolistic employer/political ruler, no individual could be actually protected against arbitrary coercion by his government.

Thus, the first alternative model of social relations in the new classless society fails to increase the aggregate negative freedom in the political sphere also. On the contrary, it undermines it. For this reason it cannot serve as *the* model for a *positive* overcoming of liberalism.

(ii) While all basic assumptions remain unchanged in the second alternative model of social relations in the new classless society, the means of production are not centralised in the hands of the state. They are made into social property owned by the society as a whole and managed, administered and controlled, on behalf of the entire population, by the collectives of employees in all economic and work units. What distinguishes this social property from a group property are the levies that each economic unit pays from its assets to a common fund.

(To put it differently, it is the interest paid for the productive use of social capital.) To make economic and work units self-managed, it is necessary to preserve their autonomy from the state. Hence, the market must not be abolished. On the contrary, it has to serve as a foundation for equal horizontal relations among economic units which exchange their output with each other. Consequently, the economic units are not subject to any binding command central plan. In such a model the only conceivable central plan could be an indicative one. The plan spells out social priorities and preferences which are followed by economic units not because the latter have been ordered to do so but because it would give them an economic advantage.

Such an arrangement preserves an unauthoritative allocation of labour, i.e. freedom of each individual to be associated with a work unit according to his choice. The arrangement also gives direct producers control over their labour and products. Of course, the old economic necessity to work remains. Equally shared by all associate producers, it is carried out by an (indirect) economic coercion rather than by an authoritative one. If there is a necessity to work, there has to be also the right to a job for everyone who wants to work. New jobs are created (a) by the already existing economic and work units, (b) by communities, (c) by the state and (d) by self-employed producers. Each newly created economic and/or work unit is, as a matter of routine, made self-managed. Job creation relies on both direct and indirect methods. Self-managed economic units are encouraged to create new jobs by tax incentives, beneficial rates of depreciation, etc. Communities and the state finance creation of new jobs from the common fund made up of the levies paid by the enterprises for the use of social assets. Though this system does not automatically bring about full employment (and which system does?), unemployment may be avoided by a shortening of working hours, an extension of paid holidays and a lowering of the retirement age; this would be in accord with Marx's concept of the realm of freedom, and that of leisure-time as a measure of social wealth.

Separation of economic units from the state administration and their autonomy from various political organs of the government could preserve pluralism of decision-making units in the economic sphere. Since economic units are autonomous not only from the state but also from each other, they have to behave as independent exchangers pursuing their economic interests, namely to get an equivalent for their output. May the particular interests of each self-managed unit always coincide with those of the society as a whole? It could hardly be so. Any social structure based on social division of labour and scarcity cannot but produce and reproduce conflicting interests. However, owing to the pluralistic economic structure and the separation of political and economic power in this model, all the conflicts may be routinely regulated by the state with as little political coercion as in any existing liberal democratic state.[23]

In the second alternative model of social relations in the new classless society, negative freedom may be preserved in, and protected by, a democratic political system based on the pluralistic self-managed market economic system. As far as the economic sphere is concerned, coercion in the broad sense (coercion by economic necessity) is democratically equalised without assuming the form of coercion in the narrow sense (coercion by other men). Hence, the equalisation is still able to preserve the freedom of labour in terms of an unauthoritative allocation of manpower. Owing to the supersession of private property, all associated producers acquire equal access to social means of production as well as equal control over their labour and products. Having gained this advantage, they may still retain their autonomy and personal independence from the government. By having acquired control over their labour and products, the associated producers are able to reduce the intensity of the coerciveness caused by economic necessity; hence, the aggregate negative freedom in economics increases. Since the model allows for pluralistic and democratic arrangements in the political sphere, it can maintain negative freedom in politics at least at the same level that has been reached by liberal democracies.

(b) STRUCTURAL LINK BETWEEN THE MARKET AND NEGATIVE FREEDOM

To argue that there is a structural link between the market and freedom is hardly a popular task. For one thing, Marxists strongly reject any notion that a market structure may serve as an economic foundation for a *meaningful* political freedom.[24] In this respect, there is no difference between the Soviet conservatives and the western New Left radicals. Moreover, most humanist Marxists have accepted Marx's anti-market prejudice as well. Second, the Marxian aversion to the market has also been shared by some liberal social scientists, namely Karl Polanyi and C. B. Macpherson.[25] And finally, after Milton Friedman published his book *Capitalism and Freedom*,[26] anyone who wanted to prove a link between the market and democracy would risk an accusation of being an arch-conservative.[27]

(i) *Karl Polanyi*

Nevertheless the link does exist, and even such an outspoken opponent of market economy as Karl Polanyi had to appreciate its existence. Polanyi approaches the market from the historical perspective. Despite the fact that the institution of the market has been fairly common since the late Stone Age, says Polanyi, its role had always been incidental to economic life. The emergence of the liberal idea of self-regulations was not only a complete reversal of the trend of development, but also 'the utopian experiment'.[28] The utopianism of the idea consists in that the market economy is, according to Polanyi, 'an economic system controlled, regulated and directed by markets alone'.[29] As an abstract model, such an economy is conceivable and Polanyi's definition acceptable; as a concrete system such an economy has never existed and, therefore, Polanyi's definition cannot serve as the point of departure for a meaningful discussion. One has never witnessed an economic system controlled, regulated and directed by markets *alone*. Even the *laissez-faire* capitalism described and analysed by Adam Smith, David Ricardo and Karl Marx relied on the market partially regulated and affected by such extra-economic means as tariffs, custom duties, taxes, corn laws, labour legislation, etc. But even if one assumed that an exclusively self-regulating market could exist, one would have to admit that it could not function smoothly without outside interference. At least since the publication of Keynes' *General Theory*, only a few economists and politicians remained believing in the validity of Say's law according to which the market *alone* can provide for a perfect equilibrium of the system. Since Polanyi defines market economy as an unlimited, absolute, exclusive and universal self-regulation, he has to admit that 'the end of market society means in no way the absence of markets'.[30] Thus, Polanyi rejects only the market which is super-imposed upon society in an absolute manner.

For Polanyi, the true criticism of market economy lies in that it is based on self-interest. He suggests that such an organisation of economic life is entirely unnatural, in the strictly empirical sense *exceptional*.[31] Here again, Polanyi does not distinguish between the particular and the general, i.e. between self-interest in the capitalist sense and between self-interest in a broader sense. Consequently, Polanyi has to identify self-interest with a monetary gain. I would argue that self-interest may consist also in such a human need as to regain (or retain) control over one's work-place, profession or vocation. If one allows that economic activity is linked not only to profitable production but to non-profitable services as well, then, logically, an economic self-interest may pursue not only maximisation of profit or material consumption but also maximisation of social security, leisure, cultural services, shorter working hours, longer paid holidays and so on. In short, one may alternatively formulate economic self-interest as one's interest in the good life, be it more money and higher material consumption, or more leisure and higher non-material consumption including social security and justice, or more meaningful work leading to self-fulfilment in one's work-place, etc.

I may further argue that one cannot really be free without a right to pursue one's self-interest. Moreover, if the economic system does not accept one's self-interest as an economic motivation, one would have to be forced to work by extra-economic means. In certain circumstances, one's self-interest may coincide with the general interests of society as a whole. To create such circumstances, one would have to apply to one's economic self-interest the same restriction which had been applied by Kant to one's right to pursue one's happiness (i.e. that one's pursuit of one's happiness does not interfere with others' pursuit of their happiness). By doing so one could formulate an abstract theoretical model allowing for an accord of the individual's self-interest with the interest of a larger community which is based on social property, earned income, distribution of material goods according to one's work and distribution of social services and education according to one's needs.

But the point is not in formulating abstract normative models. What Polanyi really rejected was not self-interest in a broader sense but self-interest in the narrow capitalist sense. Furthermore, Polanyi did not reject the market as such but the capitalist self-regulating market which has collapsed. Unfortunately, he has formulated the particular rejection of the unregulated capitalist market as the general rejection of a market economy. In doing this, Polanyi committed a mistake similar to that of Karl Marx, the mistake of not distinguishing between the general and the particular, between the essence and the appearance.

Despite this mistake, Polanyi has clearly seen and formulated the crucial dilemma of 'the great transformation'. As a radical democratic liberal, he knew only too well that freedom was a by-product of the nineteenth-century economy based on the self-regulated universal market.[32] As long as capitalism was based on free competition, its political system could have been based on a free play of pluralistic political forces. But Polanyi also realised 'that the means of maintaining freedom are themselves adulterating and destroying it'.[33] He had in mind fascism and fascisation which emerged as a result of the Great Depression. Since the exclusive self-regulating market relying on private property could not have prevented cyclical depressions, mass unemployment and monopolisation of economies, it could preserve neither free competition nor market equilibrium as the economic foundation of liberal freedom. If the self-regulating market is left unchanged and unreformed, it has inevitably to collapse. If it collapses, liberal democracies would have to be replaced by a system which is either unable or unwilling to preserve the freedom inherited from market societies. If it is reformed and changed, market freedoms would be undermined as well. What has Polanyi to offer as a solution? Just a hope. He repeatedly suggests that 'we *must* try to maintain by all means in our power [these] high values inherited from market economy which collapsed';[34] that 'every move towards integration in society *should* thus be accompanied by an increase of freedom; moves towards planning *should* comprise the strengthening of the rights of the individual in society';[35] that in 'an established society, the right to nonconformity *must* be institutionally protected',[36] etc. Moreover, Polanyi wants to extend the hitherto acknowledged volume of rights and freedoms: 'Rights of the citizen hitherto unacknowledged *must* be added to the Bill of Rights. They *must* be made to prevail against all authorities, whether State, municipal or professional.'[37] All this is laudable but not sufficient: one's goodwill is not enough to protect political rights and liberties unless there is a system whose very existence and functioning *requires* a preservation of freedoms.

Polanyi appreciates the dilemma. He knows that liberal economy gave a false direction to our ideals. He realises that we have to re-create the very principle of individual freedom. He sees the last word not in the individual but in society. He admits that 'inescapably we reach the conclusion that the very possibility of freedom is in question. If regulation is the only means of spreading and strengthening freedom in a complex society, and yet to make use of this means is contrary to freedom *per se*, then such a society cannot be free.'[38] The only way out from the dilemma would be to reformulate the very meaning of freedom itself. Polanyi says that if freedom is to be equated with contractual relations, the new society cannot be free. But if, and as long as man 'is true to his task of creating more abundant freedom for all, he need not fear that either power or planning will turn against him and destroy the freedom he is building by their instrumentality. This is the meaning of freedom in complex society; it gives us all the certainty we need.'[39] With this almost religious faith in man's virtues Polanyi concludes his book, aware that he has failed to provide us with satisfactory answers to his well-founded questions. If I read Polanyi correctly, however, he is rather inclined to contemplate trading freedom for justice and security. According to him, 'the institutional separation of politics from economics which proved a deadly danger to the substance of society, almost automatically produced freedom at the cost of justice and security'.[40] I cannot agree with this statement. For one thing, the 'deadly danger' to the substance of society has been caused not by the institutional separation of politics from economics in general, but only by the particular institutional separation of *public* politics from *private* economics. And for another, while the institutional unity of politics and economics may produce social and economic security, it would hardly produce political security and justice. On the contrary, one might expect the institutional unity of politics and economics to produce a monopoly of power detrimental to both political security and justice. If it were a question of either or, i.e. if one had only the choice between freedom at the cost of justice and security, or justice and security at the cost of freedom, one could give Polanyi credit for having preferred one evil to another. Since there is yet another alternative, Polanyi's sacrifice was unnecessary.

(ii) *Milton Friedman*
The main thesis of Milton Friedman's book on relations between economics and politics is very simple: a society which is socialist cannot also be democratic, in the sense of guaranteeing individual freedom.[41]

This thesis is derived from the model which is based on the following assumptions:

    (a) There are two basic ways of co-ordinating economic activities on a macroeconomic scale. One is central direction involving the use of coercion, the other is voluntary co-operation of individuals – the technique of the market-place.

    (b) Since socialism is, by definition, a centrally directed system without market exchange, it has to be, of necessity, a coercive system.

    (c) Since competitive capitalism (a free private-enterprise economy) is universally organised by voluntary market exchange, it is able to bring about a universal co-ordination without coercion.

    (d) Since only certain combinations of political and economic arrangements are possible, competitive capitalism is a necessary though not a sufficient condition for political freedom defined as an absence (or a minimum) of coercion by man.[42]

Before analysing Friedman's model, I wish to make three preliminary remarks.

(1) Friedman is right in suggesting that universal negative political freedom (the absence of coercion by men or its approximation) has hitherto been materialised only in those capitalist economic systems which have been evolving and functioning within liberal democratic political systems. In other words, we know of no example in time and place that universal political freedom has been in existence except in capitalist societies.

(2) Friedman is also right in suggesting that there is a link between market exchange and negative freedom. The market is not only an economic category; it is also a sociological category requiring a specific social structure, namely horizontal and contractual relations among people. No perfect market can exist without personal freedom, independence and equality of its agents. Man as an agent of market exchange must have the right to dispose of his commodity. Moreover, he must have the right to decide what equivalent he will accept in the course of exchange, which of his interests he will pursue. Every market exchange contains the principle of choice, of an alternative. In this sense, the market serves (and historically always served) as an economic basis for free and equal relations among exchangers.

(3) Friedman is also right when suggesting that a market structure is a necessary (though not a sufficient) condition for political (negative) freedom. Though political freedom is not necessary for the very existence of a market economy, it is instrumental for its prosperity. Therefore, the non-democratic market economic systems do not function too well. A negative evidence is available: all economically strong, stable and highly industrially developed wealthy market systems have for decades enjoyed an uninterrupted (or only temporarily interrupted) continuation of democratic political systems.

Although everything suggested in these three points is not wrong, neither is it true. In fact, Friedman's model is based on two dubious premises:

(a) A market economy is identified with competitive capitalism.
(b) Socialism is identified with a non-market economy relying on a coercive macroeconomic co-ordination.

If the two premises were correct, Friedman's conclusions would be correct as well. The premises are not correct, however. They do not distinguish between the essence (market) and the appearance (competitive capitalist market), between the general (autonomous enterprise) and the particular (private enterprise). They do not distinguish between the general (socialism) and the particular (state socialism). (As far as the only exception from the rule is concerned – Yugoslavia – it fits perfectly into Friedman's model: though a necessary condition, market economic structure is not a sufficient condition of political freedom.) In order to make Friedman's model acceptable, one would have to remove from it the methodological inconsistency by substituting the general for the particular:

The only known voluntary (non-coercive) way of macroeconomic co-ordination is the technique of the market-place. Since only certain combinations of political and economic arrangements are possible, the market technique is a necessary (though not a sufficient) economic condition for negative political freedom defined as an absence of coercion by men.

After having reformulated Friedman's model in such a general manner, one has to find out whether the model is applicable to socialism. To do this, it is necessary to define the very term 'socialism'. It also requires a certain level of abstraction and generalisation. Although there are many different socialist theories, concepts, doctrines, ideologies and systems in use, they share only a few common principles. The latter could be formulated as:

(a) public ownership of the means of production;
(b) social planning;
(c) distribution according to work;
(d) equality extended to the economic sphere.

If one looks at this scheme more closely, one can see that the first two traits may not be characteristic of socialism only. For instance, public ownership of the means of production had prevailed in the old Asiatic 'irrigation societies' based on slavery and could also prevail in state capitalist societies. Social planning may be introduced not only by the state capitalist systems but also by any private capitalist system during a period of emergency (e.g. war economy), by fascist systems (e.g. Nazi Germany) or by liberal states (e.g. France, The Netherlands). Hence public ownership and social planning would acquire socialist properties *only* if combined with distribution according to work and equality extended to the economic sphere, *provided that* principle (a) implies equal access to social capital, (b) implies social security and welfare,

(c) implies absence of any exploitation, and (d) implies equal distribution of, and equal access to, economic and political control.

Even if the four general conditions of the scheme are met, they may be interpreted in various ways. Thus, the public ownership of the means of production may be alternatively conceived of as a state ownership, or a social ownership, or a group ownership. The social planning may be alternatively perceived either as a substitute for the market (a command planning) or as an addition to the market (an indicative planning). Distribution according to work may be interpreted either as according to work input or work output. And finally, equal distribution of, and equal access to, economic and political power could be carried out either in a representative or in a participatory democracy.

Irrespective of all concrete alternative interpretations of the general scheme, any concept which meets the four general characteristics ought to be accepted as socialist. Before I put my socialist scheme to the test of Friedman's model, it would be proper to justify why I have chosen the following socialist arrangement.

Principle (a)

(i) Because state ownership of the means of production is, in principle, incompatible with self-management, with autonomy of economic units and with separation of political and economic power, it cannot serve as a model of democratic socialism.

(ii) Group ownership, although fully applicable to the means of production not yet really socialised, might cause serious problems if applied universally. First, it would not guarantee equal access to social capital. Second, the group nature of the ownership would have to be reflected by an income derived from the group title to capital assets and hence violate the principle of distribution according to work. (One further argument against a universal group ownership of property will be discussed below.) Thus the social ownership of the means of production appears as the most proper for the suggested socialist arrangement.

Principle (b)

Command planning is incompatible with both self-management and voluntary co-ordination by virtue of the market technique. Consequently, only an indirect, non-coercive indicative planning is applicable.

Principle (c)

Evidence was given (section 2.1) that individual labour cannot be immediately and directly socially necessary labour. Hence, distribution according to work *output* should be applied.

Principle (d)

(i) Equality is extended to the economic sphere by an introduction of social ownership of the means of production (equal access to social capital), by distribution according to work (wages, salaries, pensions), and by distribution according to needs (education and health services).

(ii) All producers (i.e. all economically active people) have equal access to participation in self-management.

(iii) All citizens have equal access to political power which *indirectly* controls the public economy through self-government at the local level and through representation (one man, one vote) at higher levels of government.

Thus, we have at our disposal an undoubtedly socialist system relying on voluntary co-ordination brought about by the technique of the market-place. If the associated producers working in autonomous self-managed economic units are to compete in the market-place, they have to enjoy equal and relatively stable conditions, rules and criteria generally and impartially applied to each economic unit and to each individual. The self-managed socialist market system could function only if economic power is separated from political power, if the government does not arbitrarily interfere with self-managed enterprises, and if the government protects general and particular interests of citizens. Since economic power is dispersed among autonomous economic units, most economic decisions are decentralised. So also should be most political decisions. As a matter of fact, the self-managed socialist market economy cannot survive without the separation of powers, without pluralism of autonomous political, social and professional associations and without a working system of checks and balances in the political sphere. If private competitive capitalism can survive and function under an authoritarian or even totalitarian political system, self-managed socialism cannot. Since it is based on public ownership, any authoritarian or totalitarian political (public) power would destroy the autonomy of economic units and the democratic principles of self-management. While one may perceive a combination of a *private* market economy and an authoritarian political (*public*) system, one may hardly perceive a combination of a *public* market self-managed economy and an authoritarian political (*public*) system. Certainly, even in the suggested self-managed socialist model, the market is only a necessary, and by no means a sufficient, condition for political freedom.

However, the link between the market, self-management and political freedom seems to be stronger than in competitive capitalism. In a strictly theoretical and logical sense, market self-managed socialism may guarantee negative freedom not only better, but also to a greater extent than the free enterprise system defended by Milton Friedman. This proposition is based on the following arguments:

(1) Once the wage-earner has sold his labour power to the owner of a private enterprise, the latter acquires social power over the former. At least during working hours, the otherwise free wage-earner loses his freedom. Though resulting from the horizontal and equal exchange act, the employer-employee relations rely on the master-servant hierarchical pattern of superiority and subordination, the masters having assumed control over labour and of all important decision-making including hiring and firing of all employees. In the self-managed socialist economic units, the employees control their own labour, their own products, and participate in all important decision-making including hiring and firing of the managers and supervisors. Consequently, they preserve their freedom even during working hours. All other things being equal, the aggregate negative freedom will increase in the market self-managed socialist system.

(2) The free enterprise system based on an unlimited private appropriation of capital leads necessarily to a monopoly of economic might which creates, at a certain point, an oligopolistic and, at least in certain branches and small countries, even a monopolistic market. The monopoly is scarcely conducive to the preservation of individual freedom. To prevent the transformation of the competitive market into the monopolistic market, a permanent governmental interference with the free market is unavoidable. However, this is exactly what Friedman so fiercely rejects. If he succeeded, the means of maintaining freedom (unregulated universal market) will eventually destroy it. If a regulation of the market, an interference with the market and an overall control over the market is exercised by the state, the means intended to prevent the degeneration (monopolisation) of the market also eventually destroy the market as the economic foundation of freedom. Viewed from this stance, the same capitalism which brought about universal political freedom is hardly capable of preserving it indefinitely.

There are the limits for concentration of social capital and monopolisation of the market in the suggested model of self-managed socialism. Though one has to assume that big enterprises will accumulate large amounts of money for expansion, any plant newly built by, or any newly created subsidiary of, the already existing socially owned self-managed unit will as a rule obtain an autonomy from its founder and immediately introduce self-management. The same principle holds for the enterprises founded by the state, local governments, etc. This arrangement is possible only within the social ownership and serves as my third argument against the universal application of group ownership to the market self-managed socialist economy.

(3) The market in the suggested self-managed model of socialist economy is neither universal nor unregulated. First, the market criteria are not applied to such social services as post-secondary schooling (equal access to higher education), health services (equal protection of the social security of each individual), etc. Second, basic macroeconomic decisions about public economy are made by public (political) means. To make such a decision-making process democratic, an equal distribution of and an equal access to political power is a *sine qua non*. For political and economic power are separated from each other; for economic pluralism is reflected by pluralism in politics; for the objectives of central (indicative) plans are binding only on the governmental agencies and not on the autonomous economic units; even the central economic co-ordination has to rely on a voluntary consensus rather than on coercion by men, on an indirect regulation rather than on direct orders or commands. In other words, the market is subordinated to, rather than superimposed on, a self-managed socialist society. On the one hand, it is strong enough to maintain the horizontal economic structure for a pluralistic democratic superstructure. On the other hand, it is restricted and regulated enough not to bring about recessions and depressions, not to sharpen income differentials and not to undermine the needed equilibrium between economic optimisation and humanisation of man's life.

On a theoretical level, Friedman's proposition is untenable. However, one should not blame Professor Friedman too severely for his methodological mistakes. For one thing, he did respond to the challenge of the historical (real) state socialism, and for another, he has taken for granted the widely spread theoretical dogma that the market and socialism are mutually exclusive.

(iii) *C. B. Macpherson*

Professor Macpherson has introduced new elements to the conventional concept of negative and positive freedom, as well as new aspects to the conventional market democratic theory. Because he is more concerned about positive freedom than about negative freedom, and yet much more about equality, he reformulated negative freedom as counter-extractive freedom, and positive freedom as developmental freedom. In order to examine his innovation, I have first to make a few explanatory remarks.

In Macpherson's terminology, developmental power is defined as 'man's ability to use and develop his capacities'. It roughly corresponds to the conventional concept of positive freedom. Extractive power, defined as 'power over others, the ability to extract benefit from others',[43] substitutes for the conventional concept of coercion. Hence, his concept of negative freedom (the absence of coercion) had to be reformulated as counter-extractive freedom. The latter is not identical with negative freedom, however. To grasp the distinction between them, I have to reproduce Macpherson's concept of transfer of power:

> If a man's power must include access to the means of labour, then his powers are diminished when he has less than free access to the means of labour. If he has no access, his powers are reduced to zero and he ceases to live, unless he is rescued by some dispensation from outside the competitive market. If he can get some access but cannot get it for nothing, then his powers are reduced by the amount of them he has to hand over to get the necessary access. This is exactly the situation most men are in, and necessarily so, in the capitalist market society. They must, in the nature of the system, permit a net transfer of part of their powers to those who own the means of labour.[44]

To translate Macpherson's liberal language into the Marxist terminology, the net transfer of power is surplus-value appropriated by the owners of the means of labour; extractive power (identified by Macpherson with coercion) is the power of the capitalists and landowners to appropriate surplus-value from the non-owners. Hence, coercion actually means exploitation, and counter-extractive freedom actually means freedom from exploitation. The absence of extractive power (coercion) is the measure of liberty.

Thus, everything's meaning has been changed: coercion means exploitation, freedom means the absence of exploitation. By definition, any non-exploitative society maximises freedom while any exploitative society minimises freedom. Because, in the capitalist market society, a man's (a worker's) powers are diminished by the net transfer of power to other men (the capitalists) and because the net transfer of power is mediated by the market, the latter cannot serve as an economic foundation of freedom. More specifically, the capitalist market society is not a necessary condition for political freedom.

Macpherson has arrived at the following conclusion:

(a) 'a non-market democratic theory which retains the ethically valuable liberal principles is, although not without difficulties, conceivable';
(b) difficulties of the attempts to reformulate liberal democratic theory while retaining market principles '*are* insuperable'.[45]

Since the liberal theorist Macpherson has argued Marx's case concerning freedom, I feel obliged to examine his concept and find out whether it is relevant for my model.

All the elegance of the concept aside, Macpherson has violated, in his discussion of the relationship between the market and freedom, the basic rule of formal logic, namely that A has to be A for both the parties of the argument. First, Macpherson's A (counter-extractive freedom) is *not* others' A (negative freedom). Second, Macpherson's definition of extractive power is logically inconsistent. On the one hand, he has defined it as 'power over others'. On the other hand, it means for him also 'the ability to extract benefit from others'. Each part of the definition has its own meaning. While the former covers coercion (by man) *per se*, the latter covers only exploitation. Power over others, which does not necessarily imply benefit for its holder, is always coercive. Extraction of benefit from others does not necessarily imply coercion: it may be either coercive, as was the case of slavery and serfdom, or non-coercive, as is the capitalist case. Hence, Macpherson's definition of extractive power is inconsistent and ambiguous.

Macpherson committed yet another lapse in his polemics against Milton Friedman. He blamed Friedman for not distinguishing between the simple economy of exchange among independent producers and the capitalist economy in which there is separation of labour and capital. Macpherson exploited the distinction for rejecting Friedman's logical link between competitive capitalism and political freedom. Friedman's suggestion was that 'the employee is protected from coercion by the employer because of *other employers for whom he can work*'.[46] Hence, the proviso of Friedman's model reads: freedom means that no one has to enter into any *particular* exchange. Macpherson seems to allow that such a proviso may be sufficient for the simple economy of exchange while insufficient for the capitalist exchange. For the latter, says Macpherson, freedom ought to mean not to enter into any exchange *at all*. Since there is no freedom to avoid exchange at all in Friedman's model (a labour force without its own sufficient capital is without a choice as to whether to put its labour in the market or not), Macpherson concludes: 'Professor Friedman would agree that where there is no choice there is coercion.'[47] One almost despairs of Macpherson's logic. For one thing, even in the simple economy of exchange, no independent producer is free not to enter into any exchange at all. If he was, the simple economy of exchange could not last long. For another, even a capitalist is not free not to enter into any exchange at all: if he was, he would cease to be a capitalist. In any market economy, liberty may consist *only* in freedom not to enter into any *particular* exchange, and this *is* a sufficient choice; as a matter of fact, this is the only kind of choice the market economy can offer.

Macpherson further suggests that 'those who in a market economy have no land or capital have no extractive power'.[48] While I agree with this statement, I cannot agree with the postscript to this statement: 'They also may be said to have, at any given time, no power (or only negligible power) of any other kind.'[49] Macpherson's preoccupation with extractive power makes him unconcerned about other kinds of power. May he indeed believe that such non-owners of land and capital as trade unions, political parties, armies, secret police, courts, various associations, mass media, etc., have no power, or only negligible power of any kind? The concept based on extractive power vs. counter-extractive freedom reduces coercion to exploitation, and freedom from coercion to freedom from exploitation only. While such a reduction points to the *class* aspect of the problem it ignores many other, more subtle aspects of coercion and freedom.

But if I for a moment assumed that Professor Macpherson is perfectly right and that his concept embraces all relevant aspects of coercion and negative freedom, then, obviously, his concept would fit perfectly in my model of *market socialist* society. Those who in a market society have no land or capital have no extractive power, says Macpherson. In my model, land and capital are *socially* owned, and no individual may use his assets (consumer goods, money) to extract surplus-value and obtain an unearned income. In this respect, no one owns land and capital. Consequently, there is not, and never may be, room for any extractive power in my model. And since Macpherson's proviso states that the absence of extractive power is the measure of liberty, my model meets his absolute ideal.

One thing is slightly unclear, however. Does Macpherson's statement (that those who in a market economy have no land or capital have no extractive power) imply that those who in a market economy have land or capital do have extractive power? If it does not, then my model meets his conditions. If it does, then obviously there would have to be something wrong with his very statement. As a matter of fact, everybody owns land and capital in my model. And since this *is* a market model, everyone owning land and capital would have to have extractive power. But if *all* were extractors, from whom would they extract benefit?

I may conclude: my *market* socialist model eliminates extractive power. Hence, it maximises counter-extractive freedom. Since it is based on voluntary (market) co-ordination, it also preserves negative freedom in the conventional sense and, consequently, approximates the absence of coercion. Thus, contrary to Macpherson's categorical suggestion 'that the difficulties of the attempts to reformulate liberal democratic theory while retaining market principles *are* insuperable', it has been proved and demonstrated that:

(1) it is conceivable and possible to reformulate liberal* democratic theory retaining such valuable *liberal* principles as the absence of coercion, absence of exploitation and equal access to the means of labour while retaining market principles; and

(2) it is even possible to formulate a *socialist* democratic theory while retaining the market principles.

What yet remains to be proved, however, is (a) that my model also maximises man's positive freedom or, in Macpherson's terminology, man's developmental power; And (b) that it is hardly conceivable to formulate a non-market democratic theory which retains the ethically valuable liberal principles, i.e. those which ought to be accepted by democratic socialism.

(c) STRUCTURAL LINK BETWEEN THE MARKET AND POSITIVE FREEDOM

Positive freedom denotes that man is free not *from* something (coercion) but *for* something. Along the lines of this simple definition, positive freedom implies participation, subjectivity, autonomy, creativity, de-

---

* Professor Macpherson might object that my model is not liberal but socialist because it is based on social rather than private property of land and capital. However, his *liberal* democratic theory is based on the absence of extractive power and the market and on equal access to means of labour. If these assumptions were met, there would be no room for private property in his *liberal* democratic theory either.

velopment and self-determination. In the Marxian terms, positive freedom means the all-round development of man. Man is, *by his nature*, the creator of his own life as well as the circumstances in which he lives. This indicates that man is the *potential* subject. Though not born as the subject, he *may* become the subject through a long process of his total (human) emancipation which implies his active participation in a gradual supersession of *all* impediments to his (human) development which is an end in itself.

Having said this, I wish to make one elucidatory note with regard to negative liberty. I have already distinguished between negative liberty in the narrow sense (the absence of coercion by men) and negative liberty in the broad sense (the absence of any coercion). This has been sufficient up to this point. Now I have to elaborate on yet another distinction. I wish to divide negative liberty into three parts:

NL^1 = the absence of coercion by men;
NL^2 = the absence of coercion by circumstances, e.g. by economic necessity;
NL^3 = the absence of any coercion.

NL^1 corresponds to negative freedom as used in conventional political concepts of freedom. NL^2 exceeds NL^1 and NL^3 approximates an ideal which is operational only in normative philosophical concepts.

Though one would have it that the precondition for one's positive freedom is NL^3, Marx emphasised NL^2. He included in his concept of negative liberty such freedoms as that from the market (the absence of man's domination by unknown spontaneous blind external forces), freedom from man's material (objective) dependence (in the sense of the dominating power of exchange-value or money), freedom from social division of labour (he was not specific enough on this point), freedom from the state (in the sense of the state being superimposed upon society), freedom from religion (in the sense of false consciousness and inner alienation), freedom from all kinds of man's external alienation and, most importantly, freedom from labour as an objectified activity imposed upon man by economic necessity (scarcity). All these newly added liberties may or may not be connected with NL^1. For instance, one may live in a market society operating either under a democratic political system or under an authoritarian political system; one may have no money $+ NL^1$, enough money $+ NL^1$, no money and no NL^1, enough money and no NL^1, and so on. Marx failed to state unequivocally and explicitly that what he wanted was NL^3 rather than NL^2. We only know that what he wanted was, first of all, positive freedom. For instance, if a social authoritative plan is able to free man from the blind forces of the market, Marx would not care whether such a plan was coercive or not. Because the authoritative social plan implies 'the associate producers rationally regulating their interchange with Nature, bringing it under their common control, instead of being ruled by it as by blind forces of Nature [i.e. by the Law of Value], and achieving this with the least expenditure of energy and under conditions most favourable to, and worthy of, their human nature',[50] then, obviously, the plan is more rational, ethical and humanistic than the market which brings about alienation, exploitation and misery. Consequently, the coerciveness of the plan is irrelevant. Of course, the plan in itself is unable to bring about the realm of freedom (positive liberty) which lies beyond the sphere of actual economic activity, but it is able to increase an aggregate amount of man's (negative) freedom. Marx did not investigate whether the increase of an aggregate amount of freedom would be caused by that NL^2 being added to the preserved NL^1 or by an increase in NL^2 being higher than a decline in NL^1. He was simply not interested in such a kind of investigation.

Marx's concept of positive freedom could seem very close to that of Kant. Both for Kant and for Marx, man is his own purpose. For both of them, man is to be free, to be himself in the sense of self-determination. And finally, in both concepts, man's human development is an end in itself. At this point, however, all resemblance ceases to be meaningful and the principal distinctions between the two concepts become transparent. While Kant's man is conceived as an abstract individual with an autonomous free will to make absolute laws for himself, Marx's man is a social being able to change circumstances only by changing himself. 'The coincidence of the changing of circumstances and of human activity or self-change can be conceived and rationally under-stood only as *revolutionary practice.*'[51] Hence, Marx's concept of man's human development is a *revolutionary* concept which can be materia-lised only under certain circumstances:

Only when the real, individual man re-absorbs in himself the abstract citizen, and as an individual human being has become a *species-being* in his everyday life, in his particular work, and in his particular situation, only when man has recognised and organised his *'forces propres'* as social forces, and consequently no longer separates social power from himself in the shape of *political* power, only then will human emancipation have been accomplished.[52]

This is, of course, quite different and rather a collectivistic concept of man's self-determination. One the one hand, in order to make the individual free, one has to make free a large social entity (a class, a nation, mankind). On the other hand, freedom of all cannot but be based on freedom of each individual. The dialectic of the individual and the social is an inseparable part of Marx's concept of liberty.[53] Thus, the right of man to liberty has to be deduced from the association of man with man rather than from the separation of man from man, from life in a political community where man considers himself a *communal being*, rather than from life in civil society where man considers himself a *private individual*. Possessive liberal individualism must be stripped off men before they enter the realm of freedom. But this has to happen much earlier than one would assume, and the instrument of this change is a revolution:

> Both for the production on a mass scale of this communist consciousness, and for the success of the cause itself, the *alteration of men on a mass scale is necessary, an alteration which can only take place in a practical movement, a revolution*; the revolution is necessary, therefore, not only because the *ruling* class cannot be overthrown in any other way, but also because the class *overthrowing* it can *only in a revolution* succeed in ridding itself of all the muck of ages and become fitted to found society anew.[54]

In its philosophic normativeness, Marx's concept of positive freedom is irrefutable. To become emancipated, man has first to be changed and re-educated through a revolution (some humanist Marxists would say through *praxis*) which is the means to both the classless society and the alteration of man, the substitution for a purgatory which opens the door to Heaven. The revolutionary alteration of man is possible only because man is both the unique individual (a part) *and* the social being controlling collectively (with others) his own powers as social powers (a whole). Owing to the dialetics of one's uniqueness and one's totality, Marx's concept of (positive) freedom does not need, as its base, NL^1, though it does need, as its base, NL^2. If NL^2 negated NL^1 the former would have to be put over the latter. In the strict normative sense, however, this cannot happen. By definition, the less perfect freedom (NL^1 based on possessive individualism) can never clash with the perfect freedom because the latter denotes a complete humanism, total emancipation of man and his self-determination. While this conclusion may be accepted in the philosophical sense, it cannot be accepted in any political and economic sense because 'the *definitive* resolution of the antagonism between Man and Nature, and between man and man . . . , between existence and essence, between objectification and self-affirmation, between freedom and necessity, between individual and species'[55] is unrealistic in political and utopian in economic terms.

As long as this philosophical concept remains a mere philosophical concept, one may either accept it or reject it. If this philosophical concept is incorporated in a political programme, in an ideology of a revolutionary movement and, consequently, pursued by those who led and won the revolution, it begins to intervene in the lives of individuals, social classes and nations. Once having been accepted as a programme for a revolutionary practice, it would necessarily have to deny liberty as the absence of coercion by men (NL^1). Even the most honest attempt to pursue this positive freedom would kill – in the name of Freedom and Humanism – any freedom at all. This is, incidentally, a well-known problem of all the concepts of positive freedom which do not pay enough attention to, or neglect, structural arrangements guaranteeing NL^1. In the name of a higher freedom, one is denied the right to pursue one's own concept of happiness, one's free autonomous will to be free, one's right to develop humanly for one's own purpose. Instead of pursuing one's own concept of happiness and freedom, one is *forced* to be free and happy by those who *know* what is one's genuinely human interest. Hence, any concept of positive freedom which is not explicitly based on NL^1 is hardly able to guarantee human freedom at all. If any *meaningful* positive freedom cannot be guaranteed without the guaranteed NL^1, however, and if the latter requires, in the condition of scarcity, a voluntary (market) co-ordination as its economic base, then, consequently, one may see the first structural *link between the market and positive freedom*.

This preliminary conclusion might be challenged, however. Even if positive freedom does not include NL^1, it might be argued that it could still be more desirable than NL^1. Would it not be better if people were *forced* to develop their *forces propres* rather than allowed to squander them freely? I cannot deny that the proposition does not lack merits. Despite its merits, however, I have to reject it in principle. A man is free, or he is not free. When debased and humanly undeveloped, he might trade NL^1 for his forced human development. When developed he would try to regain the lost NL^1. (Under favourable circumstances, one may positively develop through a forced re-education even in prison. However positive such a re-education may be, it can scarcely be called positive freedom.) Though there could be NL^1 without human positive development, there cannot be a genuinely developed human *subject* without NL^1. Developed though he might be, he would remain a mere *object*.

The search for a structural link between the market and positive liberty has not yet come to an end. I have to turn again to Professor Macpherson who has attempted to offer a radically new non-market solution[56] on how to avoid a distortion of positive freedom. Macpherson divided positive liberty into three parts:

PL^1 is individual self-direction, or self-mastery;
PL^2 is a distorted PL^1 denoting coercion by those who know the truth over those who do not know it;
PL^3 is the democratic concept of liberty as one's share in the controlling authority;

While PL^1 and PL^3 are desirable and may be complementary to each other, PL^2 is the evil which ought to be avoided. Macpherson distinguishes two kinds of the transition of PL^1 into PL^2. The conservative PL^2 results from the failure of liberal ideologists to realise that the chief impediment to PL^1 is unequal distribution of land and capital. If the same ideologists want to achieve PL^1 without the removal of the impediment (i.e. without a radical structural change), they could not but offer an elitist-authoritarian solution (PL^2). The radical PL^2 results from the radical adherents of PL^1 realising that all non-authoritarian ways to the removal of the impediment are blocked; therefore, they also decide for an authoritarian solution (PL^2). Macpherson concludes that the undesirable PL^2 is by no means inherent in PL^1 but results from a failure of the capitalist system to remove impediments to PL^1. In other words, *any* transformation of PL^1 into PL^2 is a product of bourgeois society.[57]

Since we cannot blame PL^1 for PL^2, says Macpherson, and since negative liberty is 'no longer the shield of individuality; it has become the cloak for un-individualist, corporate, imperial, "free enterprise"',[58] he sees the only way out in an alternative division of liberty with which we have already become acquainted: negative liberty has been redefined as counter-extractive liberty or the absence of extractive power of others including the state, and positive liberty has been redefined as developmental liberty which covers PL^1 and excludes PL^2. Since developmental liberty requires counter-extractive liberty, concludes Macpherson, 'it would be less easy for any theorist or leader or movement to pull positive liberty away from its moorings'.[59]

In a formal sense, this seems to offer a solution. The terms have been redefined, and become more simple: counter-extractive power (freedom from exploitation) is a *sine qua non* for developmental power which excludes PL^2 and asserts PL^1. But there is nothing new in the concept: it is but Marx's old concept translated into liberal jargon. Moreover, Macpherson's concept also excludes the market for reasons similar to those suggested by Marx (cf. my discussion of the problem in Chapter 1).

Like Marx, Macpherson confuses the market with the capitalist market. In his comment on T. H. Green's concept of positive liberty, Macpherson concludes: 'He [T. H. Green] did not see that his goal of positive liberty was unattainable along with the negative liberty he also demanded, the negative liberty of the classical liberals, central to which was freedom from interference with the operations of the capitalist market economy and with the right of unlimited appropriation. He did not see that this negative liberty, because it was available only to the few, hindered the possibility of positive freedom (PL^1) being achieved by the many.'[60] Had Macpherson realised that a market, under certain circumstances, could protect the negative liberty of the many *and* yet bring about some positive liberty to the many, he would certainly be less categorical as to his condemnation of the market and his praise of non-market libertarianism.

Strictly speaking, PL^1 requires NL^3 as its precondition. Since NL^1 and PL^3 could be arranged without any specific problems, the key which may open the door to the realm of PL^1 lies in NL^2. A mere freedom from exploitation is not enough. Even with private property abolished and maximum equality achieved, as long as social division of labour and scarcity prevail, access to positive freedom cannot but be unequal. For one thing, some activities are more favourable to one's human development than others. Second, a particular activity which may fit perfectly in the positive freedom of one individual may not fit in the positive freedom of another individual. While NL^1 could be equally applied to all, PL^1 cannot be equally applied to all without NL^2. The only element of PL^1 which could be applied equally to all without NL^2 is one's *choice* to do what one considers instrumental for one's human development. Because each individual is unique, individual concepts of positive freedom vary from one individual to the other. Consequently, only the positive freedom which implies a free personal choice of the individual can be meaningful. If so, then the measure of the individual's positive freedom is the individual himself.

Hence, PL^1 requires (i) that each individual may freely choose his own concept of human development and (ii) that he can pursue it without any limitation. While (i) presumes to remove coercion of men, (ii) presumes to remove coercion by circumstances. In other words, (i) requires NL^1, (ii) requires NL^2. If NL^2 is absent, freedom necessarily clashes with necessity. At a philosophical level, the clash could be reconciled if one redefined freedom as recognised necessity. Though helpful as a philosophical concept, the redefinition is meaningless as a political and/or economic concept. For all practical purposes, even the recognised necessity does not cease to be necessity. If it did, most of politics and economics would disappear. Most politics is decision-making concerned with priorities and preferences caused by necessity (scarcity). Economics deals with allocation of scarce resources; hence, economic decisions are also concerned with priorities and preferences caused by necessity. Man's historical experience has proved that necessity cannot be superseded by philosophical concepts. If it can be superseded at all, then it is only in the process of rational economic activity of men.

Since NL^2 is absent, and will be absent in any foreseeable future, PL^1 ought to be searched in (a) the 'realm of necessity' and (b) one's leisure. As far as (a) is concerned, certain kinds of objectified labour require creative work of those who exert them. Even if people work primarily to earn their living, they may still, under certain circumstances, also develop their capacities and satisfy their need for self-fulfilment. Creative work may be exerted in any position where initiative, judgement and decision-making is involved. The chief impediment to creative work is (1) the social division of labour in detail within a workshop and/or office, (2) centralised command type of management and (3) the absence of self-management. As far as (1) is concerned, not too much can be done without revolutionary technological changes. As to (2) and (3), an introduction of self-management which requires initiative, judgement and participation in decision-making from the employees may offer at least some elements of PL^1 even to those whose labour is otherwise alienated. (While self-management, according to Macpherson's classification, is identified with PL^3, it contains also an element of PL^1, namely self-direction.) All other things being equal, however, the most relevant step towards PL^1 consists in a shortening of the working hours and in an extension of leisure.

A crucial question arises: is private property and capitalist exploitation a greater impediment to PL^1 than the social division of labour and economic necessity (scarcity)? I suggest that it is not. Even if private property was abolished, the necessity to work in order to live would remain and the social division of labour in detail within a workshop would remain also. The only positive result of the abolition of private property will be greater equality: the necessity to work in order to live will be extended to all. The former owners of capital and land will become equal with the rest of society. While their access to PL^1 will be diminished, the access to PL^1 of the rest of society may not necessarily increase.

What about extractive power, however? Could it disappear with capitalism? In the sense that no individual could appropriate a surplus produced by other men for his private benefit, yes. In the sense that everyone would get the full value of one's product, no. No society may give the producer the full product of his labour (the case was excellently dealt with by Marx in his *Critique of the Gotha Programme*). If socialism substitutes for capitalism, the state (commune, province) rather than the capitalist would have to extract the surplus-product from the producers. If a substantial part of the social surplus-product was used for a greater equalisation of opportunity, it could equalise PL^1 within the realm of necessity in the sense that access to more meaningful occupations would be democratised. However, if the quantity of meaningful occupations remained unchanged, an aggregate amount of PL^1 would not change either. If so, the equality of opportunity could mean only one thing, namely that more people would be better prepared for a meaningful leisure owing to the generally accessible higher education. Furthermore, socialist leisure industries could be PL^1-oriented rather than profit-oriented. Socialist economy could also reasonably curb the advertising which promotes an infinite consumerism and, by a regulation of consumer credit, indirectly encourage PL^1-oriented leisure.

Given the fact that some western welfare-states (e.g. Sweden, Norway) have been able to materialise the above suggested measures without an abolition of private property, this seems to indicate that the abolition of private property *per se* is not causally linked to an extension of PL^1. The attempts to humanise meaningless labour at the assembly-lines in the plants of Saab and Volvo testify to the fact that a modest move towards PL^1 can take place even in the conditions of capitalistic exploitation.

However, both capitalism and socialism may extend PL^3 defined as one's share in a controlling authority in the economic and political spheres. One's share in the controlling authority may be either direct or indirect, i.e. through participation or through representation. It has already been argued that a participatory model can be realistically applied to a local level of control only while a representation model can be applied also to the higher levels of control. In both cases, any meaningful participation presumes that each individual is free (a) to spell out his own preferences, programmes and policies, and (b) to choose one of two or more platforms and candidates. Freedom of choice as a part of positive liberty requires NL^1 as its base. In turn, NL^1 requires, as its economic base, a voluntary (market) co-ordination. The latter, as I have already argued, is a necessary (though not a sufficient) condition of self-management which may increase an aggregate amount of positive freedom by increasing PL^3. Since self-management is undoubtedly a very important part of positive liberty; since no self-management is conceivable without an autonomy of work-places; and since no real autonomy of work-places could be guaranteed without the market – then, consequently, this is *the second structural link between the market and positive freedom.*

Thus, two structural links between the (socialist) market and man's positive freedom have been established. Furthermore, the suggested model of market self-managed socialism maximises man's positive freedom both within the limits of the 'realm of necessity' (the economic sphere) and the 'realm of freedom' (leisure). Before I turn to an examination of non-market democratic theories, I wish to make a few notes concerning the socialist market.

(d) SOME SPECIFICS OF THE SOCIALIST MARKET

(i) *The Limited Appropriation and the Twofold Character of the Socialist Market*

One of the chief humanistic objections against the market is the claim that historically, if not logically, it leads to infinite desire and, consequently, to infinite appropriation. It has been argued (among others by Marx) that as long as material wealth retained its concrete, natural form, the desire to appropriate and accumulate was limited by the usefulness of things. Once money (exchange-value) substituted for goods (use-value), the desire to appropriate and accumulate became infinite.

This proposition is perfectly true wherever and whenever money could be used by the individuals as capital. In the absence of private property,[61] however, the money accumulated in the hands of the individuals cannot be used as capital. It could be used only for the satisfaction of the personal needs of its owners and the owners' families. No one must use it, in principle, for the exploitation of other men. (This does not preclude the use of money for personal services. Since this relation denotes an exchange of labour for income rather than for capital, it is, in terms of Marxian political economy, non-exploitative.) Nor may one use it, in principle, as a source of unearned income. (If any given socialist society needs to encourage personal savings, it could pay an interest on the savings deposited in public banks.) In the circumstances, money held by individuals remains a mere medium of circulation and the measure of values. Only the money used by the socially owned economic organisations can play the part of social capital. Consequently, money's function of being the universal equivalent is also restricted to the socially owned enterprises. The individuals may spend their money less universally, i.e. only for the purchases of consumer goods, services and such personal means of production as cannot be used for the exploitation of wage-labour.

This arrangement is easily realisable. As a matter of fact, it already works in all existing socialist systems. (In the state-socialist societies, this principle is violated only by the existence of the black market which, as I have already argued, is a product of the non-market command planning systems.) It may curb, and it already curbs, the unlimited desire to appropriate and accumulate money which is unacceptable for the humanistic critics of market socialism. Because mere possession of money gives the individual neither unearned incomes nor control over other people's labour (social power), the appropriation and accumulation of money in excess of the individual's needs would be senseless.

Hence, the socialist market is of a twofold nature: the socially owned enterprises operate in the market characterised by the formula M(oney)–C(ommodity)–M′(oney) while individuals operate in the market characterised by the formula C(ommodity) – M(oney) – C(ommodity). Whereas the former market makes possible an unlimited and unrestricted social appropriation of wealth for the present and future (through accumulation) satisfaction of social and individual needs, the latter market restricts man's propensity for material appropriation to the sum total of the use-values which are conducive to the satisfaction of his needs.[62]

(ii) *Distribution, Equality and Positive Freedom*
Any realistic socialist programme relies on the distributive principle according to one's work. Although this principle is less appealing than the ideal distribution according to one's needs, it is still more appealing than the capitalist distributive principle according to one's capital.

The distribution according to work encounters several problems. I have already mentioned the most obvious one, namely whether it ought to be the distribution according to one's contribution to work input or to work output. I have decided, in accordance with the inner logic of market socialism, for the latter. Another problem of this distributive principle consists in that there is a quantitative difference between various labours. A simple quantitative difference stems from the duration of the working hours and from the labour's intensity. A more complex quantitative difference stems from various levels of the worker's skills, qualification and training (in the sense that one hour of skilled labour is a multiple of one hour of unskilled labour). Ought the differences to be reflected in one's monetary reward? If the answer is no, one would have to apply unequal criteria to unequal men which would violate the principle of class equality. If the answer is yes, one would have to apply equal criteria to unequal people which would violate the principle of social and consumer equality. Whatever is done it would preserve a certain inequality: in the first case the inequality of the measure of labour, in the second case the inequality of incomes. Provided everyone has equal access to health services, education and means of labour, the latter inequality seems to be fairer and, therefore, more acceptable than the former. Marx himself was not unequivocal enough as to the problem. In the *Critique of the Gotha Programme*, he preferred the latter inequality to the former with the qualification that it was still a bourgeois principle temporarily surviving in the post-bourgeois society. However, in *The German Ideology* (Engels also in his *Anti-Dühring*) the founding fathers of Marxism held an opposite view:

> But one of the most vital principles of communism, a principle which distinguishes it from all reactionary socialism, is its empirical view, based on a knowledge of man's nature, that differences of *brain* and of intellectual ability do not imply any difference whatsoever in the nature of the *stomach* and of physical *needs*; therefore the false tenet, based upon existing circumstances, 'to each according to his abilities', must be changed, insofar as it relates to enjoyment in its narrower sense, into the tenet, '*to each according to his need*'; in other words a *different form* of activity of labour, does not justify *inequality*, confers no privileges in respect of possession and enjoyment.[63]

In his comments on Dühring's suggestion that a better performance deserves a higher reward, Engels ironically suggested that 'Herr Dühring, too, honours himself, when, combining the innocence of a dove with the wisdom of a serpent, he bestows such touching care of the moderate additional consumption of the Dührings of the future'.[64]

Incidentally, Lenin also defended on at least one occasion the egalitarian principle 'of the equality of labour and pay'.[65] It was only a harsh economic reality which forced him later to change his mind.

Having tried to resolve the dilemma, Oscar Lange suggested a solution which would avoid an inequality of incomes and yet preserve a differentiation of incomes. True, he did not intend to equalise incomes for the pursuit of positive freedom; what he wanted to achieve was a maximisation of the total welfare of the whole population. Free choice in consumption and of occupation being assumed, says Lange, the distribution of incomes maximising the total welfare of society has to satisfy two conditions: (i) the same demand price offered by different consumers represents an equal urgency of need which is attained if the marginal utility of income is the same for all consumers; (ii) the distribution has to lead to such apportionment of the services of labour between the different occupations as to make differences in the value of the marginal product of labour in the various occupations equal to the differences in the marginal disutility involved in their pursuit. Assuming the marginal utility curves of income to be the same for all individuals, condition (i) is satisfied when all consumers have the same income. But condition (ii) requires a differentiation of incomes, since, to secure the apportionment of labour services required, differences in the marginal disutility of the various occupations have to be compensated by differences in incomes. The contradiction, argues Lange, is only apparent. By putting leisure, safety, agreeableness of work, etc., into the utility scales of individuals, the disutility of any occupation can be represented as an opportunity cost. The choice of an occupation offering a lower money income, but also a smaller disutility, may be interpreted as the purchase of leisure, safety, agreeableness of work, etc., at a price equal to the difference between the money income earned in that particular occupation and in others. Thus the differences of incomes required by condition (ii) are only apparent. They represent prices paid by individuals for different conditions of work. Instead of attaching different money incomes to various occupations, the administration of a socialist economy might pay all citizens the same money income and charge a price for the pursuit of each occupation. It becomes obvious not only that there is no contradiction between both conditions, but that condition (ii) is necessary to satisfy condition (i).[66]

Lange says that his argument holds if the marginal utility curve of income is the same for all individuals and if all individuals have the same utility scales which, he admits, does not correspond to reality. In terms of a simplified theoretical model, the two limiting assumptions are fully legitimate. In terms of a complex social reality, such assumptions would make his construction hardly applicable. What is more, Lange's solution is only seemingly conclusive. He tacitly assumes that society could pay less for intellectual jobs because of their smaller disutility or, to put it another way, charge a higher price for the pursuit of all agreeable or otherwise appealing occupations. If so, the most able would scarcely be encouraged to pursue such jobs. All other things being equal, such an arrangement would seriously undermine overall economic efficiency in the long run and, consequently, impede the future total welfare of society. If one considers skills and talents a scarce resource, it would amount to an economic waste. In terms of the development of human potentialities, the penalty charged for access to creative, stimulating, agreeable yet highly demanding, responsible and intellectually exhaustive professions would have only a dissuasive effect.

Lange's solution could be interpreted in both ways: to justify some wage differentials required by the social pursuit of efficiency as well as an egalitarian distribution of a 'social dividend' (wage) which, according to Lange, must not play any active part in one's choice of occupation. Be that as it may, Lange's solution does not solve the real problems of socialist distribution.

But one still has to make a preference. If one decides for the distributive principle according to work, the only impartial, impersonal and genuinely equal measure of economic performance could be the market principle. From the social point of view, producers ought to be rewarded not according to the individual productivity and intensity of their labours but according to the socially necessary labour determined by the market; not according to the individual quality of their individual products but according to the socially recognised quality (use-value) of their commodities by the market. If so, the difference between the more and the less productive, the more and the less intensive and the more and the less skilled labour ought to be reflected in wage differentials. Moreover, even the so-called social desirability (significance, importance, usefulness) of the individual's concrete labours ought to be measured impersonally, impartially and equally by the market demand. If some other criteria were applied instead (e.g. personal taste or preferences of the planners), one segment of the associated producers could be exploited by that one which would be receiving arbitrarily determined preferential material rewards.

Any moralist could argue that this would create different classes by income and wealth. The difference in income and wealth would not stem from any exploitation, however. It will just reflect one's greater or lesser contribution to the common welfare. One has to bear in mind that what really counts is the *class equality which has nothing in common with the wage differentials and that 'the size of one's purse is a purely quantitative distinction whereby any two individuals of the same* class may be *incited* against one another at will'.[67] As long as people are forced to work by economic necessity, the only realistic and still justifiable principle could consist in the tenet 'equal pay for equal labour'. Consequently, unequal pay for unequal labour will have to last until (a) scarcity is overcome and/or (b) the social division and unhomogeneity of labour is superseded. Needless to say, the differentials between the minimum and maximum wages can be regulated by democratic political decisions and kept within tolerable limits by progressive taxation (for instance, a 1:5 ratio between the minimum and maximum income). And finally, the minimum earnings can be guaranteed in any developed society at the level which would give even the least competitive producers a decent standard (for instance, 50 per cent of the mean or average income).

Since unequal income does not violate the universal equality of freedoms and rights in the socialist market system, there is no reason to replace it by a crude egalitarianism. Moreover, the consumer's inequality (the difference in the size of the purse) is only quantitative and does not give any (social) power to those who are better off over those who are not. What has yet to be investigated, however, is the relation between (1) inequality of the purse and accessibility to positive freedom, and (2) egalitarianism and accessibility to positive freedom.

(1) When Marx and Engels applauded the tenet 'to each according to his needs', they probably did not realise that it might be contrary to egalitarianism. If need is interpreted literally, its meaning would be closer to that of desire than to that of want. If need is related to scarcity, however, then, obviously, its meaning would have to be reduced to a reasonable amount of goods and services sufficient to satisfy the socially justified requirements of an average man. It was only in the *Critique of the Gotha Program* that Marx realised that his former scarcity-based egalitarianism was incompatible with communism *qua* humanism. Though the post-scarcity distribution according to one's needs implies a rather unequal consumption, it ought not to be interpreted as inequality; it ought to be interpreted as *variety*.

Why do I hold that distribution according to one's needs implies a rather unequal comsumption? Simply because of the infinite variety of the individuals' needs. No doubt, certain human needs are quite universal – for instance, those stemming from human instincts such as hunger, sexual desire and curiosity. There are also basic material human needs which could be more or less equally satisfied, such as the need for shelter, clothing, etc. Both the biological (instinctive) and primary material needs may be refined and consciously regulated by men through their education and socialisation. However, both education and socialisation create new human needs. If one learns to read, ski, swim, listen to music or play an instrument, one *needs* to read, ski, swim, listen to music or play an instrument. The acquired needs which have become an integral part of one's personality can be called one's inner needs. The inner needs are not only infinite but, *strictu senso*, unquantifiable. When related to the unique individual they can be expressed in qualitative terms only. The composer cannot be equal to the quantum theorist *qua* composer, though he can be equal to the quantum theorist (or, for that matter, to any other individual) as a citizen (before the law, entitled to vote and be elected), as a producer (one who contributes to the social well-being in his specific way in exchange for the goods and services which are instrumental for his own well-being), as a consumer (if he earns as much as the quantum theorist), etc. In his qualitative definiteness *qua* composer he cannot be reduced to an average quantity. If such a reduction is inapplicable to one's professional definiteness, it would be still less applicable to one's individual creativity. Whenever the individual makes the best of himself through his creative activity, he cannot be replaced by another individual. The worker at the assembly-line may easily be replaced by any other worker. If the same replaceable assembly-line man seeks self-fulfilment in his leisure as an amateur actor in an amateur theatre, or distinguishes himself as an amateur grower of refined roses, he is irreplaceable. While Milton Friedman may be replaceable as a university teacher of economics by Ernest Mandel or, for that matter, by any other competent economist, he is irreplaceable as a unique economic thinker, and vice versa.

It is obvious that each individual has specific needs in his capacity as developer of his own human energy. In the case of the poet one may need only a sheet of paper and a pencil. In the case of the scientist, one needs a well-equipped laboratory, a good library, etc. In the case of the art historian one needs to travel to famous galleries and see at least some monuments of world architecture. In the case of the top athlete, one needs access to a gymnasium, stadium, swimming-pool or ski slopes. What might be considered profligacy in the case of one individual may be a *sine qua non* in the case of another. The greater an individual's positive freedom, the more diverse and unequal are that individual's needs.

In an ideal post-scarcity utopia the variety of needs would not cause any problem since everyone will get according to one's needs. In any real post-capitalist society based on scarcity it would – unless it is offset by income differentials reflecting not only better performance, harder work, creativity, innovation, skills, knowledge and responsibility but also a discrepancy between the demand for and the supply of dirty, unpleasant and unattractive labours. For one thing, one knows only too well that, in the realm of necessity (and, consequently, of scarcity), one's willingness to perform according to, rather than below, one's ability requires certain material incentives. One also knows that the reproduction costs of a skilled producer, or of a hard-working producer in an unattractive job, are usually higher than the reproduction costs of an unskilled or less intensively working producer. (For instance, a scholar needs an additional room in his apartment (a study), has to buy specialised journals and books, travel in connection with his research, etc. A miner needs more nutritious food, longer holidays spent in the mountains or on the beach, etc.) If a higher financial reward is missing, it would be very difficult to recruit people for less attractive (or more demanding) jobs on a voluntary basis; therefore, a kind of coercion would be unavoidable. Since I reject in principle any forced labour; since it is known that a forced labour is less productive than a voluntary one; and finally, since one is also aware that any move towards a society with shorter working hours, better social services, more accessible education, sport, art, culture, etc., requires a highly efficient and smoothly functioning economy, a kind of material incentive is instrumental for the sake of a steady increase in the aggregate amount of positive freedom.

Moreover, if the producer contributes to the society according to his abilities, he expects that his needs will be satisfied proportionally to his contribution. If they were not, he would feel frustrated. As long as one lives in the realm of necessity, the very principle of equality requires that everyone able to work has to work. And if the society is unable to distribute its wealth according to one's needs, the fairest and, simultaneously, the most rational distributive principle would be according to one's work rather than according to an average ratio. If everything which could be consumed (used) either socially or individually has to be produced, then, obviously, an egalitarian distribution would imply the 'exploitation' of the more industrious by the less industrious. It is evident that, in the circumstances, a higher earned income used by the individual for the satisfaction of his needs according to his own preferences would not stem from a privilege but from one's higher contribution to output.[68]

The inequality of the purse caused by (relative) scarcity *and* different contributions to output maximises the positive freedom of the more able and industrious *without* impeding the positive freedom of the less able and industrious. While acknowledging that the arrangement is far from being ideal, I maintain that it still represents the least of the alternative evils.

(2) Having the developmental concept of man in mind, I cannot but reject egalitarian distribution. Since people are unequal in terms of their talents, faculties and abilities, their developmental potential is also unequal. Those who employ their full capacities for the sake of social well-being have the right to get a better chance to employ their full capacities for the sake of their personal development than those who, for whatever reason, are not willing to work according to the best of their abilities. As long as scarcity prevails, any attempt to separate income from one's contribution to work output would encourage parasitism, impede efficiency and slow down social development.

What to do, however, with those who do employ their full capacities for the sake of social well-being and still contribute much less to work output than their more able fellow producers? Who – in terms of their efforts – are doing their best without too much visible outcome? If one allowed that people ought to be rewarded according to their effort or, which is just another expression of the same thing, according to their contribution to work input, one would have to create almost insuperable impediments to the system's efficiency and functioning. If this were the rule, one would have to measure efficiency and outcome by input rather than by output. It would be tantamount to the rule according to which the prize is given not to the runner who finished first but to the one who tried *harder*; not to the chess player who check-mated his partner but to the one who thought *longer* about each particular move. In short, one would have to take seriously what was once suggested, with his tongue in cheek, by Henry Simons: since the talented are unavoidably favoured by being more talented, giving them higher incomes compounds their accidental and unmerited advantages.[69] Whoever finds an ethical appeal in such a redress principle and is willing to introduce it in practice as a workable economic arrangement should first be asked to pass a personal test by undergoing surgery by the man who, despite his industriousness, was unable to pass medical exams but still got his diploma and licence because of his noble efforts.

Crude egalitarianism, as well as reward according to work input rather than work output, or a bonus paid to those who are less capable than the talented, would be dysfunctional in any society pursuing maximisation of positive freedom. A net aggregate amount of positive freedom in society depends, all other things being equal, much more on the amount of goods and services available for the development of men's faculties than on equal pay for unequal labour.[70] If those contributing substantially more to work output were paid only as little as those contributing substantially less to work output, they would gradually lose their interest in good performance. Hence, economic efficiency would decline. The less efficient the system, the less it can offer to its members in terms of both material consumption and social, cultural, educational and leisure services. Even if equality of reward might be preserved, it would be a declining reward (at worst) and a stagnating reward at best; even if equality of access to positive freedom might be preserved, the more developed individuals would be unable to realise their already cultivated capacities while the less developed individuals would be unable to cultivate their potential capacities because of diminishing wealth and leisure caused by the inevitably declining efficiency of the system. In the final analysis, the unrealised though already cultivated individual capacities would degenerate while the potential individual capacities would be left undeveloped. As a result, equality would kill efficiency and impede the desired future increase of the net aggregate amount of positive freedom.[71]

(iii) *A Note on Health and Education: The Case of Distribution According to Needs*

If one thinks about various material human needs whose satisfaction is a *sine qua non* for the reproduction of man, the first idea entering one's mind is to quantify them. It is not so difficult to establish, either empirically or scientifically, the amount of calories required for different age, sex and occupation groups as well as for people living in different climatic zones; neither it is difficult to find out what proportion of man's diet should consist of proteins, carbohydrates and minerals, how many various vitamins the human body needs, etc. A similar quantification may be applied to clothing, shelter and some of man's other material needs. For the sake of man's reproduction, the quality of food, clothing, shelter and other material goods and services is secondary and, as a rule, its relevance increases only with the increased supply. If a subsistence (decent, reasonable, comfortable) level is achieved, everything which exceeds it could be considered a luxury rather than a necessity. This is not to suggest that a socialist society should not care about quantitative and qualitative improvements of living standards. This is merely to suggest that man's material needs are quantifiable, calculable and standardisable. Once a subsistence (decent) level is guaranteed for all, the care of its individual increases can be trusted to each producer and regulated — on the basis of distribution according to work output – by the individual's free consumer choice.

There are, however, yet other human needs which one would scarcely try to quantify. While the material needs of man – all individual deviations aside – approximate the average, some non-material needs are, from the individual's point of view, accidental. For instance, one person may not need medical services at all while another person might not survive without permanent medical care. What is more, each ill person needs individual attention: the same illness could have quite different effects upon different people with regard to their age as well as physical and mental fitness. In short, need for medical services is qualitative rather than quantitative: its extent and intensity depend on the merits of each medical case rather than on average consumption norms. Because of its qualitative nature, need for medical services (including prescribed drugs, spa therapy, etc.) does not meet market criteria. To make this point quite clear, I wish to illustrate it by an example. If one needs a meal, one may choose between an expensive filet mignon and a non-expensive hamburger; if one needs a dress, one may choose between an expensive woollen made-to-measure and an in-expensive cotton ready-made suit; one's need for shelter may be satisfied either by a luxurious villa or by a modest apartment. One's choice depends on the combination of one's personal preference and disposable income. If one suffers from gallstones, however, there is only one cure – surgery. The patient has no choice. Irrespective of his disposable income, he simply needs surgery however expensive it may be. While most material (quantitative) needs may be satisfied by alternative means, health (qualitative) needs ought to be satisfied by the means best reflecting the merits of any particular illness.

This is the principal difference between the quantitative needs which could best be satisfied via the market on the basis of free consumer choice, and the qualitative needs which, because of their unquantifiability, ought to be excluded from the market criteria. Since one cannot decide what kind of cure one really needs (this is decided upon by the physician); since one cannot influence either the kind of cure or its expenses; and since one cannot put one's state of health under one's full command and/or control, any socialist society concerned with the protection of one's right to health has little choice as to how to arrange medical and health services: its distribution according to one's needs seems to be not only the most just but also the most rational.

The case for free educational services should be argued from another perspective. The first argument for free educational services rests with equality of opportunity. Though natural talents are innate, most of man's potential abilities may be developed in the process of education. If distribution according to work is to be ethically justifiable, each individual ought to be given equal educational (developmental) opportunity. This entails not only free education but also a kind of salary for all well-progressing college and university students. If accepted, this principle could justify a significant reduction in income differentials for highly skilled occupations. The principle could also be applied alternatively, e.g. that only students who cannot provide for themselves would get a salary for studying, or that the rate of such a salary would be proportional both to the student's ability to provide for himself and his academic achievements, etc. If society is rich enough *and* simultaneously believes that educational equality is one of the highest social values, it might decide for a free and voluntary boarding-school system from the first grade up to Ph.D. programmes.

The second argument for free education distributed according to the individual's needs is deduced from the qualitative nature of the need called curiosity as well as from the recognition of the individuals' right to personal development. Given the variety of the individuals' talents and abilities, the free educational system would have to be flexible, diverse and differentiated enough to ensure the individuals' choice. For the individual's choices could be contrary to the social preferences, the very fact that one has the right to get education according to one's needs would not imply that one is automatically entitled to get a job according to one's educational background. The principle of free access to education is fully compatible with an open competition for any highly qualified position as well as an indirectly regulated allocation of students to various types of educational institutions and/or specialised fields by virtue of wage and salary differentials.

Having said this, I would wish to add one important qualification: as long as a given socialist society cannot afford an unlimited free access to higher education, or does not want to produce an undesired surplus of specialists, it ought to regulate admission to professional schools and specialised studies according to the applicants' talents, faculties and abilities. Even if one cannot rule out accidental errors in selecting the applicants or guarantee the absolute impartiality of the members of admission bodies, such an arrangement would still be the fairest alternative.

The third argument for free education according to one's needs is based on the principle of social redress. No individual should unreasonably suffer from his below-average inborn abilities. It has already been accepted in many developed societies that mentally retarded or physically handicapped children are entitled to special care whose costs are paid in full from the state budget in the case of families with lower incomes or in part in the case of families with above-average incomes. One may easily perceive a rich socialist society which would assume the full financial responsibility for such a redress. Since I do subscribe to the principle of economic efficiency, I feel obliged to modify the redress principle in that exceptionally talented children also be entitled to special free care. No rationally organised society should pay its full attention to the losers only. It should be also concerned about the winners. Exceptional talents are so rare that it would be unforgivable if they were neglected or if their cultivation and development were impeded because of a one-sided preoccupation with the principle of redress. Special free social care for exceptional talents may conflict with crude egalitarianism but it by no means conflicts with any democratic theory.

In principle, this is appreciated even by the egalitarians: 'The power which a democratic theory requires to be maximised is the ability of each to use and develop those of his capacities the use and development of which *does not prevent* others using and developing theirs.'[72] It is evident that special social attention paid to the most talented impedes the development of the others just as little (or as much) as special attention paid to the handicapped impedes the development of the others.[73] If the right to a special group attention is guaranteed to all who qualify for any particular category, and if the proviso is that each should be able to make the most of himself without preventing others from making the most of themselves, then, obviously, my suggestion is fully acceptable by any democratic theory. If the proviso were that no one should be able to make of himself more than *anyone* else, i.e. than the most handicapped or the least able, this discussion would have never taken place for, on one hand, there would be nothing to discuss: no political theory would have been ever written and published because all those able to write it would have had to wait as long as *everyone* could write it. The absurdity of such a proviso is only too obvious. On the other hand, one may clearly see that the emphasis on the positive (development) liberty of each must inevitably be at odds with egalitarianism.

But what to do if one took seriously the ironically meant suggestion of Henry Simons? Could the special social attention paid to the most talented be seen as a special privilege? Some would undoubtedly argue that it could and should. But if the most talented were forced to wait with the development of their potentials for the less talented, their talents would most likely vanish. The salient trait of the positive freedom conceived as the full development of *one's* personal abilities lies in that it refers to the uniqueness (quality) of each individual rather than to a quantifiable statistical average. If the special abilities of the most talented are developed only to an average level, it would actually mean that they have been curbed rather than developed at all. In other words, the most talented would be denied developmental freedom. Moreover, if each is asked to work according to his abilities, he ought to get a chance to develop these abilities. If one's abilities were curbed rather than developed, one could not work according to one's abilities either. And finally, if there is ever a hope that someone will find a cure for the handicapped, it is likely to be found by the most talented provided they get a chance to develop their unique talents in full.

My suggestion can be legitimately challenged by those courageous enough to declare that they are not concerned about an unlimited development of everyone's abilities but *only* about equalisation of unequal abilities of unequal individuals. If so, then the real social objective would consist not in maximisation of individual developmental powers but in *levelling* of individual developmental powers. The reformulated objective would bring about a less than maximum possible amount of net aggregate positive freedom, namely the maximum possible amount *minus* the unrealised abilities of the most talented.

The fourth argument for free education is derived from the fact that education is an indispensable form of socialisation. To make both the socialist self-managed economic system and the socialist democratic political system functional, individuals are expected to participate in political and economic control. To make popular participation in democratic control realistic, individuals should be taught how to evaluate information, how to make public decisions, how to evaluate the performance of public bodies. This implies that education should be combined with training and that each individual has to be offered free access to knowledge. Socialism based on self-managed economy, self-governed political communities and the principle of rotation in both self-managing and representative bodies cannot be efficient without a high level of both general and specialised education.

To sum up, health and education services ought to be exempt from the (market) distribution according to work because they satisfy unique qualitative needs of each individual which, in the case of education, also coincide with the social need to make the system economically efficient and politically functional.

(iv) *A Note on Cultural Services and Public Utilities*

In addition to the four arguments for free education, a fifth should be added with regard to art, science and culture. As a rule, the more educated (education does not necessarily mean professional training) the people, the more developed are their non-material needs. A broad education includes a cultivation of aesthetic tastes, a pursuit of critical thought, of meaningful use of leisure and an active participation in cultural, scientific, artistic and sport activities. All these needs could be considered man's inner qualitative needs which require to exempt their satisfaction from the market. While this is acceptable in principle, a word of warning is necessary. If the entire sphere of art and culture is exempt from the market, a benefactor has to be found who would subsidise or finance it. However, any model of art and/or culture which relies wholly on a benefactor is extremely dangerous. The benefactor may quite legitimately claim the right to decide what kind of artistic, scientific and cultural activities be supported. If the part of the benefactor is played exclusively by the state, art, science and culture might become too dependent on those who wield political power. Even if the part of the benefactor is played by more than one social agency, the danger would not disappear. For neither the state, nor self-managed economic units or artistic associations and cultural organisations, could guarantee artistic and cultural freedom; the most suitable model ought to rely on a combination of public subsidies and partially market-oriented artistic and cultural institutions. The same principle should apply to sciences. One has to allow – and there is plenty of empirical evidence for it – that at least some artistic or scientific innovations might not meet the prevailing tastes of the majority. If art, culture and science were entirely exempt from the market, they would depend wholly on the benefactor's tastes and preferences. Even if the part of the benefactor were played by a democratically established majority, it would not help too much: neither art nor science ought to be run by the majority principle. A work of art as well as a scientific hypothesis or theory could hardly be judged in the same way as are political issues.

Such utilities as electric power, highways, air, water and railway transport, telephones, etc., should be put under state control combined with self-management. The basic reason for this dual model lies in the very nature of public utilities. While some of them may be either profit-oriented or subsidised (e.g. telephone services, air transport), most public utilities should be exempt from the market as a matter of principle. For one thing, the state may use public utilities for social regulation of market activities of economic units. For another, by subsidising public utilities and services, the state may positively influence the structure of consumption (e.g. public transport vs. private cars).

(v) *A Note on Advertising*

No market system can properly function without advertising. What is more, no modern system may function without advertising either. On average, a modern developed economy produces about 1.5 million different commodities and goods and offers tens of thousands of various services. Advertising is necessary for obvious reasons: the public has to be informed what, where and for which price goods are available. Without a certain amount of information released to the public by virtue of advertising, life in modern society would become uncomfortable.

It is my hypothesis that it is consumer society which has brought about excessive advertising. In other words, excessive advertising is an effect rather than the cause of contemporary consumerism. In turn, consumerism inevitably had to follow completed industrialisation: mass production cannot exist without mass consumption.

It would be futile to construct a market socialist model without any advertising. (For that matter, it would be futile to construct *any* model of modern society without some advertising.) What can be done, however, is to tame advertising by keeping it within tolerable limits. If consumer credit is put under democratic social control, socialist systems could curb infinite consumerism more efficiently than if they banned advertising. By regulating the market, socialist systems may prevent the creation of some artificial consumer needs. By combining the technique of contemporary advertising with indirect taxation, socialist systems can change consumer patterns considerably. By setting a limit for tax-deductible advertising costs, socialist systems may encourage self-managed enterprises to spend funds allocated for advertising more productively.

Until now, the basic problem of most socialist systems consisted of excessive ideological advertising (propaganda) rather than of excessive commercial advertising. If a reasonable balance between the two is achieved – political pluralism *and* social regulation of the market having been assumed – advertising could cease to be both excessive and wasteful.

(vi) *The Reciprocity Principle as Psychological Need*

The socialist market based on social property implies the following principles:

1. The *Organisational* principle entails voluntarism, choice and horizontality of relations.
2. The *Communication* principle entails impersonality.
3. The *Sociological* principle entails equivalence and equity.
4. The *Competition* entails electiveness (e.g. elections, competition for a vacant position, etc.).
5. The *Democratic* principle entails participation and subjectivity of all agents of the market.
6. The *Cybernetic* (functional) principle entails self-regulation and feedback.
7. The *Reciprocity* principle entails contractual relations.

Given the absence of private property, humanistic critics might accept all the market principles except that of reciprocity based on contract. They hold that the contract principle converts desirable man-to-man relations into undesirable exchange relations. The humanistic critics of the market insist that man ought to behave vis-à-vis other men simply *qua* man rather than *qua* exchanger. Contrary to this conventional critique of the market, I would wish to argue that the reciprocity (contract) principle is a *sine qua non* for any humanistic, functional and bearable society-type arrangement. To avoid any misunderstanding or misrepresentation, I shall present my argument in an inductive manner, i.e. proceed from the particular to the general, from the concrete to the abstract.

If I need to repair my stalled car, I would call the mechanic whose particular trade is to repair cars. He will give me an estimate which I am free either to accept or reject. If I accept it, our mutual relations acquire a contractual form: the mechanic is obliged to fix my car whereas I am obliged to pay him the agreed price. If the mechanic failed to fulfil his duty, I would have the right to withhold my payment. The nature of our relation is simple and transparent: I do not bother him by asking for the service since it is his job to serve anyone who needs to fix a car. On the other hand, he does not do me any favour since I pay him the price which amounts to an equivalent of his service. If a time limit for the repair is a part of our deal, he is obliged to meet it. It should not make any difference to the mechanic if I come back tomorrow with another breakdown in my car, with yet another breakdown the day after tomorrow, etc. The mechanic would not feel that I was misusing his courtesy since he has not done me any special favour: from his point of view it is irrelevant if he repairs my car or someone else's car. We both behave as exchangers, our mutual relations are purely contractual relations. I do not care whether the mechanic is a sympathetic man or not, whether he is a vegetarian, a smoker, a liberal, a communist, an atheist, etc. I do care only about one thing: if he does a good job. The same applies to him. He also cares about one thing only: if I pay him the agreed price.

Let us imagine for a moment that our mutual relations with the mechanic were not based on the contractual (reciprocity) principle and that we dealt with each other on the basis of the man-to-man principle instead. First, when asking the mechanic to fix my car, I would have to ask him to do me a favour. When asking him to repair my car on the spot, I would have to explain why I want to get it fixed at once. If the mechanic found me personally sympathetic, he could respond positively. So far so good. But what should I do if he did not repair my car properly? Should I insist that he tries again? I hardly could because he accepted – owing to the absence of any contract based on a *quid pro quo* – no obligation as to the quality of the repair. But even if he fixed my car properly, could I come back tomorrow with another breakdown? Would he not feel annoyed? And even if he would not, what should I offer him in return for his courtesy?

This hypothetical case might be presented in many alternative ways. For instance, the mechanic did not find me sympathetic enough and therefore did not fix my car. Or he did not fix it at once. Or he did me a favour today by fixing my car properly but failed to fix another breakdown tomorrow. And so forth.

Even if there were only one positive scenario and everything went smoothly along its lines, one problem would still be left unsolved. While I may very often need the mechanic, the tailor, the physician, the dentist, etc., they may not need me at all. Certainly, someone else may need my services, but those whom I do need so often may never get a chance to find out if I repay their good services to someone else by equally good services. Let us assume that I am used to getting good services from those whom I need but that I provide those who need me with only mediocre or even less than mediocre services. Or let us assume that I am served badly by those whom I need. Could those whom I do serve expect that, having had such a bad experience with *my suppliers*, I would serve *my customers* any better? Who could check the quality of my (or their) services if the reciprocal (contractual) principle was rejected? If it was in a small community where people know each other, one may allow that no one could afford to serve other people unsatisfactorily. In the society-type organisation, however, everyone could afford it.

The market has one indispensable advantage: it automatically converts any single exchange to a common denominator (exchange-value expressed in monetary terms) which equalises one's product (service) to anyone else's product (service). By virtue of the common denominator, every single giving is at the same time also receiving. Society based on (relative) scarcity has to measure (and balance) everyone's giving and receiving; if it did not, some could live at the expense of others.

Moreover, the need for a balance between the giving and the receiving goes beyond the conditions of scarcity. Even if people do not behave as exchangers, e.g. within a family, among friends, lovers, etc., some balance between the giving and the receiving is also indispensable. If one is in love and does not think in terms of equivalence, one does still think in terms of reciprocity. If the most dearly beloved person does not give something in return to the loving person, the latter's love would not last too long. The same applies to relations between friends, between parents and children, between wife and husband. Since everyone also has a psychological need for reciprocity, for most people it would be unbearable if they were receiving from one person while giving to another person. If the principle of market exchange is removed, this would happen as a rule in any society-type organisation.

Our everyday functional relations with most other people are neutral in terms of personal sympathies or antipathies, and should remain neutral. They are impersonal and should remain impersonal. If they were turned into man-to-man relations, the society-type organisation would cease to function. Everyone would fall a victim to chance and the unpredictability of others' behaviour. The assumption that everything would go smoothly if the reciprocity (contractual) principle were removed from impersonal, functional, routine and purposeful relations among men who act in their capacity as agents of social division of labour cannot be taken for granted. Each routine and simple exchange act mediated automatically by the market would have to be substituted by the unique trade-off whose outcome would depend heavily upon each individual's momentary mood, as well as his momentary ability to cope with his unforeseeable counterpart. Whereas one can predict, with a fair degree of certainty, the standard behaviour of an average exchanger, one can hardly predict the behaviour of the stranger who ceases to behave according to the rules of his particular role (e.g. as waiter, cashier, taxi-driver, serviceman, etc.) and begins to behave just as a man. While the outcome can be accidentally marvellous in one case, it could be accidentally disastrous in another case.

Thus, the man-to-man type of relationship is hardly applicable in the *society*-type organisation. It might work only in the community-type organisation, e.g. within each self-managed work-place, in a club, among neighbours. Though the reciprocity principle can be applied without its contractual basis in the community, it could hardly be applied without its contractual basis in the society, especially if the society is based on scarcity.

One may logically argue what would likely happen if the routine market-mediated everyday exchanges were stripped of their contractual reciprocity. If the reciprocal dyads (right–duty, claim–obligation) were rejected, the everyday functioning of the society would become disrupted, the rights of the individuals would cease to be legally (contractually) protected, one's reasonable expectations would be left unfulfilled and the human situation of the average man would become unbearable. If contractual relations among exchangers were replaced by unpredictable man-to-man behavioural patterns, then an inevitable fortuity would make man permanently frustrated because of his unsatisfied psychological need for reciprocity. Hence, the humanists' conventional anti-market argument does not hold in the society-type organisation based on (relative) scarcity.

(e) IMPOSSIBILITY OF NON-MARKET DEMOCRATIC THEORY RETAINING ETHICALLY VALUABLE LIBERAL PRINCIPLES

There are at least five ethically valuable liberal principles. The first consists of negative freedom defined as the absence of coercion by other men in general and by the government in particular. If the argument that the market is a necessary (though not a sufficient) condition of negative liberty holds, then, logically, a non-market democratic theory cannot retain the ethically valuable liberal principle of negative freedom.

The second ethically valuable liberal principle lies in that man has the right to pursue his own concept of happiness. This principle implies that man has the right to become the subject, to act in his self-interest and to decide about himself. This second principle cannot be realised without the guaranteed negative freedom. Consequently, a non-market democratic theory cannot retain the ethically valuable liberal principle of man *qua* subject.

The third ethically valuable liberal principle postulates man's right to make the best of himself, to develop all his potential talents, abilities and faculties. This right requires that man has free access to all the means including the means of production which are necessary for his personal development. Since the only conceivable economic model for a strictly non-market society is that of one nation, one factory, the logic suggests that in the strictly non-market society there must be only one exclusive owner of the means of production and, consequently, also one exclusive employer (entrepreneur) only, the state. If the state is the sole employer, there is always a danger that it *might*, owing to its monopoly of employment, deny free access to the means of labour (or at least to some particular means of labour) to critics and opponents of the government. For as there is neither an alternative employer nor alternative self-employment in the strictly non-market society, a non-market democratic theory cannot suggest any real guarantee of everyone's free, universal and equal access to the means of production. Without such a guarantee, however, man's right to make the best of himself cannot be taken for granted. This is why a non-market democratic theory cannot retain the ethically valuable liberal principle of both the full and free development of man.[74]

The fourth ethically valuable liberal principle is that of equality of men. If equality is to be extended to one's participation in both direct and indirect economic and political control, a kind of self-managing economy and of pluralistic political system is necessary. Since economic self-management requires an autonomy of work-places whose preservation is, in the condition of division of labour and scarcity, impossible without the market, a non-market democratic theory cannot preserve the valuable liberal principle of equality extended to one's equal right to participate in direct and indirect economic control. And since a non-pluralistic, centralised and vertically structured economy cannot serve as a base for a pluralistic, decentralised and horizontally structured political system, a non-market democratic theory cannot preserve the valuable liberal principle of equality extended to one's equal right to participate in direct and indirect political control.

And finally, the fifth ethically valuable liberal principle may be defined as one's right to decide about the matters which have an impact upon one's life. Since work is one of the most important human activities, a practical realisation of the principle is impossible without a kind of self-management. And because self-management is, in the condition of division of labour and scarcity, impossible without the existence of the market, a non-market democratic theory cannot preserve this fifth valuable principle either.

Thus, one cannot but conclude that Macpherson's 'insuperable difficulties' of the attempts to reformulate democratic theory which would preserve all ethically valuable liberal principles apply to a non-market rather than to a market democratic theory. To prove that the market is a *sine qua non* for at least one democratic theory retaining all valuable liberal *and* socialist ethical principles, I wish to offer the following model to public scrutiny.

Part Three

Marx's Concept of Economic and Political Liberation of Man: A Challenge

6 The General Model of Democratic Socialism

The basic principles which are both necessary and sufficient for a functional *economic* structure of the model may be defined by the following set of arrangements:

1. Labour is the sole source of income.
2. The means of production are owned socially and managed by those who make use of them.
3. Social ownership of the means of production is separated from the state.
4. The social essence of capital assets is reflected by the levies which the collective users (producers) pay to social funds.
5. Producing and trading enterprises are autonomous from the state and independent of each other. They operate within the framework of the market which is regulated by a central indicative plan.
6. The institutions which provide health, education and welfare services are wholly exempt from the market.
7. The institutions which provide public services and utilities (art, culture and science included) are either wholly or partly exempt from the market.
8. The central bank is directly controlled by the state. Commercial banks can be considered public utilities for both the market and non-market sectors. Therefore, they are managed as the enterprises and institutions listed under (10).
9. The right to participate in direct management of the work units *operating in the market* is derived from labour.
10. The right to participate in direct management of the work units *exempt wholly or partly from the market* is derived proportionally from labour, ownership and consumption of the provided services and utilities.

179

11. The right to participate in indirect political control over, and regulation of, the socially owned means of production is derived from one's position as citizen.
12. Incomes are distributed according to one's contribution to work output.
13. Health and education services and social benefits for the disabled are distributed according to one's needs.
14. The dividend from the social ownership of the means of production is accumulated in the social investments fund.
15. Economic equality consists of each individual's equal access to the means of production, health and education services, social benefits and self-management. Since it does not include egalitarian distribution of incomes, individuals – while equal in their essence – are unequal in their existence.
16. The principle of self-management is limited to microeconomics only.

This set of arrangements eliminates economic exploitation, class inequality and class privilege because it gives an equal access to participation in direct management to every producer and an equal access to indirect political control over the socially owned means of production to every citizen. This model is incompatible with the hegemony of the proletariat as well as the dictatorship of the proletariat. It implicitly rejects Marx's suggestion that the proletariat is a universal class. The proletariat is not, and cannot be, a universal class. For one thing, it does not produce universally but only in co-operation with other social groups and/or classes, e.g. the intelligentsia and the peasantry. For another, the proletariat cannot satisfy its needs without exchanging its labour and products with the peasantry and the intelligentsia. As a matter of fact, this model eliminates class distinctions in the sense that *all* working people have equal access to management and control. That is why I call it *labour* self-management rather than *workers'* self-management. The only remnant of the class division is due to the social division of labour in terms of specialisation rather than in terms of the antagonistic relation between those who manage and control and those who are managed and controlled. Though this is hardly an ideal arrangement, it is still the best possible arrangement within the realm of necessity, guaranteeing a substantial extension of democracy from politics to economics.

I do not pretend that an equal access to participation in direct management is tantamount to equal participation. Those elected to self-management bodies may participate more intensively than others. Those more concerned may participate more actively than others. Neither do I pretend that the principle of one man, one vote postulates that everyone participates equally in indirect political control over the socially owned means of production. Some people will always wield more influence and decision-making power than others. I may again repeat that the maximum equality which can be ever realistically expected and achieved is equality in essence and inequality in existence.

This model could not be constructed without the concept of social ownership first formulated by the Yugoslavs. It is as instrumental for the market self-managed socialist economies as is the concept of 'operative administration' (of enterprises) for the Soviet-type command economies. One wonders why it took so much time to formulate the 'social ownership' concept. Had the concept been formulated earlier, all the discussions initiated by Barone, von Mises, Hayek, Robbins, Taylor, Lange, Lerner, Dobb and others could have resulted in less ambiguous conclusions. One also wonders why the typically nineteenth-century view identifying public property with state property and, consequently, denying any possibility of the market of capital goods in socialist economies, could survive up to this day. For one thing, there is nothing specifically capitalist about the market. For another, there is nothing specifically socialist about planning. Those who deny, as a matter of principle, the concept of market socialism, are as hopelessly ideologically biased as those who deny, on principle, any politically motivated regulation of, and interference with, the market in capitalist economies. On purely theoretical grounds, both positions are untenable.

It is worth noting that this model is rather simplified. It ignores the remnants of the yet non-socialised, individual (personal) means of production which are inevitably present in any real socialist system. If one applies to them Marx's concept of capital as the governing 'power over labour and its product', however, it could be legitimately concluded that the existence of a personal and/or co-operative type of production is fully compatible with the socialist nature of the model. And secondly, I adhere strictly to Marx's requirement that there should be an accord between the character (nature) of the means of production and the forms of their economic realisation. If the productive means yet failed to acquire social character, then, obviously, their economic realisation (i.e. ownership, control, management and appropriation) ought not to assume social character either. If it had, one would have to face the cleavage between the individual character (nature) of the productive means *and* the social character (nature) of their ownership, control, management and appropriation. The cleavage would be just a reversion of that which is characteristic of capitalism, namely that the social character of the means of production clashes with their private ownership and appropriation.

It might be argued that this model suffers from one inconsistency. While the right to participate in direct management of the work units operating in the market is derived from labour, the right to participate in direct management of the work units exempt wholly or partly from the market is derived proportionally from labour, ownership and consumption of the provided services and utilities. However, the inconsistency is only apparent. Because I assume that the market is competitive, the producers subject to market control cannot arbitrarily put their particular interest over the social interest which is being permanently created and re-created by the market. And since the market is regulated by the indicative social (central) plan, potential monopolisation of individual branches could be prevented by political control.

The case of the work units which are wholly or partly exempt from the market is quite different. In the absence of market control, there is always a danger that either the employees, or the financier of the work unit, or both, may act contrary to the needs of the consumers. To minimise such conflicts, direct management of the work units which qualify for a full or partial exemption from the market should be trusted to the boards composed proportionally of representatives of the employees, of the users and of representatives from elected political organs. For instance, the university would be run by the board made up by representatives of the staff (one-third), of the students (one-third) and of representatives from local, regional and/or national political organs; the board of the local power-station would be composed of the employees (one-third), of the public, market and household users (one-third) and of representatives from the local government (one-third). The principle of equal representation by three groups rules out arbitrary decisions.

The suggested economic arrangement retains the most valuable socialist principles: absence of exploitation; absence of private ownership of land and capital; class economic equality if not equality of the purse; income distribution according to work combined with some elements of distribution according to needs (health and education); self-management in microeconomics combined with representative democratic control over macroeconomics; central planning as an instrument of social regulation of, and social control over, the market; free choice of work-place, occupation and education combined with economic security; maximisation of both negative and positive liberty; rational economic calculation combined with maximisation of social welfare.

The suggested economic arrangement also retains the most valuable principles of liberalism: separation of political and economic power; dispersed economic power in autonomous work units; decentralised system of microeconomic decision-making; maximisation of both negative and positive liberty; competition as a means to innovation; equality of opportunity; free choice of job.

The price paid for the retention of the most valuable socialist principles is relatively small: the market has to be preserved. It is preserved in a restricted, less than universal, regulated and tamed version. I suggest that such a price paid for all the advantages of the model is negligible.

The suggested economic arrangement contains all necessary (though not sufficient) preconditions of political democracy and freedom: (1) separation of economic and political power; (2) dispersion of economic power; (3) decentralised economic decision-making; (4) horizontal type of relations; (5) voluntary co-operation mediated by the technique of the market; (6) pluralism of economic subjects; (7) free consumer, occupational and educational choice; (8) social mobility; (9) competition and electiveness; (10) pursuit of self-interest. Hence, any kind of pluralistic political superstructure is compatible with the economic structure of the model. While this holds in principle, a word of caution is necessary. Both the theoretical acceptability and practical applicability of the model depend on a satisfactory solution of the cleavage between the need for a (multi-)party system in the macro-structure (society-type organisation of the political sphere) and the undesirability of any (multi-)party system in the micro-structure (community-type organisation of the work-place).

The cause of the cleavage is obvious. Given the existence of the social division of labour and (relative) scarcity, a possible unity of interests in each community-type organisation (work unit) clashes with an inevitable conflict of interests within the society made up of autonomous work communities. While the unity of interests within each work community does not require any mediator (political party), the conflicting interests within the society cannot be democratically regulated without one or more mediators. (Even if there are some conflicting interests within the work community, they do not require the mediation of political parties.) While I have derived one's right to direct participation in the management of the work unit (economic community) from one's social role as producer, I have derived one's right to indirect participation (through representation) in the political control of society from one's social role as citizen. Consequently, I have fully appreciated the postulated cleavage. At this point, I have to offer its solution.

On a purely formal level of argument, a strict separation of microeconomics and politics (an autonomy of economic units from the state) should offer a satisfactory formal solution. A real solution is not as simple, however. Though microeconomics is separated from the state and regulated primarily by the market, it is also – as a part of macroeconomics – subject to indirect political control and regulation. Hence, the separation of economics and politics is far from being absolute. In addition, each producer is at the same time a citizen. As a producer directly participating in the management of the work unit, he is a communal being; as a citizen indirectly participating in the political control of society, he is a social being. While his communal nature does not require the mediation of political parties, his social nature does require such mediation. If a mediating element of the society-type organisation (political party) penetrated a community-type organisation, it could destroy labour self-management; if a non-mediation principle of the community-type organisation penetrated a society type of organisation, it could destroy political democracy. In other words, if political partisanship penetrated labour self-management, the intra-community relations would become subject to the society-type conflicts of interests. If, conversely, the intra-society conflicting interests became subject to the non-mediation principle prevailing in the community, then, inevitably, the one nation, one factory principle would penetrate the model whose main objective is to eliminate the one nation, one factory concept once and for all.

From whatever angle one approaches the cleavage, one inevitably faces the problem which has been left unsolved by Marx as well as the Yugoslavs. As to Marx, he failed to draw a clear dividing line between micro-structure and macro-structure. He could not understand that once the micro-concept (of the factory) is extended to society as a whole, it would have to transform itself to the macro-concept. That is why he believed that a chain of self-managed communities can coexist smoothly with the society-type organisation (a social-wide factory) without the mediating role of politics. He did not offer any political theory and/or concept of socialist society for he assumed that with the supersession of private property, politics would dissolve in economics. The community would need no mediation, be it the market or politics. This holds within the community only; the latter could live without the market as well as without political parties. The relations among the communities, however, are of a different nature than those within each community. The sum total of communities is society rather than a global community. Social division of labour and scarcity assumed, unity of interests within each community is transformed into economic and political conflicts of interests within the society. In the circumstances, the authoritative central plan expressing the interest of the society as a whole would clash permanently with particular interests of individual communities. Since no harmony of interests is possible at the level of society, only two alternatives are possible: (i) elimination of the conflicting particular interests by use of coercion, or (ii) the introduction of mediators which would regulate the conflicting interests. To regulate the conflicts, two mediators are necessary: the market mechanism for economics and the (multi-)party system for politics.

Unlike Marx, the Yugoslavs have fully recognised the indispensability of the market mediation and regulation. Because of their adherence to Lenin's concept of the party, however, they have never unequivocally appreciated the indispensability of a political mediation. Lenin understood that the one nation, one factory concept cannot but remain a society-type organisation. Though its vertical structure is sufficient to eliminate the market, it is not sufficient to eliminate social conflicts. Since there is no market which would regulate and mediate conflicting economic interests, most of the latter evolve into political interests clashing with the authoritative central plan. (The conflicting political interests caused by non-economic factors may clash with both the authoritative plan and/or the non-economic policies of the centre.) To eliminate all the interests which contradict the central plan, a guarding of the unity of interests would be necessary. Since the community/society dichotomy permanently engenders conflicts, the guardian (party) would have to eliminate them permanently rather than mediate and/or regulate them. For a mediation of the conflicts under the condition of a market self-managing socialist economic system, quite a different party would be necessary. It would have to be open to everyone, with freedom of factions, able to represent and aggregate all interests resulting from the contradictory social reality.

The only way to solve the cleavage is a separation of the *political* process within the *society* from the *economic* process within the work *communities*. Since economic self-management is derived from labour, i.e. from one's social role as producer, and strictly limited to microeconomics, each political party's organisational network and/or organised activities ought to stop at the entrance to self-managed work units. For one thing, economic activity, broadly defined, is a utilitarian activity. Its main objective is to supply the society and each individual with goods and services. To make the utilitarian activity of producers less alienated and less coercive; to free it from the governing power of a special class of managers and/or bureaucrats; to realise the social nature of the ownership of the means of production; to make labour (still caused by necessity) more meaningful and, finally, to extend positive freedom of each producer *within the realm of necessity* by his direct participation in microeconomic control, labour self-management has been introduced. It has not been introduced to substitute for *political* democracy in society – *no* self-management can simulate democracy in the political sphere – but to *supersede capital relations. Strictu senso,* socialism is impossible without a kind of self-management. Moreover, labour self-management is the only way of introducing *community*-type relations within the work-place. In the conditions of the social division of labour and scarcity it has to be based on the market which, in turn, serves as a necessary (though not a sufficient) economic foundation of democratically structured political relations. However, if *political* relations and their agents (parties) penetrate the work communities, labour self-management could be undermined. Hence, the logic of the construction reads:

(a) Capital relations (non-existence of producers' control over their labour and products) cannot be superseded without labour self-management.

(b) Under the condition of the social division of labour and (relative) scarcity, self-management is theoretically inconceivable and practically impossible without the market.

(c) The market is simultaneously a necessary (though not a sufficient) economic precondition for political democracy within the *society*.

(d) Political relations (even if democratically structured) as a phenomenon of a *society*-type organisation (structure) must not be allowed to penetrate the *community*-type organisation within the self-managed work units.

(e) Labour self-management is inconsistent either with a one-party system or with a multi-party system. It requires a non-party system. However, for *labour*, self-management is – and cannot but be – limited to microeconomics only; it represents a *community*-type subsystem within a broader *society*-type system which, conversely, cannot but be regulated/mediated by one or more political parties. The very existence of the (market-based) labour self-management requires political democracy within the given *society* and, simultaneously, serves as *the* economic basis for political democracy. However, the preservation of labour self-management also requires that the agents of political democracy in the *society* (political parties) are kept off the self-managed work communities.

Thus, the cleavage has been solved: while self-management as a community-type subsystem is inconsistent with one or more political parties, it may function only within a (multi-)party society-type system. Given the distinction between the society/community structures, marriage between a (multi-)party system and a labour self-managed system is not only necessary but also possible.

To mediate/regulate the inevitable conflicts within the society, a (multi-)party system is required. It is both theoretically conceivable and practically applicable to ensure a democratic mediation/regulation of the conflicts in both one-party and multi-party systems. While the latter alternative does not need a special explanation, the former does. It is quite obvious that it is not *any* one-party system which could democratically mediate/regulate social and political conflicts; on the contrary, only a specific one-party arrangement can serve the purpose. The specifics of the arrangement could be enumerated in the following order:

(i) The party is open to everyone.

(ii) Its organisational structure is loose and decentralised.

(iii) There is freedom of factions within the party.

(iv) The party's programme platform is able to absorb group (factional) interests.

(v) Membership in the party is simply established by the payment of an admission fee.

(vi) The party does not build any political *apparat* made up of full-time employees. (It can build a technical *apparat* – support staff.)

(vii) Each member freely competes for any elective position within the party.

(viii) Each member freely seeks the party's nomination for any elective public position.

If the specifics are met, there would be, in fact, as many parties as intra-party factions. It is reasonable to assume that three major factions would emerge: one moderate in the centre, one on the left of the centre, and one on the right of the centre. Though theoretically conceivable and practically applicable, the suggested one-party system would, in fact, be a three-party system.

Once the problem of the (multi-)party system is solved, another problem emerges: how to protect the community structure of work units from being penetrated by the elements (political parties) of the society structure? As long as the market provides the work units with politically neutral criteria for rational economic behaviour, one may assume that each self-managed unit would subject its economic decisions to its common economic interest. With respect to the composition of self-management bodies, the producers can be expected to elect those who are able and willing to pursue maximisation of the work unit's economic welfare rather than maximisation of the work unit's involvement in political conflicts brought down to the work unit from the society level. The same principle would likely apply to the criteria used by the self-management body for the selection of the manager. One must bear in mind that once the principle of social property as well as the principle of labour self-management is democratically accepted, these two principles cease to be subject to (power-)political struggle. The work unit whose members applied ideological and/or partisan political criteria to *economic* self-management might face a decline of their material well-being. To help to avoid the *partyisation* of work units, a similar principle could be applied to self-management bodies as that already applied to the civil service and/or the army in pluralistic societies, namely, that the self-managed work units are kept off the political battlefield.

Because the model limits self-management to microeconomics only, it does not provide for any body representing self-management organs at a (macro-)social level. However, labour is represented at a social level by trade unions. One has to bear in mind that the associated producers who directly control work units are not the owners of the latter; they are merely employees of the society as a whole. As employees, they are entitled to be represented by trade unions both within and without the work units. It has to be assumed that there will be always conflicts between the (self-)management and individual employees concerning hiring and firing procedures, job security, wage/salary differentials, etc. This is why there will be always a need for trade unions even within the community-type labour-managed economic units. Trade unions will also be needed for another reason. On the one hand, they should – at the society level – participate in national unification of such general terms of employment as the length of working hours, guaranteed minimum wages, length of paid holidays, pension plans, etc. On the other hand, they should represent and protect the general interests of various occupational and professional categories both vis-à-vis (self-) management and governmental bodies.

There is no need to discuss the *political* structure of the model in detail. Suffice it to say that one can derive from it a variety of constitutional, institutional and systemic arrangements which would be in accord with the economic structure of the model and, at the same time, reflect specific political cultures, traditions, ethnic composition and ideological and ethical values of the societies which would decide in favour of democratic labour-managed socialism. It is worth noting, however, that the more pluralistic are the concrete political systems, the more guarantees they could provide for the preservation of freedom.

The suggested model of democratic socialism provides for a functional combination of community/society structures; for a direct control of the socially owned means of production by the producers; for a combination of the market and central (indicative) planning; for a (multi-)party system within the society and a non-party system within the work communities; for a combination of participation with representation; for an elimination of class inequalities and privileges; for a symbiosis of individualism and collectivism. I admit that the model is structurally more complex than that based on the one factory, one nation concept. Thanks to the former's complexity, however, the structural cleavage characteristic of the latter has been eliminated.

7 Labour Self-Management Applied to Corporate Capitalism

Three crucial questions could legitimately be asked with regard to an extension of the principle of labour self-management to private capitalist economy: (1) Why should one argue that privately owned means of production be managed by labour rather than by capital? (2) Why strip the owners of their right to manage and control their means of production? (3) Could such a concept ever be reconciled with the principles of liberalism?

I freely admit that each of the three questions has its merits. If I argued from the socialist position, my answer might be found with the greatest ease: I would simply refer to the fact that private property is theft (Proudhon), or the cause of all evils and miseries (the utopian socialists), or an accumulated surplus-value extracted from those who had created it (Marx). I do not, however, wish to simplify my task in that way. Rather, I shall attempt to argue my case according to generally recognised principles of liberalism as well as the intrinsic logic of liberal democratic thought.

Capital can be viewed from two aspects: firstly, as a legal title to property and to the income from property such as profit, rent, interest and dividend; secondly, as a function, as an entrepreneurial activity which includes use, management and control of the means of production. In the first stage of industrial capitalism, both the property title and entrepreneurship were united. The capitalist was simultaneously the owner and the entrepreneur. It was only the emergence of shareholding companies that brought about separation of capital as property from capital as function. What is more, the very nature of capitalist property has changed. The share does *not* represent a title to the real (physical) property. (The corporation itself is regarded as a legal person: this means that it holds property rights.) It represents nothing more than a paper duplicate of the real capital. The owner of 10 per cent

190

of the shares issued by the stock company cannot claim any title to 10 per cent of the company's physical assets. His capital is fictitious and exists only side by side with the real capital. The fictitious capital is not a real property; it exists only parallel with the real property. It is rather a title to the dividend which, in turn, is the price for a productive use of the shareholder's money.

Contemporary capitalism is, in principle, a shareholding capitalism. As early as a century ago, Marx had appreciated this change and drew from if three important conclusions:

1. Shareholding capital is directly endowed with the form of social capital (capital of directly associated individuals) as distinct from private capital, and its undertakings assume the form of social undertakings as distinct from private undertakings. *It is the abolition of capital as private property within the framework of capitalist production itself.*

2. It entails transformation of the actually functioning capitalist into a mere manager, an administrator of other people's capital, and of the owner of capital into a mere owner, a mere money-capitalist. The dividend as a mere compensation for owning capital is now entirely divorced from the function of actual capital just as the function of the manager is divorced from the ownership of capital. *It is private production without the control of private property.*

3. Stock-company business represents the abolition of capitalist private industry on the basis of the capitalist system itself. This result of the ultimate development of capitalist production is a necessary *transitional* phase towards the reconversion of capital into the property of producers, although no longer as the private property of the individual producers but rather as the property of associated producers, as outright social property.[1]

Most contemporary Marxists would agree with their master that ownership is separated from management in stock companies. This fact is so transparently evident that there is not even any need to prove it. What is not so clear, however, is another aspect of shareholding capitalism: is ownership of capital also separated from control of capital?

To answer this question, one has first to distinguish between direct and indirect control of private capital. Most of the privately owned stock companies are *de facto* public companies.[2] Whatever the formal ownership of General Motors and other big corporations, their nature is social. If such companies decide to invest abroad instead of at home, if they lay off thousands of employees or if they go bankrupt, it is no longer a private matter of their nominal owners. Any such event has an impact upon hundreds of thousands of people and, in the final analysis, upon the social and political system as a whole. Hence, no society can afford to let its *de facto* public companies behave for the benefit of their owners only. Even in the most liberal economies, all private corporations of a *de facto* public nature are subject to public (governmental) control. At least since the Great Depression, Roosevelt's New Deal and Keynes' *General Theory*, governmental interference with, and regulation of, the private companies of a public nature has been almost generally accepted. As a rule, this public control, derived from the public nature rather than the private form of capital, is indirect. It is in accord with liberal philosophy according to which matters of public nature and concern should be controlled by public means.[3]

The case of direct control is not so simple. According to Berle and Means, there are at least five types of control of modern corporations. The first type (control through almost complete ownership) is rather rare. The second (majority control) has been declining for years. The third (control through a legal device without majority ownership) has been increasing for years. The fourth (minority control) has become a standard. The fifth (management control) tends to prevail.[4]

Even if the relation between different types of direct control changes, it hardly evolves in the direction of majority control. In addition to minority control, control through such techniques as pyramiding[5] and a voting trust, as well as management control, are typical of contemporary shareholding capitalism. Even if most of the nominal owners have no real control over the corporate assets, some of them have retained a great deal of control. In the case of Van Swerigen Brothers, 1 per cent of ownership was able to control 100 per cent of the assets. Though some ownership was necessary, the ownership itself was not enough. What was required was a special technique of shareholding (pyramiding). Without the latter, it would have been impossible to eliminate 99 per cent of the owners from the control.

If the shareholding is dispersed enough – and such cases have been and are quite common[6] – the managers may assume control over the corporation. Those Marxists who do not like such cases usually argue that, as a rule, the managers are offered a certain amount of shares, that to be appointed to the board of directors one has to own a nominal interest in the corporation, etc. (some directorships, however, are purely nominal). Yet these objections cannot change the essence of managerial control: the managers and directors control not because they own the shares; they control because they are managers and directors. If an analogy is ever possible, I would wish to offer the following. In the state socialist systems, the central planners are co-owners of the nationalised means of production. In their capacity as co-owners, they are equal to their fellow citizens. Unlike their fellow citizens, however, the planners actually control the economy. They control it not because they are co-owners, but because they are planners. The same holds in the capitalist corporation. The manager (director) who owns 0.01 per cent of the shares does have a controlling power while the ordinary shareholder owning the same 0.01 per cent of the shares has no controlling power. This is why I suggest that the direct controlling power over the means of production is, as a rule, derived from the social division of labour rather than from ownership. This is not to say that the ownership title does not play any role. It does play a rather important role in family-owned corporations; it is relevant for majority control; it is instrumental for minority control and indispensable for control through the technique of shareholding. In the three latter cases, however, only *some* owners participate in the control; in the two latter cases, only a *negligible minority* of the owners participates in control; and in the case of management control, nominal ownership of the stock is as formal as the co-ownership of the nationalised means of production in the case of the central planners in state socialist systems.[7]

To sum up, *indirect (political) control* of the nominally private capitalist corporations exercised by the state is derived not from ownership but from the public nature of the companies. *Direct management* of the stock companies is separated from the ownership. *Direct control* of the stock companies is, as a rule, derived from the social division of labour and entrusted to the experts (executives and directors) whose sole profession is to *manage*. (The professional manager can manage everything: from a government department through a university to a bank or corporation, irrespective of the concrete kind of production, services or activities of the managed unit.) In a sense, the same principle (management derived from social division of labour) applies also to indirect (political) control. It is exercised, on behalf of the society as a whole, by professional politicians and civil servants whose sole profession is to manage, control and govern. In terms of management and control, private ownership has lost its previous meaning. To put it another way, private ownership is no longer instrumental for the management and control of capitalist corporations.

Once the right to manage and – in the case of minority control,

control through a legal device and through management – also the right to control has been separated from its traditional source (title to property), it may be derived from any alternative source, not just from the social division of labour and/or the technique of shareholding. Since liberalism has already accepted the separation (if it did not, liberal capitalism would already have ceased to exist), it is just a matter of convenience which alternative would be chosen. I suggest that *labour* substitutes for both the social division of labour and the technique of shareholding. Though either of the three sources is both logically and functionally compatible with the existence of the nominally private stock companies, the former better suits the valuable principles of liberalism in general and the valuable principles of liberal democracy in particular.

According to early liberal concepts of natural rights, the right to private property was justified as an extension of man's powers. This indicated that the property owner was supposed to use land or capital in a productive way. Private property was to be connected with activity in contrast to the idleness of the landed aristrocracy and gentry. Capitalist implementation of this concept of private property was, to put it mildly, rather one-sided. Productive use of resources was made possible due to exploitation; accumulation of capital was accompanied by prole-tarianisation of the expropriated peasants and artisans; while private property extended the powers of some, it drastically reduced the powers of many.

Moreover, the same power of private property wholly dominating economics was also applied in politics. Only those who owned land, or paid a certain amount of property tax, or had an independent income, were entitled to vote and to be elected. Even matters of public concern were exempt from the control of non-owners. Justification of this pre-democratic liberal practice was deduced from private property: how could those unable to acquire private property be qualified for administration and control of public property? It was the market principle of equality used as a weapon in the battle for a universal franchise which made liberalism democratic in the political sphere. And it was through politics that the non-owners won the right to create their own associations for the pursuit of their vital economic interests.

Though liberalism logically evolved into liberal democracy, as long as private economy remained separated from public politics, the liberal logic did not allow for an extension of democracy to the economic sphere. Only when big private corporations became *de facto* public and the gradual process separating management and control from private ownership reached the point from which there was no return to the old entrepreneurial capitalism, did an extension of liberal democracy from politics to economics become possible.

Big capitalist corporations emerged not only as an enormous economic power; they emerged as an enormous *public* power.[8] They are matched by another enormous public power – that of trade unions. In a sense, they check each other.[9] (It may be also argued that, in a sense, individual big corporations in various fields and in various countries also check each other.) The system of mutual checks and balances requires an umpire wherever and whenever the mutual balance of competing powers temporarily disappears, and a political intervener whenever and wherever the competing powers are ready to reach a monoplistic agreement at the expense of the society as a whole. Because of the public nature of the corporations and trade unions, the part of the umpire and intervener has to be played by the state.

As a result, two kinds of executive wield positive economic power: the appointed (or self-appointed) corporate technocrats exercising direct control, the appointed civil servants and the elected politicans exercising (indirect) political control over the economy. The third party – the trade unions – wield only negative power. The power of corporate technocracy is authoritative rather than democratic. So is the managerial structure of the corporations and the bureaucratic structure of the civil service. To match the two powerful bureaucratic structures, the trade unions had little choice: to be a meaningful counterpart of the corporate technocracy and state bureaucracy, they also had to become bureaucratic and undemocratic. The resulting tripartite bureaucratic power prevailing in the economic sphere ceases to be subject to *democratic* public control. The scheme entails the tripartite bargaining between the executive branch of government, capital and labour rather than between the legislature, capital and labour. Public power (the state) is represented by the ruling party (the government) and the bureaucrats rather than by representatives of all the political factions elected to the legislative body. As a result, the traditionally meaningful pluralistic body of political mediation (parliament) is outmanoeuvred from the day-to-day political control over the national economy.

Under these circumstances, the producers deprived of economic control and positive power cannot feel any responsibility for the state of economic affairs. Their attitude to both the corporations and the state is rather one-sided: they demand better wages and more social services without being worried about the social consequences of such acquisitive behaviour. As long as they are deprived of any share in the controlling economic authority, their behaviour is justified: without an access to decision-making authority, they cannot be expected to behave in a responsible manner. Responsibility only goes with decision-making power and effective control. (It is worth noting that in countries with a kind of co-determination (e.g. West Germany), trade unions behave more positively than elsewhere.) In a sense, the working people behave today in the economic sphere as 'irresponsibly' as they did in the political sphere prior to universal suffrage. Having been a part of society without being granted real citizenship, they could not but feel alienated in the past. Being producers without any share in controlling economic authority, they cannot but feel alienated in the present. Without an extension of the share in public authority to all, liberalism would have never evolved into liberal democracy. Without an extension of the share in economic authority to the producers, the capitalist system can scarcely survive as liberal democracy. It is the democratic nature of contemporary liberalism which requires an extension of the universal participatory principle from politics to economics. For one thing, economics – although nominally private – is *de facto* public. For another, both direct and indirect economic control have already been separated from ownership. In these circumstances, a democratic response to this change would be self-management of the producers. If the (nominally private) public corporations are put under full state control, liberal capitalism would become state capitalism. If private control over the corporations is retained, it would lead to a vicious circle connected with tripartite labour – management – state relations.

What is the cause of the vicious circle mentioned above? If one takes a model of private corporate capitalism with strongly established welfare elements within it, one would get the following arrangements: (a) private enterprise; (b) state-operated social and public services; (c) state (indirect) supervision of the economy; (d) autonomous trade unions. The state permanently regulates all contradictions and conflicts between capital and labour as well as between various interest groups within society. The state carries this part in a democratic manner: the conflicts are regulated through negotiation, mediation and common consensus. Actually, the state's intention is not to eliminate conflicts but to keep them within the limits acceptable both by labour and capital. This attitude enables contemporary welfare-type capitalist societies to function without giving up either political democracy and social advantages or private enterprise combined with public services.

Hence, the equilibrium between labour and capital results from the combination of two principles. While economics relies on rational calculation and competitive performance, social and public services are exempt from profit criteria. The producer's income is a matter of economics while his social security is a matter of politics. The economic criterion of optimisation is combined with a political criterion of welfare maximisation.

This combination seems to be very appealing: the advantages of capitalism (performance, competition, innovation, etc.) are combined with such advantages of socialism as social security, free social services, education, and so forth. However convenient this solution may be in the short run, it is scarcely viable as a long-term proposition. The model's basic limitation lies in the manner of distribution and redistribution of incomes on the condition of private enterprise combined with socialised services.

The services provided by the state are financed from public funds. Since the economy is mostly private, the main source of the state's income rests with taxes. To finance the advantage of any welfare state combined with private enterprise, both direct and indirect taxes have to be extremely high. That is the price which the welfare state pays for its social equilibrium. About 50 per cent of the GNP is absorbed by taxation and channelled to social services. Though the high taxes are not necessarily wasted (they return to the taxpayers in the form of social benefits), they are administered by a growing bureaucracy which, step by step, assumes more and more control over the entire society. Moreover, the high public expenses place limitations upon private consumption. In a welfare state, the difference between gross and net family income is incomparably higher than in less welfare-oriented advanced countries where the share of the GNP absorbed by taxes oscillates between 25 and 40 per cent. As a result, there is permanent pressure for an increase in both private and public consumption in the welfare state and, consequently, conflicts permanently emerge between employers and employees on the one hand and between the state and employers and employees on the other. Schematically, one can describe the conflicts as follows:

An expansion of social and other public services requires that the state increase its income. Since the main source of the national and local government's income is taxes, both direct and indirect taxes have to grow. This reduces the purchasing power of wages, salaries, transfer payments and profits. Hence, both employers and employees are interested in a growth in their nominal incomes. Generally speaking, higher real incomes are limited by the rate of productivity increases and, consequently, by the increment of GNP. Whatever exceeds the growth of productivity is but a redistribution of the fixed amount available. Since the producers do not manage industries, they demand from those who control them a higher share in the gross profit. If they succeed, the managers simply add the increased costs to the prices. This is the first inflationary element. The state takes more taxes from the higher wages, salaries and profits: this is the second inflationary element. Since prices and taxes have gone up, employees would demand another rise in wages and salaries, managers would yield and the second inflationary circle would follow the first. Although the three conflicting interests are kept in balance, it is an inflationary balance which cannot last for ever.

I assume that the welfare capitalist model absorbs about 50 per cent of GNP. Some thirty years ago, a number of economists concluded that no liberal democracy and no private economy could afford taxation exceeding 25 per cent of GNP. Nowadays, 25 per cent of GNP absorbed by taxes is considered rather moderate. This is why I would not dare to suggest that the 50 per cent share of taxes in the GNP has already reached the limit, though it is obvious that the share cannot rise to 100 per cent. The critical point *is* somewhere between the present share and the impossible 100 per cent. Although it may go up proportionally with increasing social wealth, it cannot exceed a certain percentage of the GNP. The triangle of labour–capital–state (unions–employers–government) is stable only so long as productivity grows *faster* than wages, profits and taxes. Because no democratic system can offer any guarantee that this will be the case, the limits of this model are obvious. When the point has been reached at which the state is unable to guarantee a steady accumulation of capital and international competitiveness of domestic enterprises, only three alternatives to the model seem possible: (a) the state takes over the private enterprise (state capitalism or state socialism); (b) the system reverts to traditional liberal capitalism; (c) self-management of the producers is introduced.

The problem of the tripartite capitalist welfare system lies in that the state has frequently to intervene in management–labour relations to avoid monopolistic agreements between the corporations and trade unions. This is the first reason why both the size and power of bureaucracy steadily increases. Since the state is also in charge of welfare programme and general supervision of the national economy, the power and size of bureaucracy cannot but increase as well. If tripartism is thought of as the only way of regulating class conflicts in contemporary liberal democratic societies, it would have to lead, *in the final analysis*, to a kind of corporate *étatism*. Georges Gurvitch[10] pointed out this problem as early as 1942 by quoting John Dewey's famous dictum 'United States Incorporated'. Gurvitch saw the basic danger in the following:

> Stock companies, corporations, cartels and trusts are vast organis-ations of authoritarian domination, ruled by a subordinative econ-omic law which eludes the democratic law of the political state. Vast patronal associations interfere with the functioning of institutions of political democracy and reinforce the trend to 'economic feudalism'. The authoritarian organisation of shops, factories and enterprises, by submitting millions of free citizens of the democratic state to an absolutistic jural regulation and uncontrolled power, comprises the attractive forces of the old democratic symbols . . . Will not the political democracy be compelled to follow an authoritarian and ultimately a totalitarian path, in order to destroy its terrible adversary, economic feudalism? This would involve the sacrifice of democracy in order to save it, because, without political democracy, no form of democracy can survive.[11]

While I do share Gurvitch's worries about the fate of political democracy in a world dominated by gigantic national and multinational corporations, I am afraid that the state, if it takes over the corporations, would not destroy them but rather preserve them under the rule of state capitalism/socialism. The undemocratic structures of corporate and state bureaucracy are complementary to each other rather than mutually exclusive. If they unite, the employees would get squeezed in between. In the absence of self-management (as Gurvitch rightly suggested), 'individuals and groups can defend their liberty effectively against all increasing pressures only by calling upon large-scale powerful organisations to protect them against other powerful organ-isations'.[12] Moreover, individual nation-states are almost powerless vis-à-vis multinational corporations whose corporate interests prevail not only over the interests of employees and consumers but also over the interests of individual countries. As long as governments operate within the boundaries and jurisdiction of nation-states, multinational corporations cannot properly be checked by any state (governmental) power.

The very fact that the individual can be protected against powerful organisations by surrendering his subjectivity to another power-organisation is of little comfort. As long as there are three big powers – the state, capital and labour – an equilibrium might be preserved. Once the three are reduced to two, however, the whole concept would fall apart. The intrinsic logic of the triangle suggests that the only conceivable and possible reduction of the three powers to two is that resulting from a merger of capital with the state. The present-day fight between the corporate managerial technocracy and the state bureaucracy cannot be won by labour. Whatever the outcome of the managerial/bureaucratic battle for overall social control, the victims are already known: labour and (liberal) democracy. It is rather paradoxical that, in the circumstances, the only big social power vitally interested in the survival of democracy is labour. Unlike the dispersed privately owned enterprises in the era of *laissez-faire* capitalism, the contemporary gigantic corporations do not need democracy. Intra-corporate structure is authoritative, not democratic. Neither is the intra-bureaucratic structure of the civil service. Intra-trade union structure has had to become bureaucratic to match the state and corporate bureaucracy. Hence, the bureaucratisation of labour unions has been an effect rather than a cause of the bureaucratic structures of both the state and corporations. Gurvitch rightly suggests that, up to now, the establishment and maintenance of political democracy did not require an economic democracy (labour self-management). On the other hand, an economic democracy cannot be established outside the framework of political democracy. However, in the circumstances discussed above, 'the introduction of an independent economic democracy has become a necessary prerequisite for the maintenance and full effectiveness of the political democracy itself'.[13]

Corporate capitalism with its managerial control separated from ownership, or with the control of the minority ownership through the technique of shareholding, does not fit into the picture painted by the ideologues of liberalism. It gives an enormous public power to the few at the expense of the many. What is more, in the case of managerial and/or minority control of the corporations, this *de facto* public power is derived neither from real ownership nor from democratic election. Even if it is derived from real ownership, as is the case of majority ownership and/or family-owned corporations, it contradicts the liberal principle according to which *any public* power should be established through the democratic process. Furthermore, the concept of the planned sector directly controlled by the state does not fit into a liberal scheme. For one thing, if there is a disequilibrium between capital and labour, both the intensity and extent of state intervention increase. Since the system loses its former stability, the state has to become its main stabiliser. This alternative leads, in the final analysis, to state capitalism. (I would wish to stress the 'in the final analysis' qualification. Since the state has to secure a steady accumulation of capital and the functioning of its economy, it has gradually been taking over individual corporations as well as entire industries and/or services in all unstable western European economies.) For another, if there is a steady equilibrium between capital and labour, the state becomes a relatively independent machinery more and more representing the specific interests of bureacuracy (an extension of its overall control) rather than those of the civil society as a whole. In the final analysis, this alternative also leads to state capitalism. To turn the clock back to a *laissez-faire* system is just a utopian dream. Hence, labour-managed corporate capitalism should be considered an alternative to the above prescriptions.

If the right to direct management and control in *de facto* public corporations is derived from liberal-democratic logic, it would have to be given to the public power, i.e. the state. However, if the state becomes the sole manager and controller of the *de facto* public corporations, two other liberal principles would be violated, namely, that political and *direct* economic power should be separated and that the state should not be directly involved in entrepreneurship. To avoid violation of these liberal principles and yet to preserve the liberal principle that (*de facto*) public institutions should be put under public power established through the democratic (electoral) process, labour self-management of the corporations could legitimately be accepted. First, the nature of the already prevailing separation of ownership from management and control would not change. The shareholders would get their dividends (a reward for the productive use of their money), the state would get its taxes and the employees would get their wages and salaries. Second, since the employees assume the right to direct control, they will democratically elect controlling bodies, hire and fire the managers, decide about the distribution of profits, work conditions, investments, etc. The dividend paid to the shareholders would be considered a price paid for the use of others' money (interest). Hence, the net value of output would be divided between the owners and the users of capital. For as the amount of money distributed to the shareholders is always smaller than the profit (it approximates the interest rate), *a greater part of surplus-value would remain in the hands of labour.*

Hence the producers *would regain the control over their labour and products under the conditions of private ownership of capital.* The relation between the owners of capital (shareholders) and the users of capital (producers) would be analogous to that between money-lenders and money-borrowers. The dividend (interest) assigned to capital ownership would reflect scarcity of capital and would be equal for all capital-users under the conditions of a perfect capital market.[14] Moreover, the arrangement would eliminate the possibility of the financial control of corporations through the technique of shareholding (pyramiding). Consequently, the very basis of monopolisation would be seriously undermined.

There would be yet more advantages. Having assumed direct control over the management, the employees would have to demand wage and salary increases from themselves. For they operate in a competitive market, they cannot consume the whole after-dividend and after-tax profit. If they did, they would become non-competitive. The conflict between consumption and accumulation would cease to be the capital – labour class conflict, however. It would be just the conflict between the short-run and long-run interests of the producers themselves. What is more, there would be no reason for any direct state intervention in labour – management relations. In addition to this, there would be little reason for strikes and industrial unrest.

Labour self-management of *multinational* corporations may put their operations in any particular country under public control. While capital is international, labour is national in the sense that the collectives of employees of any given multinational corporation work always in one country only. What is more, labour is vitally interested in a reinvestment of the profits at home rather than abroad, in preventing an outflow of profits from one country to another, in making tax evasion by the multinationals impossible, etc. However, labour is also international in the sense of its trade union solidarity. If need be, it may agree on a common policy on an international scale (e.g. within a particular branch) to match an international co-operation of multinational corporations.

An introduction of labour self-management would also democratise and humanise undemocratic structure of the corporations. And last but not least, self-management would preserve the separation of economic and political power as well as preventing the merger of the state with the corporate management.

I have tried to argue the case for labour-managed corporate capitalism in accordance with the basic principles of liberalism. Private property would be retained. So would the dividend. Dispersed economic power separated from political power would continue serving as the economic basis of political democracy. Being exercised by democratic self-management, it would simultaneously curb the growth of state bureaucracy. By reducing (if not eliminating) labour – management conflicts, it would also undermine the trend toward state capitalism/state socialism alternatives. At the same time it would facilitate the introduction of social indicative planning indispensable in any modern industrialised society as well as *democratic* rather than bureaucratic political control over national economies. In a word, all valuable economic and political principles of liberal democracy could be fully preserved if labour-management is applied to corporate capitalism.

But this is not all. Viewed from a socialist perspective, the model implicitly offers a non-violent, gradual, reformist, democratic and – if you wish – a liberal transition to socialism. One may easily perceive that, sometime in the future, the shares would evolve into bonds and, because of inheritance tax, would lose any actual meaning within the life-span of two or three generations. Structurally speaking, labour-managed corporate capitalism can scarcely evolve into either state capitalism or state socialism. A nucleus of self-managed socialism, the work community, would already be present in the labour-managed capitalist corporation. If private shareholding is gradually replaced by the social ownership of the means of production, the transitory state-socialist stage demanded both by Marx and the Yugoslavs would be neither desirable nor necessary. If one turns back to the already quoted passage from the third volume of Marx's *Capital*, one can read it now from quite a different perspective:

In stock companies the function is divorced from capital ownership, hence, also labour is entirely divorced from ownership of the means of production and surplus-labour. This result of the ultimate development of capitalist production is a necessary transitional phase towards the reconversion of capital into the property of producers, although no longer as the private property of the individual producers, but rather as the property of associated producers, as outright social property. On the other hand, the stock company is a transition toward the conversion of all functions in the reproduction process which still remain linked with capitalist property, into more functions of associated producers, into social functions.[15]

I may conclude by answering the three questions asked at the beginning of this chapter. First, the privately owned means of production should be managed by labour rather than by capital for the sake of the preservation of liberal democracy. Second, the owners have already been stripped of their right to manage and in most cases of their right to control their means of production in nominally private joint-stock corporations. Third, the concept of labour-managed corporate capitalism suits the basic values of liberal democracy better than any of the known alternative concepts.

So far I have discussed only the theoretical conceivability of labour-managed capitalism and its compatibility with liberal democracy. What yet remains to be argued is the model's practical applicability.

To begin with, labour self-management can be introduced in the already nationalised industries, services or enterprises. Indeed, their self-management-oriented reorganisation would bring about a less radical proprietory change than did their nationalisation. (National-isation turned private ownership into the state ownership. An in-troduction of self-management would turn the state ownership into a social ownership.) In the case of the public (i.e. publicly owned) utilities and services, the same principle could be applied as that suggested for the labour-managed socialist model, namely, a proportional rep-resentation of the owners, the employees and the users in all self-management bodies. If need be, the introduction of labour-management could be *gradual*, i.e. through workers' participation as is the case of some West German industries.[16] If the latter pattern is applied, the transition would be thus: from financial/managerial control through workers'participation to labour self-management. The pattern could be employed in both public and private (though *de facto* public) enterprises. In fact, it has already been accepted *in principle* in several western European countries, is being seriously considered in Great Britain and entertained by some western European legal experts as a pattern of non-governmental public control of multinational firms within the EEC.

Second, there are also some other patterns of labour self-management reorganisation discussed by Jaroslav Vanek.[17] The first – a workers' takeover of a defunct or bankrupt capitalist firm – applies not only to stock companies but to any type of capitalist enterprise. The second type of reorganisation is one concerning the viable well-functioning capitalist enterprises. Vanek calls it the *friendly* reorgani-sation. It requires only the substitution of non-controlling but income-earning debentures for common stock and making the management of the firm responsible to the working community. In view of the fact that most communities of stockholders have surrendered most of their management rights to professional managers anyway, the reorgani-sation may, at least in some cases, represent very little *de facto* change in stockholders' exercise. Moreover, in many cases it can lead to an increase in income. Many firms not yet in bankruptcy but also not very prosperous, paying hardly any dividend, may be excellent candidates for this type of reorganisation.[18]

The third type, according to Vanek, is an *aggressive* reorganisation in which the working community forces the firm to accept self-management. Such reorganisation may be justifiable *only* in situations of very serious grievances on the part of the employees which the employers are stubbornly unwilling to remedy.[19]

Nevertheless, the general source of labour self-management re-organisation of capitalist corporations has to be looked for in the political sphere. First, if there was a major political party which accepted both the reasoning for and the principles of the model, it could be put through the legislature in a similarly democratic manner as was nationalisation and/or creation of the publicly controlled corporations in the sphere of public utilities and services (e.g. provincial and/or national electric, telephone, railway, air transport and other enterprises). Second, it would be imperative that such a party won the support of the trade unions. For one thing, the newly created self-management bodies would function parallel to the trade union bodies. For another, the introduction of labour self-management would radically change the very concept of trade unions, especially in the English-speaking countries.

An introduction of the model into a liberal system is, of course, a matter of politics. Unlike nationalisation, it is inexpensive. Since the private property of shares with the right to income is retained, there is no need for compensation. Since labour self-management is strictly limited to microeconomics, it is fully compatible with the existing constitutional arrangements of parliamentary and presidential systems. The political controversy of the model lies elsewhere. Labour self-management challenges class domination, the social power of capital, and the social and political influence enjoyed by the *functional* ruling class. Class inequality has always been defended by liberal ideologues in the name of liberty. As long as the only viable alternative to private property was seen in state property, and as long as property control and management were united, the argument might have made sense. It was just a matter of preference: either an endorsement of class (economic) inequality as the basis of (formal) political freedom, or an acceptance of class (economic) equality combined with a likely reduction of political freedom. The alternative social ownership in socialist systems and the separation of private property from control and management in corporate capitalism made the liberal case for class inequality irrelevant and the dilemma of choosing between the two evils meaningless. Hence, any contemporary attempt to preserve class inequality in the name of political freedom indicates either hypocrisy or ignorance.

It would be futile to believe that the representatives of corporate capital would give up their power without a fight. They resisted the New Deal, political control of and state intervention in corporate businesses, the nationalisation which took place in many western European countries. (As to the latter, they had a point: nationalisation gives too much power to the state.) As far as labour self-management is concerned, the advocates of corporate capital employ primarily economic arguments. They maintain that labour self-management is *by definition* less efficient than the conventional corporate management. On a theoretical level, the argument is untenable: it could be, and already has been theoretically established, that from a strictly economic point of view the labour-managed capitalist enterprises may work as well as (and even better than) those managed in the conventional manner.[20] On an empirical level, the argument is also untenable. One may refer to such conventionally managed corporations as Rolls-Royce, Lockheed, Citroën, Renault and others which could have not survived without public subsidies or nationalisation.[21]

The liberals who want to retain nominal private property of *de facto* public stock companies could find it more expedient to accept labour self-management than an impending nationalisation. The liberals who sincerely want to preserve political freedoms and other individual liberties in the future should give a second thought to the concept of labour self-management of the corporations. A stubborn insistence on the protection of class power and privileges would be counter-productive, especially if the capitalist system is unable to retain equilibrium between labour and capital, provide for a smooth functioning of its economy, curb inflation and substantially reduce the rate of unemployment. All these evils might be better dealt with by labour-managed than by the conventionally managed capitalist corporations.

It is rather surprising that some liberals who militantly promote a guaranteed minimum income, an egalitarian distribution and a maximisation of positive freedom neglect labour self-management as the most relevant means to maximisation of positive freedom and overall democratisation of modern liberal democracies. One suspects that two *sine qua non's* of labour self-management should be blamed for this: the market, and a differentiated income distribution. In the light of the various points discussed earlier in this book, it is hard to find an excuse for such an ideological prejudice.

Finally, the last relevant liberal argument against labour self-managed corporate capitalism has to be dealt with. Its essence can be formulated as follows: once the corporations have been put under the control of labour, it would be only logical if the right of the shareholders to a dividend was abolished. Well, it could be logical and it actually *is* logical from a socialist position. Indeed, if the majority of the people voted for radical social parties, this would very likely happen. But it would probably happen also *without* any labour self-management *if* the majority of the people voted for the radical socialist parties. If the leftist political parties won, they would socialise the big corporations anyway. In the absence of labour self-management, the socialisation would probably assume the form of nationalisation with its already well-known negative effects. If labour self-management were already in existence at the moment of socialist takeover, it would more likely be retained together with its democratic political superstructure. The very socialisation would have neither a logical nor a political connection with self-management; the only thing conditioned by the absence or presence of self-management would be the *form* of socialisation. Hence, labour self-management *per se* is not causally connected with socialist change.

One may suggest, with a similar degree of likelihood, another scenario: the labour-managed corporations would continue relying on mobilisation of private capital. It might happen *if* the majority of people voted liberal rather than socialist; *if* the general level of incomes kept steadily increasing, and thereby made it expedient for the producers to invest a part of their savings; *if* the system maintained social and political stability. One may suspect that, for liberals, a labour-managed corporate capitalism might be more attractive than a democratic socialism.

Be that as it may, there is scarcely one single liberal principle which would make labour-managed corporate capitalism theoretically inconceivable, politically unacceptable or practically inapplicable.

8 A General Democratic Theory of Labour-Managed Systems

/

If I now summarise the results of my analysis, I may finally formulate a general democratic theory of labour-managed systems which is aimed at maximising (1) social welfare, (2) negative freedom, and (3) positive freedom. (A theory may deal with maximisation only. Whether maximisation evolves into optimisation depends on the chosen economic and social policies.)

8.1. MAXIMISATION OF SOCIAL WELFARE

Unlike capitalist firms maximising profits, and state socialist firms maximising the fulfilment of the planned targets, self-managed work units maximise income per employee.[1] Hence, the element of labour self-management pursues, by definition, maximisation of social welfare.

All other things being equal, maximisation of social welfare depends on the amount of available goods, services and utilities, leisure included. Consequently, the level of productivity (efficiency) of labour, land and capital is decisive. While the most efficient instrument of rational economic allocation and use of scarce resources, goods and services is the market, the most efficient device for adjusting market regulation to welfare priorities is macroeconomic (central) planning. A synthesis of the plan and the market is indispensable. Of all known types of planning, only an indirect (indicative) social planning is compatible with both the market and labour self-management.

If viewed statically rather than as a process, maximisation of social welfare would require an egalitarian distribution of incomes. As skilled labour is scarce, the egalitarian distribution would scarcely be conducive to a steady increase of productivity. If applied, it would impede continuous maximisation of welfare. It would also impede maximisation of positive freedom of some; therefore, it would also be contrary to criterion (3).

Of necessity, an income distribution according to work has to be applied. To meet the requirement of equality, there should be equal pay for equal labour. Since ours is a market system, incomes have to be distributed according to work output. This does not rule out a decent socially guaranteed minimum income. If need be, a binding income-differential ratio tying the minimum and maximum rewards to each other could be adopted.

If mobilisation of individual savings for productive use in labour-managed units is deemed desirable or expedient, the users pay for such an investment a scarcity-reflecting price (dividend or interest).

Free access to medical and education services is equally guaranteed for all. Various schemes already is use in both capitalist and socialist systems could be adopted. The same applies to social benefits and transfer payments. As a matter of precaution, unemployment insurance should be introduced.

8.2. MAXIMISATION OF NEGATIVE FREEDOM

(a) ECONOMICS

Community-type industrial participatory democracy approximates the absence of NL^1 (freedom from coercion by men) within work units. Separation of political and economic power, diffusion of economic power and voluntary co-ordination by the technique of the market provide for an approximation of the absence of NL^1 within the society-type macroeconomic structure. Since the market is regulated and tamed by an indicative social plan, an element of NL^2 (freedom from coercion by *blind* market forces) is present within the realm of necessity.

(b) POLITICS

Since only certain structurally compatible combinations of the (economic and political) subsystems are possible within the system, the pluralistic, decentralized and voluntarily co-ordinated labour-managed economy creates all the necessary conditions for similar political structure with analogous checks and balances maximising NL^1 (freedom from coercion by the state).

8.3. MAXIMISATION OF POSITIVE FREEDOM

Compared with alternative managerial arrangements, labour self-management of work units maximises PL^3 (*producer's* share in the controlling authority). Because it also maximises (through the synthesis of the plan and the market) economic efficiency and (through labour self-management) social welfare with leisure included, it simultaneously maximises the prerequisite (leisure) for PL^1 (development of the individual). Labour self-management also contributes – through a more humanistic organisation of the labour process within each work unit freely decided by the producers – to maximisation of PL^1 within the realm of necessity. Free and equal access to all levels of education as well as all kinds of health services maximises PL^1 also. An approximation of the absence of coercion by men and/or the state in political and economic spheres eleminates PL^2 (the development of man by virtue of coercion). Since political democracy is combined with industrial democracy, and since free access to education equalises access to participation in political control, PL^3 (the *citizen's* share in the controlling authority) is also maximised in micro- and macropolitics.

A few words of warning are necessary, however. First, the theory is applicable to a pure, simplified labour-managed model only. Concrete labour-managed systems would likely deviate from the theory no less than *any* system deviates from its theory.

Second, the theory leaves aside the traditional capitalist firms in which the management is *not* separated from the ownership, as well as small private businesses with a few employees surviving in socialist systems.

Third, this is by no means a convergence theory. The conventional convergence theory may be realised, at best, in a negative way: corporate and/or state capitalism would become less democratic while state socialism would become more technocratic. Given the nature of both systems, the convergence theory does not offer and cannot offer any positive (democratic) solution. My theory introduces labour self-management into both systems as *one* (microeconomic) element only, without attempting to present it as an (impossible) ideal solution. Hence, it offers an innovation for, rather than a convergence of, both systems. On the one hand, my theory aims at a positive socialist overcoming of liberalism. On the other hand, it aims at a positive liberal adaptation to the realities of post-industrial capitalism.

Fourth, this theory results from a structural rather than a cultural analysis of contemporary systems. Though I am fully aware of the significance of particular political cultures for both the economic efficiency of labour self-management and the maintenance of political democracy, an application of the theory to national traditions, customs, institutions, patterns of behaviour, specific social and ethical values, religious and ideological beliefs would require another study.

Fifth, for those who might have overlooked it, one elucidatory note: if anyone can suggest a structurally viable, logically consistent, economically functional, practically applicable and theoretically conceivable substitute for the market as a *necessary* condition of efficiency *and* both economic and political democracy, it would be welcomed by no one more enthusiastically than by me.

Notes

Chapter 1

1. Concerning the law of value, Engels says in his *Outlines of a Critique of Political Economy*: 'Yet it is obvious that this law is a purely natural law, and not a law of the mind.' Cf. *Economic and Philosophical Manuscripts of 1844*, (International Publishers, New York, 1964) Appendix, p. 214. And Marx says: 'The law that regulates the division of labour in the community acts with the irresistible authority of a law of Nature . . .' *Capital*, I (International Publishers, New York, 1967) p. 358.
2. e.g. in *Capital*, I, pp. 131–2; see also K. Marx, *Early Writings*, trans. and ed. T. B. Bottomore (McGraw-Hill, New York, 1964) pp. 191–3, etc.
3. Cf. F. Engels, *Outlines of a Critique of Political Economy*, in K. Marx and F. Engels, *Collected Works*, III (International Publishers, New York, 1975) pp. 422–3.
4. Cf. V. I. Lenin, *Collected Works*, XXXIII (Moscow, 1966), p. 113.
5. Marx sees a *theoretical* possibility of crises already in the small producers' market, i.e. C–M–C. Cf. *Capital*, I, pp. 113–14.
6. F. Engels, *The Origin of Family, Private Property and the State* in Marx–Engels, *Selected Works in One Volume* (International Publishers, New York, 1970) p. 541.
7. *Capital*, I, p. 78.
8. Marx–Engels, *The German Ideology*, in Marx–Engels, *Collected Works*, V, p. 32.
9. K. Marx, *Critique of the Gotha Programme*, in Marx–Engels, *Selected Works in One Volume*, p. 325.
10. 'Division of labour and private property are, after all, identical expressions: in the one the same thing is affirmed with reference to activity as is affirmed in the other with reference to the product of the activity.' *The German Ideology*, op. cit., p. 46.
11. Engels to Kautsky, 26 June 1884, in Marx–Engels, *Selected Correspondence* (Progress Publishers, Moscow, 1955), p. 377.
12. *The German Ideology*, op. cit., p. 47.
13. A French workman, on his return from San Francisco, writes as follows: 'I never could have believed that I was capable of working at the various occupations I was employed on in California. I was firmly convinced that I was fit for nothing but letterpress printing . . .. Once in the midst of this world of adventurers who change their occupation as often as they do their shirt, egad, I did as the others. As mining did not turn out remunerative enough, I left it for the town, where in succession I became typographer, slater, plumber, etc. In consequence of thus finding out that I am fit for any sort of work, I feel less of a mollusc and more of a man.' A. Corbon, *De*

l'enseignement professionnel, 2nd ed., p. 50. Cf. *Capital*, I, p. 487, n. 2.
14. Ibid., p. 484.
15. *The German Ideology*, op. cit., p. 42.
16. Ibid., p. 256.
17. Scarcity caused by the inevitable differences between the structure of both individual and group needs and the structure of resources is sometimes called a *structural* scarcity. Cf. J. Kosta, *Sozialistische Planwirtschaft: Theorie und Praxis* (Opladen, 1974) p. 105.
18. *Capital*, I, p. 332.
19. K. Marx, *The Poverty of Philosophy*, in Marx–Engels, *Collected Works*, VI, p. 184.
20. *Capital*, I, p. 356 (emphasis added). W. Brus comments on the idea as follows: 'Marx does not find the latter prospect at all disturbing. On the contrary, the very nature of the division of labour, consciously directed from a central point of control and not by means of market mechanism of signals and incentives is basic to Marx.' Cf. Wlodzimierz Brus, *The Market in a Socialist Economy* (Routledge & Kegan Paul, London, 1972) p. 15.
21. ' . . . the exchange of products springs up at points where different families, tribes, communities come in contact; for, in the beginning of civilisation, it is not private individuals but families, tribes etc. that meet on an independent footing.' *Capital*, I, p. 351.
22. 'In practical life we find not only competition, monopoly and the antagonism between them, but also the synthesis of the two, which is not a formula, but a movement. Monopoly produces competition, competition produces monopoly. Monopolists compete among themselves; competitors become monopolists. If the monopolists restrict their mutual competition by means of partial associations, competition increases among the workers; and the more the mass of the proletarians grows as against the monopolists of one nation, the more desperate competition becomes between the monopolists of different nations. The synthesis is such that monopoly can only maintain itself by continually entering into the struggle of competition.' K. Marx, *The Poverty of Philosophy*, op. cit., pp. 195–6.
23. K. Marx, *Grundrisse*, trans. M. Nicolaus (Penguin Books, Harmondsworth, 1973) p. 241.
24. Ibid., p. 245.
25. Ibid., p. 246.
26. As Marx put it, 'by demanding the *negation of private property*, the proletariat merely raises to the rank of *principle of society* what society has made the principle of the *proletariat*, what without its own co-operation is already incorporated in *it* as the negative result of society'. K. Marx, Introduction to *Contribution to the Critique of Hegel's Philosophy of Law*, in Marx–Engels, *Collected Works*, III, p. 187.
27. *Grundrisse*, op. cit., p. 248.
28. Ibid., p. 158.
29. Ibid., pp. 158–9.
30. Ibid., p. 159.
31. In fact, Marx answers this question only in a negative way: 'It is just as pious as it is stupid to wish that exchange-value would not develop into capital, nor labour which produces exchange-value into wage labour.' Ibid., p. 249.

32. Ibid., pp. 157–8 (emphasis added).
33. Karel Michňák, *Ekonomie a fetišismus* [The Economy and Fetishism] (Prague, 1965) p. 44.

Chapter 2
 1. K. Marx, *Critique of the Gotha Programme*, op. cit., p. 323.
 2. F. Engels, *Anti-Dühring* (International Publishers, New York, 1939) pp. 337–8 (emphasis added).
 3. *The German Ideology*, op. cit., pp. 46–7.
 4. K. Marx, *Grundrisse*, op. cit., pp. 171–2.
 5. G. Kozlov, 'Sotsialism i tovarno-denezhnyie otnosheniya', *Voprosy Ekonomiki*, No. 11 (Moscow, 1960) pp. 18–19 (emphasis added).
 6. *Critique of the Gotha Programme*, op. cit., p. 324.
 7. Ibid., p. 324.
 8. *Capital*, I, p. 42 (emphasis added).
 9. 'But all science would be superfluous if the outward appearance and the essence of things directly coincided.' K. Marx, *Capital*, III, p. 817. Because Marx was an essentialist, he did violate the rules of his own method. One may speculate, however, that K. Popper and his followers would absolve Marx of his inconsistence and dismiss my criticism at this point.
10. *Capital*, I, p. 351.
11. Ibid., pp. 354–5 (emphasis added).
12. 'Where there is division of labour on a social scale there the separate labour processes become independent of each other.' Engels to C. Schmidt, 27 Oct 1890, in Marx–Engels, *Selected Works in One Volume*, p. 694.
13. Cf. Radoslav Selucký and Milada Selucká, *Člověk a hospodářství* [Man and the Economy] (Svobodné Slovo, Prague, 1967); Radoslav Selucký, *Czechoslovakia: The Plan that Failed* (Nelson, London, 1970); Radoslav Selucký, *Economic Reforms in Eastern Europe* (Praeger, New York, 1972).
14. Cf. Lev Kritsman, *Die heroische Periode der grossen russischen Revolution* (Verlag für Literatur und Politik, Wien–Berlin, 1929).
15. Ludwig von Mises, 'Die Wirtschaftsrechnung im sozialistischen Gemeinwesen', *Archiv für Sozialwissenschaften*, (Apr 1920). Its English translation is available in F. A. von Hayek (ed.), *Collectivist Economic Planning*, (Routledge, London, 1935). Cf. also L. von Mises, *Gemeinwirtschaft* (Jena, 1934) p. 98.
16. e.g. F. A. von Hayek, 'The Nature of the Problem' (Chapter I) and 'The Present State of the Debate' (Chapter V) in *Collectivist Economic Planning*, op. cit.; L. C. Robbins, *The Great Depression* (Macmillan, London, 1934) p. 151.
17. Cf. E. Barone, 'The Ministry of Production in the Collectivist State', in Hayek (ed.), *Collectivist Economic Planning*, pp. 286–9.
18. F. M. Taylor, 'The Guidance of Production in a Socialist State', presidential address delivered at the 41st annual meeting of the American Economic Association, Chicago, 27 Dec 1928; reprinted in B. E. Lippincott (ed.), *On the Economic Theory of Socialism* (McGraw-Hill, New York, 1964) pp. 41–54.
19. Oscar Lange, in Lippincott (ed.), *On the Economic Theory of Socialism*, op. cit., pp. 57–142. A. L. Lerner (cf. his articles 'Economic Theory and Socialist Economy', *Review of Economic Studies*, II, Oct 1934; 'A Note on

Socialist Economics', ibid., IV, Oct 1936; and 'Statics and Dynamics in Socialist Economies', *Economic Journal*, XLVII, June 1937) came to a similar conclusion. This is why the solution of the problem is often referred to as the Lange–Lerner solution.

20. 'The solution by trial and error is based on what may be called the *parametric function of prices*, i. e. on the fact that, although the prices are a resultant of the behaviour of all individuals on the market, each individual separately regards the actual market prices as given data to which he has to adjust himself. Each individual tries to exploit the market situation confronting him which he cannot control. Market prices are thus parameters determining the behaviour of the individuals.' Lange, op. cit., p. 70.
21. Ibid., p. 95.
22. Capital, III, p. 820.
23. McLellan, *Marx's Grundrisse* (Macmillan, London, 1971) p. 135.
24. Marx–Engels, *The Communist Manifesto*, in *Selected Works in One Volume*, p. 45 (emphasis added).
25. 'In all appropriations up to now a mass of individuals remained subservient to a single instrument of production. In the appropriation by the proletarians, a mass of instruments of production must be subservient to each individual and the property of all. The only way for individuals to control modern universal interaction is to make it subject to the control of all.' L. Easton and K. Guddat, (eds.), *Writings of the Young Marx on Philosophy and Society* (Doubleday, New York, 1967), pp. 467 f.
26. K. Marx, *Early Writings*, pp. 153–4.
27. Ibid., p. 155.
28. K. Marx, *Economic and Philosophic Manuscripts of 1844*, in Marx–Engels, *Collected Works*, III, p. 325.
29. Ibid., p. 324.
30. Cf. Chapter 1, note 32. The term 'thing' means, in the context, money.
31. Already Aristotle knew that 'it is more necessary to equalise appetites than property'. Cf. Aristotle, *Politics* (Penguin Books, Harmondsworth, 1972), p. 74.
32. McLellan, *Marx's Grundrisse*, p. 142 (emphasis added); in M. Nicolaus's translation of *Grundrisse* cf. p. 705.
33. McLellan, ibid.; Nicolaus, pp. 705–6. The idea of social wealth measured by leisure was taken by Marx from an anonymous pamphlet, *The Source and Remedy of the National Difficulties. A Letter to Lord John Russell*, published in London in 1821, p. 6.

Chapter 3
1. 'The state exists *only* as the *political state*.' K. Marx, Introduction to *Contribution to the Critique of Hegel's Philosophy of Law*, in Marx–Engels, *Collected Works*, III, p. 118.
2. 'The abolition of the state only has a meaning for communists as a necessary result of the suppression of classes whose disappearance automatically entails the disappearance of the need for an organised power of one class for the suppression of another.' K. Marx, review of E. Girandin, *Socialism and Taxes* (Paris, 1850), quoted from David McLellan, *The Thought of Karl Marx* (Macmillan, London, 1971) p. 192.

3. Marx–Engels, *Manifesto of the Communist Party*, in Marx–Engels, *Selected Works in One Volume*, p. 53.
4. Cf. *The German Ideology*, in Marx–Engels, *Collected Works*, V, p. 61.
5. F. Engels, *The Origin of the Family, Private Property and the State*, in Marx–Engels, *Selected Works in One Volume*, p. 588. Cf. also K. Marx, *The Eighteenth Brumaire of Louis Bonaparte* (Progress Publishers, Moscow, 1972) p. 105. On another occasion Engels observes: 'Society gives rise to certain common functions which it cannot dispense with. The persons appointed for this purpose form a new branch of the division of labour *within society*. This gives them particular interests, distinct, too, from the interests of those who empowered them: they make themselves independent of the latter and – the state is in being.' Cf. Engels to C. Schmidt, 27 Oct 1890, in Marx–Engels, *Selected Works in One Volume*, pp. 695–6.
6. K. Marx, *Capital*, III, p. 383.
7. Marx–Engels, *Collected Works*, III, p. 155.
8. Ibid., p. 153.
9. Cf. A. Labriola, *Essays on the Materialistic Conception of History* (Charles H. Kerr, Chicago, 1908) p. 137. An excellent characterisation of the modern bourgeois state was given at the May 1963 Conference of the A. Gramsci Institute in Rome by Tamburrano and Goen in their paper entitled 'The Role and Structure of the State in Contemporary Capitalist Society'. For instance: 'The workers demand the legalisation of collective contracts while the manufacturers ask for anti-strike laws; civil servants want higher salaries and tenure; peasants ask for guaranteed quotas at fixed prices and for public subsidies; trade unions demand participation in corporate decision-making; families with children want higher allowances; tenants ask for protection against landlords and landlords for protection against tenants . . .. The state yields and does not yield – its stand depends on the instantaneous economic situation and, first of all, on the influence of individual pressure groups – but it does intervene, it is *obliged* to intervene . . ..' Quoted from *Kapitalismus našeho věku* [Capitalism in Our Age] (Prague, 1966) p. 262.
10. Marx, Introduction to *Contribution to the Critique of Hegel's Philosophy of Law*, in Marx–Engels, *Collected Works*, III, p. 47.
11. Cf. Lewis S. Feuer (ed.), *Marx and Engels, Basic Writings on Politics and Philosophy* (Anchor Books, New York, 1959) p. 317.
12. Marx–Engels, *Selected Works in One Volume*, p. 679.
13. Ibid., p. 331.
14. 'Das Ziel der Assoziation ist der Sturz aller privilegierten Klassen, ihre Unterwerfung unter die Diktatur der Proletarier, in welcher die Revolution in Permanenz erhalten wird bis zur Verwirklichung des Kommunismus, der die letzte Organisationsform der menschlichen Familie sein wird.' Cf. 'Weltgesellschaft der revolutionären Kommunisten', in Marx–Engels, *Werke*, VII (Dietz Verlag, Berlin, 1969) p. 553.
15. The relevant part of the speech was reported in *The World* of 15 Oct 1871 as follows: 'Aber bevor eine solche Veränderung [i.e. the abolition of class rule and oppression – R.S.] vollzogen werden könne, sei eine Diktatur des Proletariats notwendig, und ihre erste Voraussetzung sei eine Armee des Proletariats. Die arbeitende Klassen müssten sich das Recht auf ihre

Emanzipation auf dem Schlachtfeld erkämpfen. Aufgabe der Internationale sei es, die Kräfte der Arbeiter für den kommenden Kampf zu organisieren und zu vereinen.' Ibid., xvii, p. 432.

16. Marx–Engels, *Selected Works in One Volume*, p. 52.
17. I am aware of only one exception. In a short article 'On Crises and Counter-Revolution' published in *Die Neue Rheinishe Zeitung*, No. 102, 4 Sep 1848, Marx stated the following: 'Jeder provisorische Staatszustand nach einer Revolution erfordert eine Diktatur, und zwar eine energische Diktatur.' Cf. Marx–Engels, *Werke*, v, p. 402. However, the statement refers to *any* post-revolutionary period rather than to the dictatorship of the proletariat and, secondly, the article was commenting on the 1848 bourgeois rather than a socialist revolution.
18. F. Engels, *Anti-Dühring* (International Publishers, New York, 1939) p. 279.
19. Marx–Engels, *Correspondence 1846–1895* (Martin Lawrence, London, 1934) p. 486. Although the ending of the sentence is somewhat ambiguous, its meaning seems to be unequivocal.
20. Rosa Luxemburg, *The Russian Revolution and Leninism or Marxism?* (University of Michigan Press, Ann Arbor, 1961) p. 77.
21. Ibid., pp. 76–7.
22. Ibid., p. 69. And further: 'The public life of countries with limited freedom is so poverty-stricken, so miserable, so rigid, so unfruitful, precisely because, through the exclusion of democracy, it cuts off the living sources of all spiritual riches and progress . . . . Without general elections, without unrestricted freedom of press and assembly, without a free struggle of opinion, life dies out in every public institution, becomes a mere semblance of life, in which only the bureaucracy remains as the active element. Public life gradually falls asleep, a few dozen party leaders of inexhaustible energy and boundless experience direct and rule. Among them, in reality, only a dozen outstanding heads do the leading and an elite of the working class is invited from time to time to meetings where they are to applaud the speeches of the leaders and to approve proposed resolutions unanimously – at bottom, then, a clique affair – a dictatorship, to be sure, not the dictatorship of the proletariat, however, but the dictatorship of a handful of politicians, that is a dictatorship in the bourgeois sense, in the sense of the rule of the Jacobins.' Ibid., pp. 70–2.
23. *History of the Communist Party of the Soviet Union (Bolsheviks)* (Foreign Languages Publishing House, Moscow, 1943) p. 356. This book was edited by a Commission of the CC of the CPSU, but some of its chapters were written by Stalin and afterwards included in his works. The diction of the quoted paragraph is so typically Stalin's that there is no doubt that he formulated it.
24. Cf. F. Engels' introduction to Marx's 1891 edition of *The Civil War in France*, in Marx–Engels, *Selected Works in One Volume*, p. 262.
25. 'The first decree of the Commune . . . was the suppression of the standing army, and the substitution for it of the armed people. The Commune was formed of the municipal councillors, chosen by universal suffrage . . . responsible and revocable at short terms. The majority of its members were naturally working men, or acknowledged representatives of

the working class. The commune was to be a working, not a parliamentary, body, executive and legislative at the same time. Instead of continuing to be the agent of the Central Government, the police was at once stripped of its political attributes and turned into a responsible and at all times revocable agent of the Commune. So were the officials of all branches of the Administration . . .. The whole of the educational institutions were opened to the people gratuitously, and at the same time cleared of all interference of Church and State. Thus, not only was education made accessible to all, but science itself freed from the fetters which class prejudice and governmental force had imposed upon it.' K. Marx, *The Civil War in France*, op. cit., p. 291.

26. Marx–Engels, *Selected Works in One Volume*, p. 339.
27. Ibid., p. 338.
28. 'To prevent possible misunderstanding, a word. I paint the capitalist and the landlord in no sense *couleur de rose*. But here individuals are dealt with only in so far as they are the personifications of economic categories, embodiments of particular class relations and class interests. My stand-point, from which the evolution of the economic formation of society is viewed as a process of natural history, can less than any other make the individual responsible for relations whose creature he socially remains, however much he may subjectively raise himself above them.' K. Marx, *Capital*, I, p. 10.
29. F. Engels, *Socialism: Utopian and Scientific*, in *Selected Works in One Volume*, p. 430.
30. F. Engels, *The Origin of the Family, Private Property and the State*, ibid., p. 589.
31. F. Engels, *Socialism: Utopian and Scientific*, ibid., p. 429.
32. Marx–Engels, *The Communist Manifesto*, ibid., p. 52.
33. Ibid., p. 292 (emphasis added).
34. K. Marx, *On the Jewish Question*, in Marx–Engels, *Collected Works*, III, p. 168.
35. K. Marx, *Capital*, III, pp. 330–1.
36. Ibid., pp. 386–7.
37. Paradoxically enough, one of the keenest defenders of the orchestra model, N. I. Bukharin, had to pay very heavily for his unsubstantiated belief that 'the process of overcoming class oppositions, of "servile hierarchy" (Marx) and of the dying away of the state will create a self-discipline which little by little will not only push out the relics of class compulsion but also of authoritarianism in general'. N. I. Bukharin, 'Marx's Teaching and its Historical Importance', in *Marxism and Modern Thought*, trans. R. Fox (Routledge, London, 1935) p. 79. The absence of structural guarantees of personal independence of individuals put Bukharin eventually before the firing squad.
38. K. Marx, Preface to *A Contribution to the Critique of Political Economy*, in Marx–Engels, *Selected Works in One Volume*, pp. 182–3.
39. Cf. F. Engels, letter to J. Block, 21 (22) Sep 1890, ibid., p. 692.
40. Cf. F. Engels, letter to H. Starkenburg, 25 Jan 1894, in Marx–Engels, *Correspondence 1846–1895*, p. 516. The term *Verkehr* is here translated literally as transport; what Engels meant was a broader meaning of the German word which should be translated as commerce or intercourse.

41. Cf. Easton and Guddat (eds.), *Writings of the Young Marx on Philosophy and Society*, p. 480.
42. The concept is not too popular among some contemporary Marxists. Henri Lefebvre is one of those who dislike it: 'One widely recognised schema distinguishes various levels of praxis: The base or foundation (productive forces, techniques, organisation of labour); structure (production and property relations); superstructures (institutions, ideologies). This schema is in keeping with some of the texts by Marx.' Cf. H. Lefebvre, *The Sociology of Marx* (Vintage books, New York, 1969) p. 51. One cannot resist saying that Lefebvre's suggestion is as ludicrous as if the economist said: One widely recognised schema distinguishing between use-value, exchange-value, value and surplus-value may be found in some of Marx's writings.
43. 'Soon we were on the field of Natural Science, and Marx ridiculed the victorious reaction in Europe that fancied it had smothered the revolution and did not suspect that Natural Science was preparing a new revolution. That King Steam who had revolutionised the world in the last century had ceased to rule, and that into his place a far greater revolutionist would step, the electric spark. And now Marx, all flushed and excited told me that during the last few days the model of an electric engine drawing a railroad train was on exhibition in Regent Street. 'Now the problem is solved–the consequences are indefinable. In the wake of the economic revolution the political must necessarily follow, for the latter is only the expression of the former.' In the way that Marx discussed this progress of science and mechanics, his conception of the world and especially that part later on called the materialistic conception of history became so clearly apparent that certain doubts I had hitherto entertained vanished like snow in the sun of spring.' Wilhelm Liebknecht, *Karl Marx, Biographical Memoirs* (Greenwood Press, New York, 1968) pp. 57–8.
44. Cf. K. Marx, *Theses on Feuerbach*, in Marx–Engels, *Selected Works in One Volume*, p. 29.
45. Cf. K. Marx, *Critique of the Gotha Programme*, ibid., p. 324.
46. F. Engels, *On Authority*, in Feuer (ed.), *Basic Writings on Politics and Philosophy*, p. 483.
47. K. Marx, *The Civil War in France*, in Marx–Engels, *Selected Writings in One Volume*, p. 292.
48. Ibid., p. 292.
49. Ibid., p. 292.
50. Marx on Bakunin (1875), quoted from McLellan, *The Thought of Karl Marx*, p. 195.
51. Ibid., p. 221.
52. Ibid., p. 222.
53. Ibid.,
54. Cf. K. Marx, *On the Jewish Question*, in Marx–Engels, *Collected Works*, III, p. 167.
55. 'Thus, while the refugee serfs only wished to be free to develop and assert those conditions of existence which were already there, and hence, in the end, only arrived at free labour, the proletarians, if they are to assert themselves as individuals, will have to abolish the very condition of their

220 *Notes to pages 81–93*

existence hitherto . . . namely, labour.' Or: 'Labour *is* free in all civilised countries; it is not a matter of freeing labour but of abolishing it.' Marx–Engels, *The German Ideology* (Progress Publishers, Moscow, 1968) pp. 96, 224.

56. 'In order to assert themselves as individuals, they must overthrow the state.' Ibid., p. 96.
57. 'Circumstances make men just as much as men make circumstances.' Ibid., p. 51.
58. Cf. McLellan, *The Thought of Karl Marx*, p. 25.
59. Ibid., p. 195.
60. Ibid., p. 222.
61. *The German Ideology*, op. cit., p. 88.
62. Ibid., p. 85.
63. Ibid., p. 93.
64. Ibid.
65. Ibid., p. 93.
66. As long as there are relations of superiority and subordination, one may accept the following propositions: 'A superior power which is exercised to the benefit of the subordinate and which, because in accordance with his will, is accepted by him, is called authority.' Cf. Ferdinand Tönnies, *Community and Association* (Routledge & Kegan Paul, London, 1955) p. 21.
67. Cf. *The Communist Manifesto*, in Marx–Engels, *Selected Works in One Volume*, p. 53.
68. Cf. F. Engels, *Anti-Dühring*, p. 338.

Chapter 4
1. Cf. *Bulletin of the International Institute of Social History*, No. 1 (Leiden, 1951) quoted from Bertram D. Wolfe, *Marxism: 100 Years in the Life of a Doctrine* (Dial Press, New York, 1965) p. 214.
2. Ibid.
3. F. Engels, Introduction to Marx's *The Class Struggles in France*, in Marx–Engels, *Selected Works in One Volume*, p. 664.
4. Ibid., p. 661.
5. Ibid., p. 660.
6. Ibid., p. 664.
7. Ibid., p. 666. Despite all these unequivocal evolutionary assertions, Engels made this important qualification: 'Does that mean that in the future street fighting will no longer play any role? Certainly not.' Ibid., p. 663. And also: 'Of course, our foreign comrades do not thereby in the least renounce their right to revolution. The right to revolution is, after all, the only *really* "historical right", the only right on which all modern states without exception rest . . ..' Ibid., p. 665.
8. Wolfe, *Marxism*, p. 223.
9. Marx's letter to H. M. Hyndman, 8 Dec 1880, in Marx–Engels, *Selected Correspondence* (Progress Publishers, Moscow, 1955) p. 334.
10. 'If you say that you do not share the views of my party for England I can only reply that the party considers an English revolution not necessary but – according to historic precedents – *possible*.' Ibid.

11. Cf. Marx–Engels, *Selected Works in One Volume*, p. 649.
12. In her polemics against Bernstein, Rosa Luxemburg argued that Marx's suggestion had referred to the attitude of the proletariat *after* its victory, 'for, obviously, it can only be a question of buying out the old dominant class when the working class is in power'. Cf. *Selected Political Writings of Rosa Luxemburg*, ed. and introduced by Dick Howard, (Monthly Review Press, New York and London, 1971) p. 120. Rosa Luxemburg's argument has its logic: it is very likely that Marx really meant 'after the victory of the proletariat'. It would have to be a peaceful victory, however. One may hardly imagine that a victorious working class would ever think about such a concession to its adversaries if its victory had been won in a bloody revolution.
13. Some words were deleted by an editor of *Die Neue Zeit* when the text was published for the first time (vol II, No. 27–28, 1894–5). However, even the restored original text from which I have quoted seems to be unequivocally clear. For a discussion concerning the controversy, cf. Wolfe, *Marxism*, pp. 222–3, and D. Howard's editorial footnote on pp. 383–4 of *Selected Political Writings of Rosa Luxemburg*.
14. Cf. E. Bernstein, *Evolutionary Socialism* (Schocken Books, New York, 1961).
15. I. Kant 'On the Maxim: Good in Theory, but Bad in Practice', quoted from Irving Fetscher, 'Marx's Concretisation of the Concept of Freedom', in Erich Fromm (ed.), *Socialist Humanism* (Doubleday, New York, 1965) pp. 260–1.
16. K. Marx, *Capital*, I, p. 176.
17. Not only him. In his brief biographical sketch 'Karl Marx' written in 1913 for the *Granat Dictionary*, Lenin also used the title '*The Marxist Doctrine*', with the subtitle 'Marx's Economic Doctrine'. At this point, Lenin proved to be a faithful disciple of Kautsky. Cf. V. I. Lenin, 'Karl Marx', in *Selected Works in Three Volumes*, I (Foreign Languages Publishing House, Moscow, 1960) pp. 27 ff. Engels would have disagreed with both of them: 'But all concepts of Marx (*Auffassungsweise*) are not doctrines but methods. They do not provide complete doctrines but starting points for further research and methods for that research.' F. Engels, letter to W. Sombart, 11 Mar 1895, quoted from Branko Horvat, *An Essay on Yugoslav Society* (IASP, New York, 1969) p. 90.
18. K. Marx, *The Poverty of Philosophy*, quoted from K. Marx, *Selected Writings in Sociology and Social Philosophy*, ed. and trans. T. B. Bottomore (McGraw-Hill, New York, 1964) p. 91.
19. K. Kautsky, *The Class Struggle* (Erfurt Program) (C. H. Kerr, Chicago, 1910) pp. 98–9.
20. Ibid., p. 150.
21. Ibid., p. 49.
22. K. Kautsky, *The Labour Revolution* (Allen & Unwin, London, 1925) p. 260. Kautsky was aware of yet another type of economy without money: 'Besides the rigid allocation of an equal measure of the necessaries and enjoyments of life to each individual, another form of socialism without money is conceivable, the Leninite interpretation of what Marx described as the second phase of communism: each to produce of his own accord as much as he can, the productivity of labour being so high and the quantity

and variety of products so immense that everyone may be trusted to take what he needs. For this purpose money would not be needed. We have not yet progressed so far as this. At present we are unable to divine whether we shall ever reach this state. But that Socialism with which we are alone concerned today, whose features we can discern with some precision from the indications that already exist, will unfortunately not have this enviable freedom and abundance at its disposal, and will therefore not be able to do without money.' Ibid., pp. 260–1.

23. Ibid., p. 259.
24. Cf. K. Marx, 'Provisorische Statuten der internationalen Arbeiter-Assoziation', in Marx–Engels, *Werke*, XVIII, p. 14.
25. 'Bureaucracy *versus* democracy is in fact centralism *versus* autonomism; it is the organisational principle of revolutionary Social-Democracy as opposed to the organisation principle of opportunist Social Democracy. The latter strives to proceed from the bottom upward, and, therefore, whenever possible and as far as possible, upholds autonomism and "democracy", carried . . . to the point of anarchism. The former strives to proceed from the top downward, and upholds an extension of the rights and powers of the centre in relation to the parts.' V. I. Lenin, *One Step Forward, Two Steps Back* (Progress Publishers, Moscow, 1969) pp. 192–3.
26. Marx–Engels, *Selected Works in One Volume*, p. 46 (emphasis added).
27. Quoted from Wolfe, *Marxism*, p. 195.
28. Marx–Engels, *Selected Works in One Volume*, p. 446.
29. Cf. K. Kautsky, *Aus der Frühzeit des Marxismus* (Prague, 1935) p. 271.
30. Cf. Gustav Mayer, *Friedrich Engels, A Biography* (Chapman & Hall, London, 1936) p. 275.
31. Cf. Marx–Engels, *Collected Works*, VI, pp. 585–8.
32. Cf. General Rules of the International Working Men's Association, in Saul K. Padover (ed.), *On the First International* (McGraw-Hill, New York, 1973) pp. 13–15.
33. Rosa Luxemburg, *Selected Political Writings*, p. 291.
34. V. I. Lenin, *The State and Revolution*, in J. E. Connor (ed.), *Lenin on Politics and Revolution* (Pegasus, New York, 1968) p. 228.
35. '. . . although commodity production still "reigns" and continues to be regarded as the basis of economic life, it has in reality been undermined . . . .' Cf. ibid., p. 120.
36. V. I. Lenin, *Selected Works* (Moscow, 1967) II, p. 692.
37. V. I. Lenin, 'Left-Wing Childishness and Petty Bourgeois Mentality', in *Lenin on Socialist Economic Organisation* (Progress Publishers, Moscow, 1971) pp. 145–6.
38. V. I. Lenin, 'The Immediate Tasks of the Soviet Government', ibid., p. 128.
39. V. I. Lenin, 'Left-Wing Childishness and Petty Bourgeois Mentality', ibid., p. 146.
40. The latter alternative was quite acceptable for Lenin. In his polemics with Tomsky at the Ninth Congress of the Party, Lenin said: '. . . Soviet socialist democracy and individual management and dictatorship are in no way contradictory, and the will of a class may sometimes be carried out by a dictator, who sometimes does more alone and is frequently more necessary.' V. I. Lenin, *Collected Works*, XXX (Progress Publishers, Moscow, 1965) p. 476.

41. V. I. Lenin, *The State and Revolution*, in *Lenin on Socialist Economic Organisation*, p. 72.
42. 'Industry is indispensable, democracy is not. Industrial democracy breeds some utterly false ideas.' V. I. Lenin, 'On the Trade Unions', in *Collected Works*, XXXII, p. 27.
43. 'But this "factory discipline", which the proletariat, after defeating the capitalists, after overthrowing the exploiters, will extend to the whole of society, is by no means our ideal, or our ultimate goal. It is only a necessary *step* for thoroughly cleaning society of all the infamies and abominations of capitalist exploitation, and *for further* progress.' V. I. Lenin, *The State and Revolution*, op. cit., p. 72.
44. Cf. 'Economics and Politics in the Era of the Dictatorship of the Proletariat', in *Lenin on Socialist Economic Organization*, p. 233.
45. Cf. *Capital*, III, p. 820.
46. F. Engels, *Socialism: Utopian and Scientific*, in Marx–Engels, *Selected Works in One Volume*, p. 432.
47. *The State and Revolution*, in *The Essential Left* (Unwin Books, London, 1971) p. 232.
48. A. Gramsci, *Selections from the Prison Notebooks* (International Publishers, New York, 1971) p. 261.
49. V. I. Lenin, *Collected Works*, X (Moscow, 1962) p. 246.
50. V. I. Lenin, 'Proletarian Revolution and Renegade Kautsky', in *Collected Works*, XXVIII (Moscow, 1965) p. 237.
51. Cf. V. I. Lenin, 'The Trade Unions, the Present Situation and Trotsky's Mistakes', in *Collected Works*, XXXII (Moscow, 1965) p. 21.
52. 'The despot always sees degraded people', noted Marx in his letter to Arnold Ruge in May 1843. Cf. Marx–Engels, *Collected Works*, III, p. 138.
53. Cf. V. I. Lenin, *Collected Works*, XXIX, pp. 388, 419.
54. Cf. V. I. Lenin, 'The Trade Unions, the Present Situation and Trotsky's Mistakes', op. cit., pp. 21 ff.
55. V. I. Lenin, 'Fourth Anniversary of the October Revolution', in *Lenin on Socialist Economic Organisation*, pp. 233–4.
56. V. I. Lenin, 'The Importance of Gold Now and After the Complete Victory of Socialism', ibid., pp. 343–4.
57. 'In the case of socialised production the money capital is eliminated. Society distributes labour power and means of production to the different branches of production. The producers may, for all it matters, receive paper vouchers entitling them to withdraw from the social supplies of consumer goods a quantity corresponding to their labour time. These vouchers are not money. They do not circulate.' K. Marx, *Capital*, II, p. 358. 'With the seizing of the means of production by society, production of commodities is done away with . . . .' Cf. F. Engels, *Socialism: Utopian and Scientific*, in Marx–Engels, *Selected Works in One Volume*, p. 432. Both these suggestions are remarkably similar to the Soviet credit reform described by G. Kozlov. Both are based on the same false assumption that labour expended according to the social plan is *a priori* immediately social labour.
58. *Lenin on Socialist Economic Organisation*, p. 340.
59. Ibid., p. 341.
60. 'Direct transition to communism would be possible if ours were a country

with a predominantly – or, say, highly developed – large-scale industry, and a high level of large-scale production in agriculture.' V. I. Lenin, *Collected Works*, XXXII, p. 323.

61. 'Left-Wing Childishness and Petty Bourgeois Mentality', in *Lenin on Socialist Economic Organisation*, pp. 145–6.
62. Cf. Stalin, *Collected Works*, XI (Moscow, 1954) p. 152.
63. It was true not only for Bukharin or Preobrazhensky, but also for Lenin himself. Incidentally, the belief that money is incompatible with socialism was so strong that G. Sokolnikov, then People's Commissar of Finance, opened his address to the First All-Russian Congress of Economic Councils with the following apology: 'Finances will not exist in socialist society. Therefore, I do apologise both for their existence and for my address . . . .' Cf. G. Sokolnikov, *Finantsovaya Politika Revoliutsii* [Financial Policy of the Revolution] (Moscow, 1923) p. 114.
64. '. . . the New Economic Policy *does not change* the integrated economic plan, *nor does it exceed* its framework, it merely changes the *ways* of its implementation.' V. I. Lenin, *Polnoe Sobranie Sochinenii*, LIV (Moscow, 1965) p. 101.
65. 'Bookkeeping, as the control and ideal synthesis of the process [of production] becomes the more necessary the more the process assumes a social scale and loses its purely individual character. It is therefore more necessary in capitalist production than in the scattered production of handicraft and peasant economy, more necessary in collective production than in capitalist production.' Karl Marx, *Capital*, II, p. 135. 'Accounting and control – that is mainly what is needed for the "smooth working", for the proper functioning, of the first phase of communist society.' V. I. Lenin, *The State and Revolution*, in *Lenin on Socialist Economic Organisation*, p. 71.
66. Cf. Laszlo Szamuely, *First Models of Socialist Economic Systems* (Akademiai Kiado, Budapest, 1974) p. 77.
67. Lenin agreed only with workers' control *prior* to the nationalisation of private capitalist enterprises. After the revolution, his policy may be best summed up in the following tenet: '. . . from workers' control to the creation of the Supreme Council of the National Economy.' Cf. V. I. Lenin, *Sochineniya*, XXII (Moscow–Leningrad, 1929) p. 394.
68. Cf. *Manifesto of the Communist Party*, in Marx–Engels, *Selected Works in One Volume*, p. 52.
69. K. Marx, 'Konspekt von Bakunin "Staatlichkeit and Anarchie"', *Werke*, XVIII, p. 634.
70. Ibid.
71. Ibid.
72. K. Marx, *Critique of the Gotha Programme*, in *Selected Works in One Volume*, p. 330.
73. F. Engels, *Socialism: Utopian and Scientific*, ibid., p. 428.
74. Marx to Ruge, Sep 1843, in *Collected Works*, III, p. 143.
75. Cf. *Economic and Philosophic Manuscripts of 1844*, in *Collected Works*, III, p. 295.
76. Ibid., p. 247.
77. In his letter to Bernstein (25 Oct 1881) Engels explains that Marx was the author of the *draft* programme of the French Workers' Party: 'Its preamble

was dictated (to Guesde) word for word by Marx in the presence of Lafargue and myself right here in my room.' Engels calls Marx's formulation, from which I have quoted the introductory sentence) 'a masterpiece of cogent argumentation rarely encountered and couched in a few words for the masses . . .'. Marx–Engels, *Selected Correspondence* (Progress Publishers, Moscow, 1965) p. 344.

78. Cf. Rules of the Communist League, in Marx–Engels, *Collected Works*, VI, pp. 585–8; General Rules of the International Working Men's Association, in Padover (ed.), *On the First International*, pp. 13–15.

79. I am using the most recent Yugoslav concept of delegations as defined by President of the Federal Assembly M. Todorovic in his report on the final draft of the SFRY Constitution: 'The essential change introduced by the delegational system lies in the fact that decision-making in the broader socio-political communities (i.e. regions, provinces, etc.) is no longer exercised by some kind of general political representatives but through a type of political institution which ensures that interests formed in the base of society are directly represented in the centres of political power. Delegations and delegates are not general political representatives vested with a general political mandate expressing some kind of general political rights of electors, but are instruments of the working class organised politically and on a self-management basis . . ..' Cf. *The Constitution of the Socialist Federal Republic of Yugoslavia* (Belgrade, 1974) p. 34.

80. Ibid., p. 163.

Chapter 5

1. Cf. F. Engels, 'Über die Assoziation der Zukunft', in Marx–Engels, *Werke*, XXI, p. 391.
2. Cf. *The Communist Manifesto*, in Marx–Engels, *Selected Works in One Volume*, p. 53.
3. Cf. *Capital*, III, p. 820.
4. *The German Ideology*, op. cit., p. 48 (emphasis added).
5. So was the consumption of the capitalists who, as Marx approvingly quotes from Dr Aikin's book, 'lived like misers and were far from consuming even the interest on their capital'. K. Marx, *Capital*, I, p. 594.
6. 'First, the shares of past and present labour in a commodity decline equally. Second, the share of present labour declines faster than the share of past labour (present labour declines, past labour remains constant); thus, there is a relative increase in the share of past labour. Third, the share of past labour declines faster than the share of present labour (past labour declines while present labour remains constant); thus there is a relative increase in the share of present labour. Fourth, the share of past labour grows absolutely, while the share of present labour declines more rapidly, and thus there is a relative increase in the share of past labour. And fifth, present labour grows absolutely while past labour declines faster; thus, there is a relative increase in the share of present labour.' Cf. M. Hájek and M. Toms, *Dva modely růstu* [Two Models of Growth] ČSAV, (Prague, 1965) p. 30.
7. Cf. *The Communist Manifesto*, op. cit., p. 45.
8. K. Marx, *Moralising Criticism and Critical Morality*, in *Collected Works*, VI, p. 319.

9. F. Engels, Introduction to K. Marx, *The Class Struggles in France, 1848–1850*, op. cit., p. 656.
10. F. Engels, *Principles of Communism*, in Marx–Engels, *Collected Works*, VI, p. 349.
11. F. Engels, *Speeches in Elberfeld*, ibid., IV, p. 246.
12. Ibid., p. 249.
13. F. Engels: *Socialism: Utopian and Scientific*, in Marx–Engels, *Selected Works in One Volume*, p. 432. This and other statements and predictions of Engels must not be taken too seriously. For instance, he quite sincerely suggested that 'the weapons used have reached such a stage of perfection that further progress which would have any revolutionising influence is no longer possible'. Cf. *Anti-Dühring* (International Publishers, New York, 1939) p. 188.
14. K. Marx, Preface to *The Critique of Political Economy*, in Marx–Engels, *Selected Works in One Volume*, p. 183.
15. '. . . The worst thing that can befall a leader of an extreme party is to be compelled to take over a government in an epoch when the movement is not yet ripe for the domination of the class which he represents, and for the realisation of the measures which that domination implies. What he *can* do depends not upon his will but upon the degree of contradiction between the various classes, and upon the level of development of the material means of existence, of the conditions of production and commerce upon which class contradictions always repose. What he *ought* to do, what his party demands of him, again depends not upon him or the stage of development of the class struggle and its conditions. He is bound to the doctrines and demands hitherto propounded, which, again, do not proceed from the class relations of the moment or from the more or less accidental level of production and commerce, but from his more or less penetrating insight into the general result of the social and political movement. Thus he necessarily finds himself in an unsolvable dilemma. What he *can* do contradicts all his previous actions, principles, and the immediate interests of his party, and what he *ought* to do cannot be done. In a word, he is compelled to represent not his party or his class, but the class for whose domination the movement is then ripe. In the interests of the movement he is compelled to advance the interests of an alien class, and to feed his own class with phrases and promises, and with the asseveration that the interests of that alien class are its own interests.' F. Engels, *The Peasant War in Germany*, in Feuer (ed.), *Basic Writings on Politics and Philosophy*, p. 435. Having written this, Engels commented on Thomas Münzer. Had Marx's and Engels' party seized power in the mid-nineteenth century, this comment could have been applied to Marx and Engels themselves.
16. F. Engels, 'Draft of a Communist Confession of Faith', in Marx–Engels, *Collected Works*, VI, p. 96.
17. Cf. Isaiah Berlin, *Two Concepts of Liberty* (Clarendon Press, Oxford, 1958).
18. This refers to disfranchised people prior to an introduction of universal suffrage; to alien residents in liberal democracies; to those who as yet have not reached the voting age.
19. 'It is one of the civilising aspects of capital that it enforces this surplus-labour in a manner and under conditions which are more advantageous to

the development of the productive forces, social relations, and the creation of the elements for a new and higher form than under the preceding forms of slavery, serfdom, etc.' K. Marx, *Capital*, III, p. 819.

20. K. Marx, *Capital*, I, p. 356.

21. F. A. Hayek, *The Constitution of Liberty* (A Gateway Edition, Chicago, 1972) p. 21.

22. e.g. C. B. Macpherson, *Democratic Theory* (Clarendon Press, Oxford, 1973) p. 151.

23 'Being made impersonal and dependent upon general, abstract rules, whose effect on particular individuals cannot be foreseen at the time they are laid down, even the coercive acts of government become data on which the individual can base his own plans. Coercion according to known rules, which is generally the result of circumstances in which the person to be coerced has placed himself, then becomes an instrument assisting the individuals in the pursuit of their own ends and not a means to be used for the ends of others.' F. A. Hayek, op. cit., p. 21.

24. That is to say, for a meaningful *socialist* political freedom. A link between the market and formal liberal freedom was recognised by Marx in his *Grundrisse*, op. cit., p. 245; by Engels in his *Socialism: Utopian and Scientific*, in Marx–Engels, *Selected Works in One Volume*, p. 417; and Lenin admitted a connection between the market and liberal freedom in his *Economics and Politics in the Era of the Dictatorship of the Proletariat*: 'General talk about freedom, equality and democracy is in fact but a blind repetition of concepts shaped by the relations of commodity production.' Cf. *Lenin on Socialist Economic Organisation*, p. 241.

25. Cf. Karl Polanyi, *The Great Transformation* (Beacon Press, Boston, 1957); C. B. Macpherson, *Democratic Theory*, and also *The Real World of Democracy* (Canadian Broadcasting Corporation, Toronto, 1965).

26. University of Chicago Press, 1962.

27. I have already been labelled a 'Friedmanist' by a somewhat bewildered reviewer of my *Czechoslovakia: The Plan that Failed* (Nelson, London, 1970) in *Canadian Slavonic Papers*, XIV (4) (1972) p. 717.

28. Polanyi, *The Great Transformation* p. 250.

29. Ibid., p. 68.

30. Ibid., p. 252.

31. Ibid., p. 249.

32. He seems in agreement with the link between free market competition and liberal freedoms as formulated by Engels: 'The mode of production peculiar to the bourgeoisie known since Marx as the capitalist mode of production, was incompatible with the feudal system, with the privileges it conferred upon individuals, entire social ranks and local corporations, as well as the hereditary ties of subordination which constituted the framework of its social organisation. The bourgeoisie broke up the feudal system and built upon its ruins the capitalist order of society, the kingdom of free competition, of personal liberty, of equality before the law, of all commodity owners, of all the rest of the capitalist blessings. Thenceforward the capitalist mode of production could develop in freedom.' F. Engels, *Socialism: Utopian and Scientific*, in Marx–Engels, *Selected Works in One Volume*, p. 417.

33. Polanyi, *The Great Transformation*, p. 254.

34. Ibid., p. 255 (emphasis added).
35. Ibid. (emphasis added).
36. Ibid. (emphasis added).
37. Ibid., p. 256 (emphasis added).
38. Ibid., p. 257.
39. Ibid., p. 258.
40. Ibid., pp. 254–5.
41. Friedman, *Capitalism and Freedom*, p. 8.
42. Ibid., pp. 11–15.
43. Macpherson, *Democratic Theory*, p. 42.
44. Macpherson, *The Real World of Democracy*, p. 43.
45. Macpherson, *Democratic Theory*, p. 77.
46. Friedman, *Capitalism and Freedom*, pp. 14–15 (emphasis added).
47. Macpherson, *Democratic Theory*, p. 146.
48. Ibid., p. 43.
49. Ibid.
50. *Capital*, III, p. 820.
51. K. Marx, *Thesis on Feuerbach*, in Marx–Engels, *Collected Works*, V, p. 4.
52. K. Marx, *On the Jewish Question*, ibid., III, p. 168.
53. 'Man, much as he may therefore be a *particular* individual (and it is
    precisely his particularity which makes him an individual, and a real
    individual social being), is just as much the *totality* – the ideal totality –
    the subjective existence of imagined and experienced society for itself; just as he
    exists also in in the real world both as awareness and real enjoyment of
    social existence, and as a totality of human manifestation of life.' K. Marx,
    Economic and Philosophic Manuscripts of 1844, ibid., III, p. 299.
54. Marx–Engels, *The German Ideology*, ibid., V, pp. 52–3 (emphasis added).
55. K. Marx, *Early Writings*, p. 155.
56. Cf. his *Democratic Theory*, especially the essay on Berlin's Division of
    Liberty, pp. 95–119.
57. Macpherson even excuses Stalin for Stalinism: 'The transformation of
    radical $P1^1$ into PL^2 which comes with Stalinism, comes, it appears, only
    after long-continued and intensive refusal of the beneficiaries of unequal
    institutions, on a world-wide scale, to permit any moves to alter the
    institutions in the direction of more nearly equal powers.' Ibid., p. 115.
58. Ibid., p. 116.
59. Ibid., p. 119.
60. Ibid., p. 114.
61. I use the term 'private property' in its Marxist sense, i.e. as private
    ownership of the means of production. For a private ownership of
    consumer goods or individual means of labour, the term 'personal property'
    is far more appropriate. 'But no economist would think of it [my frock-coat]
    as my private property, since it does not enable me to command any, even
    the smallest amount of other people's labour.' Cf. Marx–Engels, *The
    German Ideology*, in *Collected Works*, V, p. 230.
62. Such a market cannot make man an infinite appropriator. This has been
    explicitly recognised even by Macpherson: 'While the postulate of man as
    infinite consumer does not necessarily make him an infinite appropriator,
    only a simple additional minor premise is necessary to convert him into

that. The premise required is merely that land and capital must be privately owned to be productive.' Cf. *Democratic Theory*, p. 30. Moreover, the market *without* private property does not necessarily have to make man an infinite consumer, as Macpherson rightly allowed, and the concept of man as a consumer of utilities does not logically carry with it a postulate of *infinite* desire (cf. ibid., p. 27). In the suggested market socialist society man is both a consumer of utilities *and* a producer of goods and services. Hence, each new desire could be satisfied only if the consumer/producer is willing to increase the output.

63. *The German Ideology*, in Marx–Engels, *Collected Works*, v, p. 537.
64. F. Engels, *Anti-Dühring* (International Publishers, New York, 1939) p. 328.
65. V. I. Lenin, *The State and Revolution*, in *Lenin on Politics and Revolution*, p. 228.
66. Lange, in Lippincot, op. cit., pp. 101–2.
67. K. Marx, *Moralising Criticism and Critical Morality*, in Marx–Engels, *Collected Works*, VI, p. 330.
68. I agree with Hayek that we should not try to assess one's merits: 'It is only the value of the result that we can judge with any degree of confidence, not the different degrees of effort and care that it has cost different people to achieve it.' Cf. his discussions of reward according to merit in *The Constitution of Liberty*, op. cit., pp. 93–100. The quotation is from p. 96.
69. Henry C. Simons, *Personal Income Taxation* (University of Chicago Press, 1938) pp. 12–13, quoted from Arthur M. Okun, *Equality and Efficiency: The Big Tradeoff* (Brookings Institution, Washington, D.C., 1975) p. 44.
70. Educational and health services are undoubtedly conducive to an increase of a net aggregate amount of positive freedom. They consume not only some percentage of GNP but also a lot of material goods. For instance, the largest consumer of electricity in the Boston area is MIT; the second largest consumer of electricity in the Boston area are the affiliated hospitals of Harvard. Cf. Lester Thurow, 'Zero Growth and the Distribution of Income', in A. Weintraub, E. Schwartz and J. R. Aronson (eds.), *The Economic Growth Controversy* (IASP, New York, 1973) p. 145.
71. This problem is discussed from a different angle by Arthur A. Okun. If the view is taken that no inequality is tolerable unless it raises the lowest income, then, according to this criterion, society is (for instance) 'worse off if the lowest-income family loses one dollar, no matter how much everybody else in the society gains'. If one accepted this principle, one would have to prefer a society which guaranteed every family $14,000 a year to that which provided 99 per cent of families with $20,000 and 1 per cent with $13,000. Cf. *Equality and Efficiency*, p. 93.
72. Macpherson, *Democratic Theory*, p. 55 (emphasis added).
73. Macpherson might retort that I have misrepresented his case by quoting only the second part of his egalitarian principle of morally justifiable rights which translates right into power while ignoring the first part which reads: 'It must be asserted that the rights of any man which are morally justifiable on any egalitarian principle are only those which allow all others to have equal effective rights; and that *those are enough* to allow any man to be fully human.' (ibid.) Of course, this formulation *may* imply that no one must get anything which is not available to anyone else. If *this* was the meaning of the

formulation, then, evidently, the first part of the principle contradicts the second, and Macpherson would have to be asked to reformulate it according to the principles of logic. Incidentally, it seems absurd to interpret the egalitarian principle of rights in the way suggested above: it would imply, for instance, that no one has the right to orgasm unless everyone has the same *effective* right.

74. In his defence of the strictly non-market society, Macpherson suggests that any affluent socialist non-market system may eliminate this danger by introducing a guaranteed minimum annual income to everyone regardless of employment (*Democratic Theory*, p. 154). One wonders how such a fierce advocate of positive freedom could have so betrayed his ideal of the free development of man which cannot be guaranteed without man's guaranteed free access to the means of labour.

Chapter 7

1. *Capital*, III, pp. 436–8 (emphasis added).
2. 'The corporate organisations of business and labour have long ceased to be a private phenomenon. That they have a direct and decisive impact on the social, economic and political life of the nation is no longer a matter of argument.' Wolfgang Friedman, *Law in a Changing Society* (Columbia University Press, New York, 1972) p. 333.
3. 'The extension of public power and control, and the increasingly "public" role of nominally private organisations that control essential aspects of social life, is an inevitable consequence of the eclipse of *laissez-faire* in the contemporary industrialised and urbanised society.' Ibid., p. 366. 'It [shareholding] establishes a monopoly in certain spheres and thereby requires state interference.' Marx, *Capital*, III, p. 438.
4. Cf. A. Berle and G. Means, *The Modern Corporation and Private Property* (Macmillan, New York, 1948) p. 70. In 1930, of the 200 largest U.S. companies, 44 per cent were under management control, 23 per cent under minority control and 21 per cent under control through a legal device. Ibid., p. 94.
5. This involves the owning of a majority (or a controlling minority) of the stock of one corporation which in turn holds a majority (or a controlling minority) of the stock of another; this chain is theoretically indefinite. The classical case is that of Van Swerigen Brothers who were able to control with an investment of less than $20 million combined assets of $2000 million. Ibid., pp. 72–3.
6. For instance, as of 13 December 1929, the largest single shareholder of the Pennsylvania Railroad Company owned a 0.34 per cent and the 20 largest stockholders owned together only 2.70 per cent of shares. Cf. ibid., p. 85. Similar cases were quoted by R. W. Goldsmith, R. C. Parmelee *et al.* in *The Distribution of Ownership of the 200 Largest Nonfinancial Corporations*, U.S. Congress, Temporary National Economic Committee, Investigation of Concentration of Economic Power, Monograph 29 (U.S. Government Printing Office, Washington, D.C., 1940) pp. 684–5. For instance, the largest stockholder of the AT & T in 1937 was the Sun Life Assurance Co. of Canada with 0.63 per cent of the shares.
7. Separation of nominal ownership from real control is particularly visible in

North America. According to Peter F. Drucker, employees of American business today own – through their pension funds – about 25 per cent of equity capital, which is more than enough for control. Cf. P. F. Drucker, *The Unseen Revolution* (Harper & Row, New York, 1976) p. 1. Unlike Drucker, I cannot interpret this state of affairs as the coming of socialism to America. This substantial nominal ownership does not give the employees any real controlling power over the corporations. The purpose of pension funds is that of social security rather than that of social control. Incidentally, the social security function of shareholding is becoming more and more common. It also contributes to the dispersion of shareholding: to avoid a risk, the shareholder invests in several corporations to secure a steady income.

8. 'Power over the public is public power.' R. H. Tawney, *Equality* (Harcourt, Brace, New York, 1931) p. 231.
9. Cf. the concept of 'countervailing power' formulated by J. K. Galbraith in his *American Capitalism: The Concept of Countervailing Power* (Houghton Mifflin, Boston, 1952).
10. Cf. his 'Democracy as a Sociological Problem', in *Journal of Legal and Political Philosophy*, I (1–2) (1942) pp. 46–71.
11. Ibid., pp. 61–2.
12. Ibid., p. 66.
13. Ibid., p. 59.
14. Cf. J. Vanek and A. Vahcic, 'Self-Management, Workers' Management and Labour Management in Theory and Practice: A Comparative Study', unpublished paper, Cornell University, Ithaca, N.Y.
15. K. Marx, *Capital*, III p. 437.
16. 'Tied to Allied efforts to restructure German industrial power, codetermination originated in steel in 1947 and was extended to coal in 1951. In steel and coal, labour representatives constitute half of the board of directors (which then mutually selects a neutral director) and the personnel director of the enterprise is controlled by labour through his or her appointment. The Works Constitution Act of 1952 established works councils in all enterprises over five workers and economic committees in those over one hundred workers. The Act also prescribed one-third labour representation on boards of directors outside steel and coal." G. D. Garson, 'Recent Development in Workers' Participation in Europe', in J. Vanek (ed.), *Self-Management: Economic Liberation of Man* (Penguin Books, Harmondsworth, 1975) pp. 164 ff. Note that codetermination was introduced for the sake of *democratisation* of the post-Second World War German key industries.
17. Jaroslav Vanek, 'Education for the Practice of Self-Management in the United States', unpublished manuscript, Cornell University, Ithaca, N.Y., 1976.
18. Ibid., pp. 18–19.
19. Ibid., p. 19.
20. Cf. Jaroslav Vanek, *The General Theory of Labour-Managed Market Economies* (Cornell University Press, Ithaca, N.Y., 1970).
21. A good point has been made by a British Labour MP and former research fellow in management sciences, Eric Moonman, who recently argued for

workers' representation on company boards from the standpoint of efficiency. First, says Moonman, the workers' participation could spark off not only a widespread improvement in communications inside industry but also provide the stimulus needed to sharpen up management's approach to its job. Second, the worker-directors as experienced trade union representatives will be considerably more demanding in seeking explanations of poor performance than the average shareholder who rarely bothers to turn up even at the annual meeting and then meekly accepts whatever explanations the board of directors cares to give him. Third, it has been recognised that the workers' well-being is far more closely allied to the company than is that of an average shareholder. Cf. E. Moonman, 'The Ineptitude of British Managers', *New York Times*, 1 May 1977, p. F3. Moonman's argument seems more persuasive than that presented by a French executive ('Our free economy system would end on the day when company management was no longer appointed and dismissed by capital') and is complementary to that presented by a German executive ('Every social group . . . remains stable only if a majority of its members feel involved'). Cf. *Atlas World Press Review*, June 1977, p. 39.

Chapter 8

1. In his *General Theory of Labour-Managed Market Economies*, Vanek convincingly argues that maximisation of income per labourer is a natural operating principle in labour-managed and income-sharing systems. Cf. Vanek, op. cit., pp. 3 ff.

Index